Hunters are hunted as saboteurs pro
Pack of trouble looms as the hunts saddle up
PROBE INTO POSSIBLE FIREARMS OFFENCES
Police seize guns held by Hunt
by Staff Reporters
NTS FACE
V FOES
lls farmworker's pet fox
ent clashes as saboteur
ng hunt stewards
aces the Force
egal confusion
illed
r fox
anger
badger setts
Fury as hound killed on road
Hunt calls in ex-SAS squad to stop saboteurs
Beaufort Hunt braced for saboteur sorties
Plan to disrupt fox hunt course
Beagle festival turned into a wrestling match as antis met hunters
Saboteur threat to hunting festival
ANGER AT HUNT POW-WOW
MATTHEW ACTON
Hunters are a menace
Hunt and the ca
what YOU sa
No remorse as hunt saboteur is trampled
By Nicholas Schoon

CIS
0400

First published 2021 by Hunt Saboteurs Association
ISBN 978-1-3999-0391-2

Written by Dazza Scott

Dedicated to everyone taking direct action against animal abuse
and to those animals who have lost their lives at the hands of hunters

CONTENTS

1960S: THE BEGINNINGS OF THE HUNT SABOTEURS ASSOCIATION

Father Eugene Sheehy

In the Beginning....

Resistance towards hunting with hounds dates back a considerable amount of time. As far back as the nineteenth century, the Irish Land Leagues (groups of tenant farmers who believed that the people who farmed the land should also own it) believed that their rich landowners had no place riding across it for their own murderous pleasure. Fervent Land Leaguer, Father Eugene Sheehy, once even gathered together the local hurling team and prevented John Gubbins (a wealthy landowner and racehorse breeder in County Limerick) and his hunting colleagues from hunting across the district after Gubbins evicted a number of his tenants. In 1891, vegetarian and anti-vivisectionist Henry Salt founded The Humanitarian League, which before its closure in 1919, called for a ban on all hunting for sport. The Humanitarian League campaigned against a variety of issues such as vivisection and corporal and capital punishment but its longest running campaign was against stag hunting, which included monitoring the hunts, recording any incidents of cruelty and leafleting on the issue. This pressure even forced the Royal Buckhounds, who were kenneled at Ascot, to disband in 1901. However, the modern animal liberation movement only really gathered serious momentum in the latter half of the twentieth century.

The early 1960s was a tumultuous time for social justice movements. The anti-war movement was in full swing and struggles for black liberation, gay rights and women's rights (to name but a few) were garnering widespread support. It was amongst this backdrop that the seeds of the animal liberation movement were planted and direct action against one particular form of animal abuse - that of hunting with hounds - has its roots firmly grounded in the youthful ambition of this period. Founded in 1924, the League Against Cruel Sports (an organisation whose mainstay is evidence-gathering, undercover investigations and political lobbying) had established a number of wildlife sanctuaries in Somerset and Devon to provide a barrier to the stag hunts operating in the South West. This included the Baronsdown wildlife sanctuary, which is located close to Dulverton and to this day provides a much-needed refuge for many species of wildlife under threat from the numerous hunts and shoots littering the Exmoor countryside.

Despite later distancing itself from more confrontational tactics, the League was at this point even endorsing direct action. In August 1958, members of the League made their first venture into hunt sabotage in a high profile attempt to lay a false trail using a 'secret chemical' at a meet of the Devon and Somerset Staghounds. *The Daily Telegraph* reporter on the scene later described the action:

> *Members of the League were out early yesterday morning spraying the roads around Cloutsham, from which the hunt had started. They used an anti-pest spray behind a Land Rover. It rained after the first effort and they returned an hour later and sprayed again. When I arrived two hours before the hunt started the 'secret' chemical smelled strongly of aniseed.*

After failing to kill, hunt master, Louis Murphy tried to save face by claiming that hunt supporters, in chasing the stag, had destroyed the animal's scent. However, Ernest Hemmingway, the League's chairman, knew the truth and fired off a victorious response: "The fact that the hunt had to call off their hounds after they had lost a deer [...] shows only too well how thoroughly the League's volunteers had done their job. This is only the beginning. We shall hit other stag hunts in the same during the next few months." The action is widely regarded as the first organised sabotage of a hunt in the UK and the League enjoyed extensive good publicity as a result.

Garnered by its radical new chairman, Raymond Rowley, the League shifted its focus northwards and eastwards from Somerset and membership of the organisation began to increase dramatically. For instance, in November 1962 alone, after laying false trails at meets of the North Warwickshire Hunt and the Albrighton Woodland Hunt, the League added 400 new members to their books. Gwen Barter, a prominent League militant, was busy making headlines: in March 1962, she brought the Norwich Staghounds to a halt by climbing onto the front of the deer-cart. In February that same year she also prevented the East Kent Hunt from digging out and killing a fox when she sat on the foxhole. "There was nothing we could do", confessed the huntsman, "we just stopped digging out the fox and went away."

Despite these notable direct interventions, however, the League suffered from a distinct lack of dynamism since its inception, with no legislative success and a largely elderly and inactive membership. There were growing calls for a more direct approach within the anti-hunt movement and even former Tory MP, Howard Johnson, voiced the hopes of many when he told the League's 1963 AGM; "I have a vision in the coming stag and fox hunting season of whole numbers of you sitting in the roadway at meets of the hunt doing exactly what the anti-nuclear demonstrators do". Indeed, later that year, Rowley did take 100 activists on a 'dawn attack' with more 'secret chemicals' to use against the Old Berkeley's Boxing Day meet at Amersham. But, it was becoming apparent that an organisation more fundamentally based on direct action was needed.

Hunt Saboteurs Association Origins

The aptly named Hunt Saboteurs Association (HSA) was founded in December 1963 by a 21 year old freelance journalist by the name of John Prestige. Despite *The Guardian* newspaper's claims that the League and the HSA colluded to form a new direct action group, both Rowley and Prestige maintain that no formal meeting ever took place and Prestige holds the widely accepted view that the HSA was born out of a frustration over the League's general lack of effective action. Financed by a small legacy of Prestige's, two early donations of £500 from ex-Liberal MP for West Ham Count Maurice de Bendern and anti-hunt campaigner Claire Monk, and a membership fee of two shillings and six pence (£10 for life membership), the association enrolled 100 members within the first week of its inception and received a total of around 1000 letters within its first ten days.

A national committee was established that included Prestige's father and racing car designer Robin Jackson, with the ex-palladium dancer Joyce Greenaway as its secretary. A headquarters was soon set up on Fore Street in Brixham, Devon. Capt. Robert Churchward, an ex-Joint Master of the South Shropshire Foxhounds who had seen the light and now spent his time campaigning against his former colleagues, was quick to praise the new organisation, stating, "the Hunt Saboteurs Association is to be congratulated on its achievements during the past few months. You have certainly struck a great blow for the cause of abolition". Churchward provided the early organisation with wildly enthusiastic recordings of horn calls, holloas and 'tally ho backs' which most of the HSA novices found extremely amusing but later proved to be invaluable in training saboteurs on how to intervene in a hunt.

Prestige led a small group to the South Devon Hunt's meet near Torquay on Boxing Day, 1963 on what was somewhat of a 'dry-run' for future actions. "We did so well that day that they cancelled the hunt", Prestige recalls. "The local butcher gave us 50 pounds of meat and we fed it to the hounds. We used hunting horns. Nothing like that had ever really happened before and it caused absolute chaos. We did a lot of research on horn blowing and did the job very, very well. The police were completely bemused".

The first official hit of the newly-formed Hunt Saboteurs Association was on 10th January 1964 when the HSA again struck at the South Devon Hunt. According to the report in the association's first news bulletin:

> *A group of thirty supporters, employing various tactics, brought utter confusion to the hunt. Raw meat was thrown to the hounds as they gathered at the outset of the hunt. Phantom fanfares on hunting horns, the laying of false scents, and the blocking of lanes by saboteurs' cars to cut off the horsemen all played a vital part in the operation. A Master of the South Devon Foxhounds claimed that we had failed in our objective, but it is significant that the hunt broke up early and returned empty-handed – no fox had been taken and there wasn't even a 'near-miss'.*

Above: Gwen Barter at the Norwich Staghounds, 1962

Above: Street HSA pose for the press. Left to right: Anna Smith, Terry Fricher, Joyce Cebo, Sandra Munday, Carol Holden, 1964

Other hits were also reported in the bulletin including ones against the Chiddingfold Farmers Hunt, the Dartvale and Haldon Harriers, the Hambledon Hunt and the Surrey Union Hunt.

First Arrests

Very soon after the emergence of this new form of direct action, however, came the movement's first arrest. Norman Redman, the leader of the Littlehampton group, was fined £15 at Godalming Magistrates Court for 'insulting behaviour whereby a breach of the peace may be occasioned' and bound over for two years after feeding meat to the Chiddingfold Farmers Hunt's hounds on 15th February 1964 at their meet at Ewhurst, Surrey. The 30 saboteurs present had used acetone and other chemicals on the ground to dull the hounds' sense of smell, the first time that they had experimented with this tactic. Despite their best efforts, the hunt did manage to kill once. Infuriated at their interference, a 'small army' of hunt supporters attacked the saboteurs for interfering with the hunt. According to the news bulletin:

> *Huntsmen, wielding whips and sticks, literally attacked a number of saboteurs. One woman was punched, several of the girls were 'man-handled', two were knocked into a ditch and horses jumped over them. Neutral bystanders - including pressmen and photographers - were appalled at the treatment meted out.*

Although Prestige was also throwing meat to the hounds, the police decided to arrest only Redman, who was doing the same just a few yards away. None of the hunt supporters were arrested. In later years, saboteurs would take such arrests as customary but at the time the fledgling movement took the ruling very seriously and Prestige was moved to write a letter to Redman forbidding him to break the terms of his sentence. 'We CANNOT allow you to take any active part in sabotage' it read. Interestingly, Prestige was threatened with arrest for 'depositing litter on a public highway' for using the same tactic a month earlier in Devon. With growing irritation at the HSA's insistence that he should not actively take part in sabotage until the terms of his binding over were met and a feeling of being disowned by the movement, Redman bizarrely took up an offer to ride with the Crawley and Horsham Hunt a couple of years later. Upon news of this, the London and Littlehampton groups organised a hit against the hunt and even had the satisfaction of witnessing Redman fall head first from his horse into a thorn bush!

Early Tactics

Tactics were refined and included skilled use of the hunting horn to throw the hounds into disarray, holloaing to fool the hunters that a fox had been seen where there was none and using sprays to mask the scent of fleeing quarry.

A secret concoction known only as 'Chemical X' was made up for the purpose and consisted of amyl acetate (paint stripper), Jeye's fluid and water. Antimate or 'bitch spray', a commercially available liquid designed to be sprayed on the hindquarters of bitches on heat to cover their distinctive smell and stop them from mating, was also used to mask the fox's scent.

The basic tactics employed by saboteurs to disrupt hunting with hounds has changed very little over time, mainly due to the fact that those used in the early days proved to be very effective. As the methods of hunting have remained the same, so too have most of the strategies against it.

One welcome refinement, however, was the ditching of the highly noxious 'Chemical X' in favour of other forms of scent dulling liquids. The most widely used is citronella, a non-toxic essential oil obtained from lemongrass leaves that when used covers the musky smell of fox in a sweet citrusy fragrance.

First HSA Press Release

On 4th April 1964, West Country saboteurs took on their first stag hunt, of which the following report also featured in the HSA's first news bulletin:

> *Fifteen hardy saboteurs should certainly be awarded medals for courage and devotion to duty for their tenacity and engagement. In the teeth of a Force 7 gale and surrounded by a swirling blizzard of snow, an advance guard of three HQ members spent all night at Dunkey Hill Gate - the highest point of bleak Exmoor. The objective was to outwit the Devon and Somerset Staghounds by exposing their practice of 'harbouring' stags for the hunt in convenient coverts or woods.*
>
> *Intelligence sources had previously pinpointed the likely hiding places, and the party spent all night visiting each spot. Using various explosive devices and a number of other strategies the party flushed the harboured stags out of the woods. To do this they had to outmaneuver sentries posted by the hunt, but despite the wariness of the opposition it would appear that the saboteurs were highly successful.*
>
> *Only one stag was spotted by the hunt. One saboteur got between the stag and the hunt and managed to lay a smoke screen. The stag got away and the hunt got nothing.*
>
> *Special mention must be made here of three HQ members who formed the advance squad – John Prestige and his two able lieutenants, Barry West and Leo Lewis. Their exploits on Exmoor during their all night vigil in Arctic conditions are in the best 'Commando' tradition.*

Much of the press, although somewhat ambiguous in their stance on fox hunting, had little sympathy for the cruelty of stag hunting. *The Bristol Evening Post* even thought the hit newsworthy enough to devote its entire front page to it, with the words, 'HUNT SABOTEURS SET UP SMOKE SCREENS' printed in large type across the newspaper. *The West Somerset Free Press* was no less enthusiastic in its reporting of the hit:

> *On Saturday morning, after a briefing session in a Dulverton café, the saboteurs, young men and girls, mostly wearing jeans and anoraks, drove to the meet, but did not attempt any diversions. Soon the 'field operation' was in full swing. Thunder flashes roared – one saboteur let one off in a tree as the Master passed the bottom of Eastwater – and there were intermittent counter-blasts on an alien hunting horn. When the hunted deer came round the bottom of Cloutsham with a lone hound in pursuit, the saboteurs were galvanised into feverish activity. One youth ran after the hound shouting, while another lit two flares that belched a billowing cloud of pink smoke. By the time the smokescreen had built up to its full strength both he stag and the lone hound had disappeared. But the 20 or so saboteurs were not to be deterred and some time later desultory bangs could be heard down in the Horner Valley.*

A few weeks later, the saboteurs returned to the Devon and Somerset Staghounds near Corners Gate. The hunt was again unsuccessful, but not entirely down to the actions of the saboteurs. Thick fog had descended that brought the visibility down to just 50 yards and the group was forced to abandon their efforts to flush the harboured stag from the wood he was in. This also meant that the hunt were unable to find any stags. However, in the early morning mist, the group of saboteurs bumped into Bob Nancekivell, a joint master of the hunt. A strange exchange then took place in which Nancekivell agreed to participate in a public debate on stag hunting. *The Western Morning News* later interviewed the master who said of the saboteurs: "I shook hands [..] and told them they would always be welcome at the meet.

Above: Bristol HSA, 1966

Above: Dave Wetton's sausage dog, Becky, outside the London saboteurs' headquarters in Tooting, 1965

The saboteurs seemed to be quite reasonable chaps. I think they want something to do to let off steam. My personal view is that they could not have behaved better". True to his word, the strange debate eventually took place two years later when Nancekivell would travel to Bristol to meet with Dave Wetton and Ian Pedlar.

Within four months of its founding, the Hunt Saboteurs Association formed groups in Portsmouth, Street, Weybridge, and Littlehampton. Run by Joyce Cebo, the Street group had 40 members in its ranks by December 1964 and was regularly sabotaging both the Mendip Farmers Hunt and the Sparkford Vale Hunt. A group in Bournemouth was being formed; another in London, and Derek Lawrence was busy trying to turn Midlands LACS over to the HSA. Ian Pedler joined the moribund Bristol branch of the League Against Cruel Sports, revitalised it and then set up an HSA group from its ashes. Large joint hits took place on the Waddon Chase Hunt and the Surrey Union Hunt where saboteurs used smoke bombs and rook scarers in addition to their usual tactics for added dramatic effect. Twelve months after founding the HSA, Prestige estimated there had been 120 hits altogether, mostly in the West Country.

First Serious Violence Against Sabs

The HSA's honeymoon was relatively short-lived, however, as hunt supporters became increasingly violent towards saboteurs. The first serious incident of hunt violence occured on 2nd May 1964 as the Street and Brixham groups (totalling nine saboteurs) visited the Culmstock Otterhounds at Colyford. During the break for lunch, and after the saboteurs had been with the hunt for around two hours, the hunt surrounded their vehicles, smashed the windows and even attempted to throw lit matches into the petrol tank as there were no locking caps at the time. Whilst this was occurring, the occupants were assaulted with otter poles and whips. Leo Lewis, the driver, was pulled from his car and beaten by four men, breaking his jaw in the process.

The attack prompted the following statement from the HSA:

> *The incident took place during the lunch break of the Culmstock Otterhounds' meet at Colyford, Devon. Twenty saboteurs had been with the hunt for two hours when the assault took place. One of our cars was sandwiched between a Land Rover and another car. About 20 followers attacked our members with brass-tipped otter poles and whips. They bashed and dented the car roof and bonnet, let down the tyres and even tried to turn over and set it on fire whilst our members were still inside. The car driver, Leo Lewis, café proprietor of Paignton, was dragged from the car. He was struck with poles and punched heavily in the face Three of our girls in the car were slashed with whips and punched. They were terrified, as the attackers seemed to go berserk. One of the assailants shouted: "that will teach you a lesson to interfere with our sport".*

A week later, 70 saboteurs turned out in retaliation against the same hunt and sent them home in disarray after one Brixham saboteur waded in front of the pack with a smoke flare in each hand.

However, the damage inflicted by the subsequent court hearing was far reaching. Whilst Trevor Glasper, the hunt's whipper-in, was successfully convicted of attacking Lewis and fined £10 and three other hunt members were found guilty of common assault and each given £3 fines, seven saboteurs were bound over for a year for disturbing the peace after giving evidence. It was not the last time the courts would use this tactic and it took the aggrieved seven (who included Lewis and Prestige) so much by surprise that none of them took any further part in hunt sabotage. Prestige had in any case become disillusioned by the politicisation of the HSA as a result of 'left wingers' joining the anti-hunt movement and resigned as chairman.

The guilty verdict proved to be the nail in the coffin for the Brixham group, with the Street group following suit not long after.

The folding of the Brixham group threw the HSA into disarray and national emphasis moved to Surrey and Gloucestershire. By 1965, the only effective links that remained between the local groups were between Weybridge, Littlehampton and Bristol.

More violence was to come in February 1965 when three Bournemouth saboteurs were attacked with an axe and a starting handle by thugs from the Sparkford Vale Harriers. Although a hunt supporter was fined £15 for breaking a saboteur's guitar with the axe, eight saboteurs were fined £10 each for 'threatening behaviour' that mainly consisted of throwing flour bombs. During the same month, Marcus Lipton, the Labour MP for Brixton, attempted to outlaw the stag hunts operating in the South West by introducing the Protection of Deer Bill. Although the bill was unsurprisingly not successful, it did provide a glimmer of hope to those on the ground that there was at least some political will in bringing an end to hunting with hounds.

With the collapse of the Brixham group, the chairmanship of the HSA was offered to national committee members Robin Jackson, his daughter Janet, and Joyce Cebo, all three of whom declined. National organisation gradually fell to Dave Wetton's London group, being the most active by 1967 and having sabotaged 20 fox hunts, four cub hunts, two hare hunts and seven otter hunts in the 1964/65 season alone (an impressive feat at a time when communication and transport were much bigger problems than they are today). An 'operational base' for the London division of the HSA was set up at 5 Recovery Street, Tooting.

Otter Hunt Equality

Wetton had first joined the HSA in 1964 at the age of 20 and had taken over the running of the new London group from Janet Jackson. On becoming leader, Wetton soon overturned Jackson's ruling that women weren't allowed on otter hunts due to the threat of violence (this of course, excluded herself). As he later described, "the group's main tactics at the time included holloaing, horn blowing, aniseed and creosote drags and the use of smoke canisters which cost between 2s 11d and 23s 3d (15p and £1.16). Acetone sprays were eventually superseded by Antimate sprays. Meat had generally been discarded, both for vegetarian principles and the fear of contravening the Perishable Goods Act (in case any of it remained uneaten)."

It was this London group who were also the first to experiment with high frequency sound as a method of sabotage and the group was prolific in the amount of action that they were able to achieve. On 19th March 1966, the group even sabotaged two different packs during the same day. Of the morning's hit against the Old Berkeley Foxhounds at Amersham, the group wrote:

> *We definitely annoyed them this time despite not being able to draw the hounds away. They got wise to our holloas and kept doubling back on themselves. The car supporters were the most annoyed, and some even seemed on the verge of tears (females included). At one point in a wood the dogs were only about 30 yards behind a fox and in cases like, with a well-trained pack, we stand little chance of stopping them (neither does the huntsman), although we did spray aniseed across their path but they went straight through it. The fox escaped, though and we left early in order to hit [the Eton College Beagles].*

Above: Dave Wetton calling hounds, c.1965

Above: Dave Wetton protesting at a BFSS (British Field Sports Society) AGM at the Piccadilly Hotel, 1965

Opposite: Cicely Norman protests at a meet of the Devon and Somerset Staghounds, March 1957

The group of twelve saboteurs then duly headed to Rose Hill near Henley-on-Thames to hit the Eton College Beagles:

> *They were completely confused after our arrival. We sprayed the dogs, who were screaming after a hare, with Antimate spray (perfectly harmless) and they lost the scent completely. Eventually the police were sent for and we had to promise not to go on to the private land. By this time, though, their hunting day had been practically ruined and as far as we could ascertain, they did not actually hunt any more. On leaving, we saw them coming down towards us on the road, so let them have a few horn blasts and holloas, and managed to turn them back on their tracks again, the kennelman's adjectives echoing back loud and clear until they disappeared from view.*

Pop singer, Lady Lee even joined the group on one occasion against the Cowdray Foxhounds in 1965, the same hunt at which saboteurs had the amusement of witnessing a local homeowner throw a bucket of water over one of the riders just the week before.

A Growing Force

Although the first year of the HSA's existence ended with no more than half a dozen groups with no real central organisation, things were soon to grow. Between 1965 and 1966, new groups from Warwickshire, Hampshire, Cambridge, Northampton, Brighton, Hertfordshire, Yeovil and Essex University sprang into action and the first Northern hit occurred in October 1966 when a group from Keighley sabotaged a meet of the Airedale Beagles at Silsden. The University of Essex Anti-Bloodsports Society had first emerged in 1965 with the intention of organising a system of anti-bloodsports associations in universities throughout the country and as such was not officially involved in direct action. However, the group was revived in 1967 and soon became a fully-fledged hunt saboteur group. On the whole, these local groups acted autonomously but did meet up for the occasional joint hit. There was even talk of a Dumfriesshire group around this time but no contact was ever made.

The latter half of the decade proved to be quieter than the early eagerness of the HSA's formation. There were of course still hits on both fox and otter hunts, but these were not as regular as before. Some new wildlife protection groups did begin to appear at the end of the 1960s, primarily due to a lack of central organisation, such as the South London League Against Cruel Sports group (which later became Wild Animals Protection Society), Direct Action Against Bloodsports (DAABS) and the Dorset-based Campaign for the Relief of Wildlife (CROW) who Wetton once described as 'a great bunch of hippies who often got thrown in the rivers by the otter hunters!' CROW's first strike was against the Purbeck Beagles on 17th October 1970. The action received national coverage in the press amid hysterical and fictitious accusations of hounds being blinded by hair lacquer sprays which in actual fact were harmless Antimate sprays, as was later clarified on *Radio Bristol*. As well as sabotaging hunts, CROW's activities also included other forms of helping wildlife, such as rescuing oiled-up seabirds and cleaning litter from local rivers used as rubbish dumps.

During this period of relative quiet, it was Wetton who tirelessly provided the energy and took up a lot of the work involved in ensuring the continuation of the HSA. On 14th May 1968, Marcus Lipton tried another attempt at abolishing stag hunting when he introduced the Stag-Hunting with Hounds (Abolition) Bill, but unfortunately failed once more.

As the 1960s came to an end, anti-hunting groups were becoming frustrated with the general inertia towards stopping hunting with hounds. However, this was short-lived and with a new decade came a renewed enthusiasm for direct action in the name of animal rights.

DEMANDS
OUT LAW THIS
CRUELTY
CRUEL SPORTS
PLEASE HELP IN REMOVING THIS BLOT
RTT 585
Popular

STAG HUNTING

Above: A stag killed by the Devon and Somerset Staghounds, 26th August 1982

Save Our Stags

Of all types of hunting with hounds, perhaps the most cruel and despised bloodsport is that of deer hunting. Stag hunting remains a strange subsection of the hunting fraternity as the number of staghound packs in the UK in recent years stood in the single digits, whereas the number of foxhound packs averaged at around two hundred. Due to the nature of the bloodsport, each hunt was able to attract a vast number of supporters, far greater than that of fox hunts. Nevertheless, this abhorrent activity could not be allowed to continue unchallenged and there were many who ventured into the wilds of the South West to stop the deer hunters in their tracks.

Following on from the successes of earlier hits against stag hunts in the West Country, a number of saboteurs in the area joined forces and formed the Save Our Stags (SOS) campaign in 1973. The main driving force behind SOS was Ian Pedlar, who had had the idea of forming a splinter group within the HSA that solely focused on the issue of deer hunting, after being inspired by the Save Our Seals Campaign led by Northampton HSA's Rorke Garfield. Having learnt much about how best to disrupt deer hunting from numerous hits during the previous seasons, meetings were held with many HSA groups across the West Country and later an inaugural meeting took place in Crewkerne to finalise plans for the upcoming campaign. The original committee comprised of Ian Pedlay, Brian Roach, Sue Smith, Marley Jones and Patrick Hirst, who acted as the liason officer with the HSA.

The press were generally sympathetic towards the anti-deer hunting lobby with the *Sunday Mirror* praising the launch of SOS with a front and centre page spread entitled, 'DEER HUNT HORROR'. The article, dated 11th March 1973, described a horrific ordeal in which a stag was chased for twelve miles over the Quantock Hills before being killed in the small Somerset village of Williton.

Bloodied Quantocks

SOS began life campaigning against stag hunts generally but towards the end of the 1978/79 season had become involved in a war of attrition against the Quantocks Staghounds. The group had made it their stated aim to shut down the hunt after a meet on 28th April 1979 in which the hunt had chased a stag for seven hours straight. Hunt riders rode down and whipped saboteurs throughout the day and instigated three pitched battles which led to fifteen activists requiring hospital treatment. A saboteur witnessed the kill at 7.56pm whereby three attempts were made to shoot the stag before the animal's throat was eventually slit. The AGM of the Quantock Staghounds was later stormed by ten hunt saboteurs who released stink bombs and smoke flares. Despite numerous scuffles within the Taunton Castle Hotel, all ten managed to escape without arrest.

With the SOS so publicly focusing on one particular hunt, supporters of the Quantock Staghounds became evermore infuriated. During the 1979/80 season, the tyres of SOS's vehicles were slashed, the windscreens smashed and on a few occasions brake pipes were cut and sugar poured into the petrol tanks. Retaliation came from the ALF who damaged any vehicle that was found to have connections with the hunt. The SOS also took measures to prevent themselves from becoming the victims of attack, as Ian Pedlar describes in his book, *Save Our Stags*:

> *Another toy we played with during this period was a Land Rover that had been fitted with a ramming-bar. With two sockets welded each side of the bonnet, complimented with a V-shaped contraption similar in shape to the cow-pushers familiar on early American trains which could be slotted into place whenever needed, it made a fearsome weapon. It was only used twice and then abandoned on advice of the police who gently pointed out something along the lines of "next time" and "throw the key away."*

The violence continued to escalate the following season as two brothers who supported the Quantocks Staghounds would drive across the hills on motorbikes to find any saboteurs and report back to the main bulk of the supporters to head that way and give them a hiding. Almost every week between the 1979/80 and 1982/83 seasons saw at least one hit of Quantock Staghounds by SOS. Mass hits were organised every four to six weeks with HSA groups from as far as Luton, Merseyside, and the West Midlands meeting at Bridgewater before driving in convoy across the Quantock Hills.

The courageous acts of SOS were many, as one of the group, Marley Jones, recalled in the American magazine, *Agenda*:

> *The most exhilarating moment I had was on 1st January 1981, during a meet of the Quantock Staghounds. We saw hounds and riders streaming past us over the brow of a hill in fast pursuit of a red deer hind.*
>
> *We were able to circle the hill and race on foot into the combe where we thought she was heading, and arrived just in time to see her coming towards us at full speed. She was covered in sweat, out of breath, her tongue hanging to one side. We froze until she passed, and then we saw the hounds almost upon her. We charged behind her, covering the ground with false scent and at the same time pushing the hounds back with our hands.*
>
> *At this point the hunt master and a number of riders appeared and we were forced to retreat. But the hind was safe! I think that as long as I live the elation felt by all of us will stay with me.*

Another exceptional day was to occur on 20th April 1981 when the Quantock Staghounds were forced to change their Easter Monday meet from the Quantock Hills to a location in the centre of Exmoor in a vain attempt to avoid saboteurs. SOS successfully split the pack with over half of the hounds called in the wrong direction and not recovered until late in the evening. Around 30 riders from the hunt also entered the League's Gilmore Farm sanctuary, close to Dulverton. Having spotted that they had been photographed doing so, the riders then attempted to smash the saboteurs' camera. A further fight soon broke out as hunt supporters smashed the windscreen of an anti-hunt van taking reinforcements to the original fracas. The fight turned particularly nasty and during the battle a number of riders were even dragged from their mounts and seriously injured.

The Last Stand

During the 1982 season, the hunt took the decision to stop hunting on a Saturday due to the disruption caused by antis. Contrary to many pro-hunt rumours, many on the anti-hunt side worked full time and as such very few saboteurs were able to attend midweek actions. As opposed to the more confrontational tactics employed at the weekends, the four or five saboteurs who sabotaged the staghounds midweek often opted for more covert operations such as sneaking through woods the night before a meet to flush out a harboured stag from where he was being kept to be hunted. The repeated violence faced by saboteurs did eventually take its toll as many veterans went into retirement, worn down by constant injuries as a result of their hard work protecting wildlife. As such, the last full scale attempt to disrupt a stag hunt was made on 14th April 1984 as SOS pitted themselves against the Devon and Somerset Staghounds. Perhaps as was to be expected, fighting broke out almost immediately when the hunt left their meet at Brendon Two Gates, near Simonsbath. A police helicopter flew above the saboteurs as ten people were injured in the melee. Fortunately, however, although the hunt did manage to locate two stags, both were able to escape with their lives.

Above: A stag is killed by the Devon and Somerset Staghounds, 29th October 1981

Ian Pedlar said of the day:

> *The end came some miles from the meet, near the village of Winsford, when the entire mounted field charged the saboteurs. Most antis remained in their vehicles whilst riders lashed out with their crops. Angry and frustrated, I stood my ground and started lashing back with the battered walking stick that had been my constant companion throughout the SOS campaign. I would be joined by a solitary saboteur (a magnificent fellow with a bright yellow Mohican haircut I was later informed answered to the name Sunflower) and we maintained a 'back to back' until the last rider had passed. This 'last stand' had proved prophetic, for it confirmed what we had known for some time: that day of the stag hunt saboteur was over, but it had allowed us to bow out in style.*

This hit proved to be the final action on the day of hunting itself for the group, although night time excursions to flush harboured deer still occurred up until 1987.

Although some hits on stag hunts did continue to happen, these were by no means common. The violent nature of these hunts coupled with the sheer numbers of supporters that they attracted meant that sabotaging them was no mean feat. Stag hunts also understandably attract some of the very worst types of people as is typified by serial animal abuser John Norrish, who was the huntsman of the Tiverton Staghounds between 1995 and 2012 until he was jailed for four years in 2012 for raping a female follower of the hunt at their July 2011 ball.

Left: A young child examines the body of a stag just killed by the Devon and Somerset Staghounds, 8th October 1981

Opposite Right: The huntsman of the Devon and Somerset Staghounds carves up a body of a stag at Wheddon Cross, 25th August 1981

1970S: A GROWING MOVEMENT

HOWL NO. 1 5p
Hounds off our wildlife
MAGAZINE OF THE HUNT SABOTEURS ASSOCIATION
11 BRUNSWICK ROAD, KINGSTON, SURREY

Hi there!

Welcome to the first edition of the Hunt Saboteurs Association magazine.

We hope that this will go some way towards bridging the communications gap amongst our own members and also outline some of our activities to our many supporters.

HOWL is essentially a newsletter, wherein we can compile all those interesting snippets from local papers that you send in.

It's also a viewsletter, not grinding it's own axe, but a platform where all those concerned with animal welfare can air their opinions on different aspects. So please let us have lots of articles, cuttings, cartoons or letters. We want to make No. 2 even better.

Good anti-huntin'.

Dave & Hilde

SABOTEURS V. SEAL HUNTERS

THE WATERS of the Wash, so recently threatened by a huge oil slick, have seen yet another dark stain drifting across the waters. But this time there was no panic, no questions in Parliament, no clean-up squad. For the slick was blood. And it was spilt with the sanction of the law in a clinical, deadly but perfectly legal game. The name of the game – Seal Cull.

Rorke Hospitalised

Rorke Garfield, East Anglia H.S.A. organiser has gone into hospital for the fourth time for an operation on his wrist, after he was whipped by Nally of the Oakley Hunt last October. He has spent £150 in legal costs, trying to sue Nally for compensation. He has received £65 from an appeal in the last newsletter.

He is also trying to raise funds for a landrover, a boat, and a diving suit, for next year's seal cull on the Wash. Amongst his schemes to raise funds locally was a sponsored cannon tow!

Rorke is desperately short of money, having also spent £123 on sabotage materials recently. Any donations would be like manna from heaven. Please send whatever you can spare direct to Rorke at 65 Lower Thrift Street, Northampton.

FACT

25 otters were killed in Britain in 1971 (16 of these were in Scotland and Wales). Eastern Counties have killed one this year, Border Counties have murdered four.

HUNTS A PEST?

BOVVER BOYS ACTIVE

Above: The first issue of *HOWL*, 1973

Hounds Off Our Wildlife

By 1970, the number of hits against fox hunts averaged 200 per season. The Hunt Saboteurs Association was starting to formalise its structure and held its first recorded General Meeting in July 1971. 25 people attended and a constitution was approved. A biannual newsletter was also established in the same year to tell the public of the deeds done in the name of direct action. Adverts were placed in *Private Eye*, *The Vegetarian* and the *New Musical Express* looking for new recruits. Membership of the HSA doubled to over 800 in 1972, after *The Guardian* published a long and sympathetic article written by Jill Tweedie when she accompanied a group sabotaging an otter hunt. Although by 1974 the membership was back down to 300, this did include some famous members such as Monica Hutchings and Sir Patrick Moore. The network of anti-hunt activists was slowly growing too as the HSA was now able to boast of seventeen active groups across the country. It was decided that a proper magazine was needed to promote hunt sabotage, provide tactical and legal advice as well as news from the frontlines. The first issue of *HOWL* (*Hounds Off Our Wildlife*) was published in late 1973 with Dave McCalden as editor. The committee meetings were then held at various places across London including the Peace News offices on Caledonian Road, Kings Cross, occasionally sharing the space with other radical organisations such as the Gay Liberation Front.

The London group remained by far the most active at this point in time, visiting many packs throughout the South East and beyond. In the 1970/71 season alone, the group managed to hit twelve different hunts including the West Kent Hunt, the Essex Union Hunt, the Fernie Hunt and the Eridge Hunt. At the Eridge's opening meet the 13 saboteurs in attendance (including four Tunbridge Wells Young Libs) had to do what they could in the face of the 500 hunters in attendance. On 8th May 1971, the group travelled over to Suffolk to hit the Eastern Counties Otterhounds at Chelsworth. The saboteurs outnumbered the hunters 28 to 20 and had much success with the horn and the spray despite the hounds sadly managing to kill a moorhen. Two months later (and with many hits in between), on 17th July, the group headed to Snelsdon to sabotage the Buckinghamshire Otterhounds. The day proved to be a successful one, with the saboteurs holloaing and immediately the hounds veering away from the river and towards the next field entrance where a saboteur was waiting with packets of extremely foul-smelling sardines. The group of saboteurs split but five managed to stay with the hunt until they finished at 5.30pm. One saboteur had even been taken ill during the day and had fallen asleep behind a roadside hedge, only to stumble out when the rest of the group drove by!

The Yeovil group was also very active at the time, first venturing out on 31st October 1970 on an observation mission to the Seavington Hunt. The following Saturday, on their first day actually interfering with a hunt, the group headed to Yetminster, Dorset and experimented with trailing fox manure in order to confuse the hounds - but this had very little effect. They did, however, manage to keep up with the Blackmore Vale Hunt for three hours and successfully holloaed to confuse the hunt.

Whilst saboteurs were out in the fields, some were also attempting to gain political progress in the fight against bloodsports. On 26th November 1969, Labour MP Arnold Shaw introduced the Deer Hunting and Hare Coursing (Abolition) Bill after a series of letters from former stag hunter Richard Hall, detailing the gruesome practices of the stag hunts were printed in the national press. One excerpt read:

> *On one occasion a stag's right eye was shot out and it hung down its face; it turned away and trotted down the road to a stream, crying as it went. The pack of hounds were uncontrollable and got past the hunt servants and boiled over the stag, ravaging it all the time until whipped-off and a second shot killed it.*

However, the second reading of the bill failed even to reach a debate as pro-hunt Conservatives filibustered the previous bill, to deny time on the stag hunting issue. Clearly rattled by a growing movement to outlaw their bloodsport, the three staghound packs organised a joint meet and rally in Crowcombe, Somerset on 10th March 1970. On the day, around three hundred riders as well as over two thousand supporters were in attendance to hear speeches about how they were 'animal lovers in practice and not just in theory'. When *The Somerset County Gazette* asked master Sir Bernard Waley-Cohen if he was surprised that no counter demonstrations were made by hunt saboteurs, he replied with the thinly veiled threat: "Not in the least. They know very well what happens to them down here. They know that if they come and try to make a nuisance of themselves by one of those indecent and undesirable hullabaloos, very short shrift will be given them." In actual fact, a few hunt saboteurs did attend the meet after spending the morning trying to flush deer from the surrounding woods. Sadly, however, the hunt did manage to kill a young stag after a two hour chase.

1973 also saw the HSA undertake one of its most successful campaigns of its then ten year existence when various local groups, coordinated by Northampton saboteur, Rorke Garfield, sabotaged the annual seal cull in the Wash. The campaign attracted very favourable press coverage and as a result strong public support. After two weeks of the campaign, the cull was ended with the hunters falling 47 seals short of their quota of 380. Largely due to the huge public support the campaign gained, Home Secretary, Roy Jenkins, announced the following year that licences would not be granted for the 1974 cull, just a few days before the killing was due to start.

Television Breakthrough

The first major breakthrough for the HSA came in the form of the BBC's *Open Door* programme. With the HSA being more active than ever, it was decided to apply for a slot on the programme. The application was successful and Iain MacNay and Dave Wetton were invited to their first meeting with the TV team on 7th November 1975 where they were informed that due to a vacancy suddenly arising, they were to go out just fifteen days later. A frantic rush to find decent footage ensued as most of the BBC's clips of hunt sabotage were missing. Bob Smith, the cameraman for the Wild Animals Protection Society was kind enough to let them use his 8mm films of hare coursing and the WAPS in action but after the *Open Door* team went through them, they were told that much of the quality was too low. Time was fast running out but an unlikely saviour soon came in the form of the Tickham Hunt. On Saturday 15th November, 40 saboteurs from WAPS, Weald, Brighton and Essex went to take on the Tickham Hunt along with a BBC camera crew at their meet in Stockbury, Kent. Throughout the day, the group was managing to distract a few of the hounds but when the hunt entered Detling Aerodrome, they succeeded in taking control of the whole pack. Unsurprisingly, this infuriated the hunt and a large brawl broke out which left some of the saboteurs needing treatment at Maidstone's West Kent Hospital. The incident made national headlines and suddenly the HSA had its material for the show. Two saboteurs who had been there on the day, Fred Piddock and Jenny Simpson, were taken to the recording studio to record their version of events and share the benefits of hunt sabotage. Before long, the big day arrived. It was 22nd November and the 20 minute programme consisted of a mixture of Wetton, McNay and Sue Hough, old BBC archive footage and some of WAPS's 8mm footage as well as the interviews with Piddock and Simpson.

Despite the British Field Sports Society (a pro-hunt lobbying organisation and the precursor to the Countryside Alliance) trying its hardest to prevent a second showing of the programme, it was nevertheless repeated a week later. The reaction was astonishing with the HSA receiving around 3,000 responses. The only other *Open Door* programme to get a bigger response was their show on cystitis! The majority of the responders became members and as a result the HSA was able to set up many local groups in places they had never existed before.

Above: Saboteurs put up a sign saying 'BEWARE SADIST!' by a road near a meet of the Surrey Union Hunt, 10th April 1976

Above: Dave Wetton calls the hounds away from the Enfield Chace Foxhounds, 16th November 1974

Opposite page: Saboteurs follow behind a supporter of the Croome and West Warwickshire Foxhounds, 24th November 1979

The police continued to prove themselves to be distinctly biased in favour of those who killed animals for fun, perhaps because many of whom had very powerful positions within society, being rich landowners, judges, barristers, politicians, etc. Both the police and the law courts time and again chose to stifle lawful, non-violent disruption and instead turn a blind eye to the criminal violence dished out. One of the vast number of incidents proving this occurred in Sussex in December 1979 when three members of the East Sussex and Romney Marsh Hunt attacked a group of saboteurs. Two of the hunt supporters, Kevin Barton and Michael Bullen were later found guilty of causing actual bodily harm yet evaded punishment by being given an absolute discharge. On refusing to be bound over, Keith Bird and Mervyn Dallas, who were two of the saboteurs that were subjected to the assault, were sentenced to six months imprisonment after the court evoked the Justices of the Peace Act, which dates from 1361! After spending a night inside, the pair reluctantly agreed to be bound over.

The Band of Mercy

Whilst the activities of the HSA took place largely on the day of hunting, there were those who felt that different tactics were needed to prevent the hunt from even going out. During 1973, a group named the Band of Mercy started a campaign of trashing hunt vehicles from the Whaddon Chase, the Vale of Aylesbury and the Puckeridge and Thurlow. The Band of Mercy arose from the Luton hunt saboteur group, a particularly militant group that Ronnie Lee and others set up in 1971. The Band of Mercy was also responsible for the animal liberation movement's first known act of arson. On 10th November 1973, two of the group set fire to a vivisection laboratory that was being built by Hoechst Pharmaceuticals near Milton Keynes. The blaze caused £26,000 of damage, but the pair returned six days later to burn what remained of the building. This form of economic sabotage received mixed reactions at first by some hunt saboteurs but as time went on, more and more activists began to see the benefits of such actions. At this early stage of the organisation, and of the movement as a whole, the HSA was worried that such overt law breaking would bring the anti-hunt movement into disrepute and even went so far as to offer a reward of £250 for information on the Band of Mercy (not, it must be noted, to hand over to the police but to be 'dealt with' internally). Later years would see the HSA grow closer to more radical groups such as the Animal Liberation Front, inviting members to write to animal liberation prisoners and publicising ALF raids through *HOWL*.

Expelling the Fascists

At this point in time, the HSA was largely an apolitical organisation, focused solely on wildlife protection and having a membership from a wide variety of political ideologies. Rather incredulously, committee member Dave McCalden was even also a member of the National Front. However, for most this was a step too far and a dispute broke out with some arguing that McCalden's fascist sympathies were bringing the HSA into disrepute whilst a small minority held the view that no one should be expelled on the grounds of their political ideology. This came to a head at the 1979 AGM whereby a motion that called for the expulsion of McCalden was passed with 84 votes in favour, 15 against and 10 abstentions - McCalden was dismissed as a result. Another motion was also put forward that no National Front members should be allowed to serve on the HSA committee. It was resoundingly passed with 109 votes in favour, 4 against and 9 abstentions. The latter motion also included some other points that there was to be 'no racism or nationalism ever to be used in HSA campaigns' (this was passed unanimously) and that the HSA would support the formation of a Vegetarians Against the Nazis group (this was passed with 64 votes for, 18 against and 38 abstentions). Later, in 1985, Milton Keynes-based Margaret Flynn was dismissed as a member of the HSA after her links with the Nazi organisation, November 9th Society were unearthed (it is important to note that Flynn soon denounced the group, after leaving her husband who ran the Milton Keynes branch,

FO
TO
EFK 209L

before going on to become a Labour councillor and dedicated animal rights activist). Also in 1985, Michael Fishwick, the then treasurer of the Norwich branch of the National Front was expelled from Norwich HSA as a result of his fascist sympathies. During this period there were rumours of fascist infiltration of hunt saboteur groups and of the animal rights movement more generally, however the press spun the situation out of all proportion and only a handful of such cases were ever found (and the fascists expelled when they were). Such incidents moved the HSA to solidify its anti-fascist position by adding a clause in its 1987 constitution that;

> **Membership or support of racist or nationalistic organisations that knowingly oppress humans or any sentient creature will preclude membership of the Association.**

In the early 1990s, the Belfast group was split apart when a self-confessed fascist, Stuart Pierce, attempted to join the group. He tried to convince other saboteurs to lean towards far right views, even sending a copy of the fascist magazine, *Final Conflict,* to groups in Essex. He didn't get very far as the vast majority of groups had (and still do have) a 'no compromise' approach when it comes to the far right. However, in order to officially counter any further attempts of infiltration, the HSA decided at its 1993 AGM to affiliate with Anti-Fascist Action, an organisation that both confronted fascism physically and ideologically. Indeed, the vast majority of hunt saboteurs have throughout the years also been active in anti-fascist struggles, with many HSA groups and anti-fascist groups overlapping somewhat in terms of personnel. In 2014, as a new anti-fascist umbrella organisation was becoming established (the Anti-Fascist Network) the HSA affiliated with the group to further solidify its anti-fascist roots.

The 1974/75 season saw 131 'strikes' (as they were then called) against hunts involving around 40 active groups. The East Midlands group was founded around this time and organised many forays into the countryside to hit the South Notts Hunt among others.

Desecration

In the latter half of the 1970s, one action in particular caused much uproar within the hunting fraternity. In the early hours of Sunday 23rd January 1977, a group of anti-hunt activists travelled to Saint Kentigern's Church in the Cumbrian village of Caldbeck where the grave of the famed huntsman, John Peel (1776 – 1854), was located. The grave is a shrine to fox hunting fanatics who view the man as some kind of legendary hero. Indeed, the year before the attack was the bicentenary of Peel's death and the hunting media was full of stories championing the life of this prolific killer, accompanied by photographs of his headstone decked out with all kinds of hunting memorabilia. Buoyed by the plethora of tributes to a man most hunters view as a father of fox hunting, the activists dug a hole into the grave and toppled the headstone, breaking off a small corner. A taxidermy fox head, bought from an antique shop, was left along with a note that read:

> **John Peel, John Peel come blow your horn,**
> **Come blow your horn till your face turns blue,**
> **No rest for the thousands of foxes you've torn,**
> **But at least this one's got the last laugh on you.**

The hunting community was furious. Immense pressure was put on the local police to find the perpetrators as the media was whipped into a frenzy with an inaccurate claim that Peel's remains had been exhumed and thrown in a cesspit. This was of course untrue, but rumours spread like wildfire across the hunting world and the chase was on to catch those involved. At Forton Services on the M6, a police officer happened to be checking number plates of vehicles to see if any were stolen and came across a car belonging to an anti-hunt protester. The entry on his computer read; 'Member animal liberation anti-bloodsport supporter CR0 TX 47 11.1.77. Refers'. Police officers followed the lead and raided the Gloucester bedsit of Mike Huskisson. A detective sergeant kindly allowed Huskisson to remove the film from his camera found in the flat but as Huskisson faked a blunder and began exposing the film, it was grabbed back. Crucially, half a frame of an innocent photograph of the group, taken the

Opposite page: Hunt saboteurs look after a stray hound from the Enfield Chase Foxhounds, 15th January 1977

Above: A run-on by hunt saboteurs to protest against the parade of hounds at the Stow-on-the-Wold show, 24th July 1976

Opposite page: Hunt saboteurs gather before attending the Zetland Foxhounds on 12th January 1980

same day as the incident, remained unexposed. Police traced the photograph back to Workington, some 25 miles south of Caldbeck, and found twelve possible combinations of the partly visible number plate of a car in the image, only one of which belonged to a green Fiat. The Fiat's owner happened to be visiting Workington and when contacted, gave the police the exact date the photograph was taken. Mike Huskisson, aged 24, along with Gary Treadwell, aged 21, and David Hough, a 48 year old company director were imprisoned for the act which caused just £70 of damage yet created huge outrage within the hunting community.

As well as the desecration of John Peel's grave, the 1976/77 fox hunting season saw the Warwickshire Hunt's point-to-point course trashed, the BFSS's offices broken into and files stolen, and at least 14 hunt kennels visited by ALF campaigners. In the hunting fields, however, the HSA was able to report that an average of 20 hunts were hit each week over the season and new groups in Exeter, Poole and Ireland also sprang into action during this period.

New Constitution

A new constitution was agreed in 1977, which along with numerous clauses on how the committee of the HSA was to be run, also contained four 'rules' for its members:

1. **Members shall not strike or in any way cruelly treat a hunt animal.**

2. **Members shall not offer violence to persons, nor intentionally provoke persons to violence and shall make every effort to avoid any situation which is bound to lead to a violent reaction against themselves whilst acting, or purporting to act, in furtherance of the policy of the association.**

3. **Comments to local press people may only be made by a recognised group officer or representative. Official comments on HSA policy should only be made by the Chairperson, Secretary, Treasurer or Press Officer of the Executive Committee.**

4. **Members should follow the Country Code as strictly as possible.**

In order to follow the 'Country Code' members were to:

1. **Guard against all risk of fire.**
2. **Fasten all gates.**
3. **Keep dogs under proper control.**
4. **Keep to the path across farmland.**
5. **Avoid damaging fences, hedges and walls.**
6. **Leave no litter.**
7. **Safeguard water supplies.**
8. **Protect wildlife, wild plants and trees.**
9. **Go carefully on country roads.**
10. **Respect the life of the countryside.**

Whilst the majority of these were easily and readily adhered to, such as protecting wildlife, not leaving litter, etc. trespassing was obviously necessary in order to effectively stop a hunt and therefore saboteurs tended to wave such rules when an animal's life was in danger. Ten years later, as the efficacy of the HSA led to an increase in violence by hunt supporters, the organisation chose to subtly relax its official policy on the issue of violence by altering the constitution so as to state:

> **The intention of the Association shall be at all times non-violent although genuine self-defence is the right of any person, the Association condones self-defence when necessary.**

Such was the effect of the HSA on the sick activities of hunters that fox hunter Douglas Leslie felt it necessary to write the following compliment in the 1978/79 issue of *Baily's Hunting Directory*:

> *I feel myself bound to mention for yet another year, the undesirable activities of the self-styled 'Hunt Saboteurs', who still persist in defiling the countryside wherein we enjoy our sport. Their record throughout the year has been quite deplorable, and although many of them are now living behind prison bars at the rate payer's expense, their very presence at a meet is sufficient to ruin a day in the minds of many who love the country for what it is.*

This was music to the antis' ears!

OTTER AND MINK HUNTING

TOYOTA

CVJ 753V

Saving the Mustelids

With the fox and hare hunting season spanning most of the autumn and winter, otter, and later mink, hunting fills the gap in the summer months for bloodsports enthusiasts to get their twisted kicks. Despite naturalists noting a decline in the otter population from the 1950s onwards, 1,065 otters were killed by the 11 otterhound packs in England and Wales between 1958 and 1963.

Otter hunts had been sabotaged since the very early days of the Hunt Saboteurs Association, with the London group (along with others) visiting the likes of the Courtenay Tracy Otterhounds, Bucks Otterhounds and the Cheriton Otterhounds, to name a few. On 11th September 1965, three members of the group attended a rather daunting triple meet of the Crowhurst Otterhounds, the Kendal and District Otterhounds and the Eastern Counties Otterhounds at Udimore near Hastings which comprised of around 80 hunt supporters. However, it seemed someone else was keen to stop the Eastern Counties from killing too:

> *[We] sprayed as much as possible but [the] situation [was] somewhat explosive since some unsporting 'bounders' (at least their word did begin with 'b') had apparently put the ECOH hound van out of action for a while just a few weeks earlier. Wonder who that was! No otters caught this day, which must have been a pity for the K and DOH as they'd come all the way from the Lake District.*

In 1976, the Mid Wales Wildlife Conservation group was very active against the Border Counties Otterhounds, a particularly ruthless band of animal abusers. In June of that year, the hunt and its supporters violently set about five of the antis present at one meet, as they're two children looked on. In retaliation, the HSA mustered 90 saboteurs to hit the hunt the following Saturday (June 26th) at Llandinam, near Newtown. Unfortunately, however, security had lapsed and the hunt were forewarned that a large contingent of saboteurs was due that day. Soon after the hunt set off, the hounds caught the scent of an otter on the edge of a nearby lake. Saboteurs rushed in to confront the hunt staff but suddenly, out of the wooded slopes to their left, came 50 or so hunt supporters armed with four foot staves who swiftly ambushed the unprepared saboteurs. Jaws and noses were broken as the saboteurs were pushed back onto the road, caught totally unawares at the level of violence dished out. By the time the group reached the road, the police had arrived but viewed the scene with complete disinterest. "We're only local police, we don't want to get involved" was their reply when asked if they would take statements from the many bloodied activists. The day proved to be a wake up call for the movement as such pacifist action was simply no match for burly farmhands more than keen to attack anybody interfering with their 'sport'.

From Otter to Mink...

After the otter was given protected status in 1978 following severe persecution from hunters, the vast majority of otter hunts simply changed their name and started hunting mink instead. Despite many terriermen and other members of fox hunts taking part in the 'sport', it is by no means as widespread as other bloodsports. For example, there were only an estimated 21 mink hunts operating in Britain by the summer of 1985 and this number has only gone down since. Mink hunters are an extremely shy breed of wildlife abuser. Meeting times and places are very rarely advertised and as each hunt covers a vast area of land, finding meets can often be a tricky task.

1986 proved to be a vintage year for those involved against the riverside bloodsport as local groups (mainly from the South) continued their campaign. On July 19th, the Exeter group paid one of many visits to the Devon and Cornwall Minkhounds after a tip off from a rural sympathiser that they were meeting at Fingle Bridge on Dartmoor. On arrival the saboteurs met a few bewildered hunt supporters but crucially, no hounds. A second tip off soon reached its way

Above: Brighton HSA and Tunbridge Wells HSA stop the Kent and Sussex Minkhounds

Opposite page top left: Cotswold HSA arrive at a meet of the Three Counties Minkhounds, 7th May 1983

Opposite page top right and bottom: Saboteurs descend on a meet of the Three Counties Minkhounds, 7th May 1983

Above: Saboteurs from Leeds, Manchester, Liverpool and Nottingham surround the Dove Valley Minkhounds' van and stop any attempt at hunting, 1993

Opposite page top: Ytene supporters try to overturn a saboteurs' van near Keevil after the day's hunting was stopped prematurely, 1992

Opposite page bottom left: Saboteurs follow the Ytene Minkhounds near Great Somerford, Wiltshire

Opposite page bottom right: New Forest saboteurs stay in the river to avoid arrest at the Ytene Minkhounds, 1991

to the group that the hunt was actually just down the road at Drewsteignton and within minutes a saboteur was sat on the bonnet of the hound van preventing it from leaving until their minibus arrived to block it in. After an hour's delay, 15 police officers escorted the opposing sides to a new meet near Okehampton but due to the unsolicited horn blowing and hollas coming from the group of antis, the hunt once again failed to catch anything.

Taking on the Ytene

The Dorset-based Ytene Minkhounds bore the brunt of anti-hunt activity and the 1991 season proved no different. They were subjected to consistent and effective sabotage throughout the summer, with the North Dorset, Bath, Bristol, Yeovil, Winchester, New Forest, West London, Bournemouth and Oxford groups all paying the group of blood junkies a visit. The first hit, on 4th May, saw 60 saboteurs prevent the hunt from even leaving their meet at Fifehead Magdalen. Just over a week later, 130 saboteurs trashed an evening meet and the huntsman, Tony Smart, was forced to blow for home after only an hour. During the summer of 1992, the Ytene encountered saboteurs on 24 occasions which included virtually every Saturday meet. This particular hunt had a fearsome reputation at the time, with many violent thugs from within the hunting community travelling down to Dorset simply to fight with the antis. This did not deter saboteurs, however, as activists from all across the country would join their southern comrades to lend support whenever they could. For example on one occasion, when a large number of hunt thugs were about to launch an all out attack on members of the local group, they were suddenly forced to reconsider when saboteurs from the Bolton, Liverpool and Oxford groups stormed onto the scene. The hunters withdrew and packed up straight after. Scuffles were a common occurrence when the hunt were met with antis but the sustained campaign against the Ytene achieved great successes and saved the lives of many mink. Saboteurs were always willing to put themselves in harm's way to protect these mustelids. This was particularly demonstrated at one meet when a dig-out had to be abandoned after the spades that the hunters were using to get at a mink who had gone to ground ended up at the bottom of the River Frome.

Blockades of the kennels were a common occurrence and the Ytene eventually decided to give up trying to hunt on a Saturday and instead took to meeting at random times to avoid saboteurs.

The 1990 season saw even more pressure mounted onto the mink hunting community despite the usual difficulties in obtaining meets. On one hit, due to the fact that they were severely outnumbered by supporters of the Four Shires Minkhounds, four members of Oxford HSA chose to run ahead of the hounds as they worked their way up the River Enlode near Shipton under Wychwood and sprayed and beat the riverbank. This meant that the mink were safe and virtually no contact was made with the hunt staff. There was a very different feeling at a hit against the Northamptonshire Minkhounds, however, and more than a hundred saboteurs from thirteen groups faced a group of hunters half that size along with a small army of police officers, including a helicopter and an officer from Essex on the animal rights squad who was over on an intelligence gathering mission. Despite the huntsman saying that he had had two day's notice of the planned sabotage, no attempts were made to change the meet and the day was spent by saboteurs calling his pack in various directions with little interference from the police. Another joint hit was later organised against the same hunt at Cattingham, although this time the hunt didn't even leave the kennels on advice of the police.In the North, the West Yorkshire Minkhounds would occasionally see saboteurs and, in 2000, good news came in the form of the Mid Cheshire Minkhounds disbanding.

A Revival

Renewed pressure was applied to mink hunts in the 2010s. On Saturday 10th May 2014, over 60 activists successfully sabotaged two mink hunts in the Midlands. A blockade of

Top: Tony Smart threatens saboteur Joe Hashman

Bottom: A Bristol saboteur stands next to a member of the Three Counties Minkhounds, 17th August 2017

Opposite page: Ytene huntsman, Tony Smart, is surrounded by saboteurs, 24th July 1993

the Dove Valley Minkhounds' kennels stopped their day's activities from even starting. As one van-full of saboteurs stayed at their kennels to ensure they didn't attempt to sneak out, the rest headed for the Northamptonshire Minkhounds who were hunting on the River Kym, near Kimbolton, on the Bedfordshire/Cambridgeshire border. As the group descended on the hunt, hounds were spotted chasing a hare but upon becoming aware that he was not alone, the huntsman simply gathered up the hounds and finished hunting for the day. Just two weeks later, the Devon and Cornwall Minkhounds suffered their first hit in over ten years as saboteurs as far away as Berkshire and South Wales forced the hunt to pack up early without any chance to even find any mink. Not long after, on 31st May 2014, dozens of saboteurs gathered at the kennels of the Dove Valley Minkhounds. Whilst in Devon a further 40 saboteurs attended a meet of the Culmstock Minkhounds at Exebridge. Both packs abandoned hunting for the day. On the same day, other saboteurs covertly monitored the Northamptonshire Minkhounds, who didn't leave their kennels, presumably due to the fact that a large number of saboteurs had gathered not too far away. Eight mink hunts were sabotaged during May 2014, meaning that after only one month of the season it was already the mink hunters' worst season in over a decade. Saturday 9th August saw hunt saboteurs disrupt a joint meet of the Three Counties Mink Hunt and Teme Valley Minkhounds at their meet in Aston Cantlow, Warwickshire, which took the number of packs sabotaged that summer to 11, over half of the mink hunts then active within the UK.

Mink hunting has suffered a terminal decline in recent years and many packs are prone to simply packing up when faced with the presence of saboteurs. This was certainly the case on 19th August 2017 when saboteurs from Bath, Bristol, South Wales and Severn Vale visited the elusive Three Counties Mink Hunt at Michaelchurch Escley in Herefordshire. After the saboteurs' arrival, the hounds were simply boxed up and driven all the way back to their kennels in Kinnersley, Worcestershire. From the start of the 2018 season until June that year, the Northants Minkhounds, The Dove Valley Minkhounds and the Culmstock Minkhounds had all suffered visits from saboteurs.

Long gone are the days of mass hits and pitched battles against mink hunts and their followers. Since the bloodsport was outlawed in 2005 with the arrival of the Hunting Act, mink hunts have been forced underground and have become extremely elusive. Their following has dwindled to a small hardcore of supporters. As such, finding out the locations and times of meets is still often a difficult task. Despite this, local saboteur groups continue to hit mink hunts during the summer months.

HARE HUNTING

Top: Saboteurs steal the pack at the Northumberland Beagling Festival, 1989

Bottom: Clinkard Beagles pack up early, January 1992

Opposite page top: The Surrey and North Sussex Beagles are halted in their tracks by North Downs HSA, 1986

Opposite page bottom: Saboteurs wrestle with the Aldershot Beagles hunt staff, 1986

Next double page: Saboteurs ruin the Northumberland Beagling Festival, 1989

In Defence of Lagomorphs

Throughout the years, saboteurs have also taken action against beagle packs, harrier packs and on occasion basset packs who hunt another iconic British mammal; the hare. Beagle packs (and basset packs) differ from foxhound packs in that they are hunted on foot rather than on horseback and as a result are much easier to keep up with in the field and effectively stop. This makes thwarting the hunt's efforts much easier as it is far harder to cast hounds across open fields with a bunch of antis walking alongside you. However, this does come with a slight drawback in that both hunt staff and supporters, having had their efforts frustrated and, having often traded insults with the saboteurs standing next to them throughout the day, have had a tendency to resort to fisticuffs. In recent years (especially after the Hunting Act came into force), however, the beagler (much like the mink hunter) has become a very shy and elusive breed and as such the main difficulty in sabotaging beagle packs has been actually finding them, as they more often than not simply pack up upon sighting any saboteurs. Since the formation of the HSA, beagling has suffered a huge loss of support, with most hunts now made up of only a handful of people. For example, when the Kent-based Bolebroke Beagles were hit in 2018, the whole hunt comprised of a huntsman and two very young whipper-ins with just a few very elderly supporters lurking about.

Harrier packs are hunted on horseback in a very similar way to fox hunts and will chase both hares and foxes. As opposed to other quarry, a hare will more often than not run in large circles as they tend not to want to leave their familiar territory. These circles will become ever smaller as the hare tires, only breaking off from the circle in a last ditch attempt to avoid being caught. Whereas in fox hunting the hounds are cast through woodland, scrub and other areas in which foxes inhabit, hare hunting takes place across open fields where hares are most likely to be found. The brown hare population has declined by an estimated 80% over the past 100 years (the population was estimated at 817,500 in the UK as of 1995) and although the two major factors causing this are shooting parties and habitat loss, hunting hares with hounds has only added to the decline of these wonderful animals. Indeed, the hare is the only 'game' species in England and Wales not protected by a closed hunting season.

Northumberland Beagling Festival

Each year, a number of beagling festivals take place that in essence involve a number of packs getting together and hunting over a week-long period. Of course these have proved to be a prime target for sabotage and over the years both the Alston and the Northumberland beagling festivals have had their fair share of national hits against them. The lure of such a large group of animal abusers in one place proved too much for the HSA and in 1987 the organisation launched a campaign against the Northumberland Beagling Festival. At this point in time, the festival was at its peak, with up to five separate hunts a day and often up to 18 or 20 meets in the week. However, after continued sabotage, it was decided that the number of meets per day would be cut to two during the 1992 festival.

Despite the official festival being advertised to start on 21st September, some savvy local saboteurs thought better and managed to hit the Holme Valley Beagles on the morning of the 16th September, the week before. The Wick and District Beagles, who had travelled up from Bristol, were found the following morning but sadly the host pack (the Newcastle and District Beagles) killed that afternoon.

The event was a showpiece for the BFSS and on the first advertised day (21st), around 80 stewards were bussed in from the Borders and Humberside at an estimated cost of £15,000. Two TV crews were in attendance at the meet on the moors above Redesdale, along with the local MP and a police horsebox as well as a police helicopter circling overhead. Having to contend with the 150-strong crowd of supporters, the opening meet proved a tough one for the saboteurs as the Newcastle and District chopped a leveret very close to the crowd gathered at the meet, all according to plan.

Above: Saboteurs from Bath, Cotswolds and Swindon stop the RAC Beagles for two hours as they are forcibly removed from Major Gregory Phillips' land, 26th January 1985

Below: Saboteurs at the Alson Hare Week, 2014

The rest of the week also proved frustrating due to the large number of stewards present and the fact that public footpaths and access land were blocked. Despite this, much disruption was caused and many hares were certainly saved from hunts who had travelled a long distance to take part, such as the Newmarket Beagles who had made the journey from Essex and the Bolebroke Beagles from Kent. The latters' hearts sank as they spotted their nemeses, Tunbridge Wells HSA, who often sabotaged the pack down south and had also made the significant journey to Northumberland.

By 1993, the event only lasted four days and could only boast of one hunt per day. After seven solid years of campaigning, festival organisers were forced to abandon the 1994 festival completely. Rupert Gibson, a master of the Newcastle and District Beagles and the organiser of the festival was even quoted in a 1992 edition of *The Northern Echo,* making the obvious connection that;

> *The trouble is that we are seen by some of these people as a set of murdering bastards.*

It seems Gibson hit the nail on the head!

Alston Hare Week

Another beagling festival known as the Alston Hare Week would also receive unwanted guests throughout its existence. Although this orgy of pre-season hunting had largely escaped attention from saboteurs, a handful of brave activists did disrupt the entire week of killing in 1991 amid constant violence. Later, after rumours began to circulate that thirteen hares had been killed at the 2013 event, the HSA knew that something had to be done and in 2014, 20 saboteurs quietly made their way to Cumbria. A motorbike driven by one saboteur followed the hunters from their hotel to the first meet of the week at a remote farm. When the main body of saboteurs arrived the beaglers had nothing to do but to stand around before walking back down the road to pack up.

One evidently perceptive hunter summarised the situation quite well when he was overheard saying, "the antis have turned up and there's fucking loads of them!" With the use of a drone and an army of spotters, the saboteurs were able to find and turn up at each meet in the week, ensuring that no animals were killed - a miraculous reversal of the 2013 death toll. In 2015, with the aid of the Hare Preservation Trust, the HSA decided to go public with its campaign against Alston and distributed a leaflet to every house in the town, appealing for information about the event. The plan worked as the very real threat of sabotage and the knowledge that beagling hits were becoming more common (the Severn Vale Beagling Festival had suffered a national hit in February that year) persuaded the event's organiser, Simon Becket, to cancel 2015's Alston Hare Week completely. The 2016 event also suffered a similar fate. The Weardale and Tees Valley Beagles, who hosted the festival, were at this point a 'professional' pack, in that they had their own kennels and a paid employee to feed and hunt the hounds. However, due to the fact that the HSA had completely decimated the Alson Hare Week (the Weardale and Tees Valley Beagles' biggest money-earner), the hunt was forced to sell their kennels and resort to becoming an 'amateur' pack.

Although the Northumberland and Alston festivals received the most saboteur activity, other hare killing festivals were also duly wrecked by antis. For example, the 1990 North Wiltshire Hare Week was totally ruined by a mixed contingent of saboteurs from the Bath, Bristol, West Midlands, Cotswolds, West Somerset and Vale and Valleys groups. Clearly startled by the arrival of the sixteen antis present and worried that the Sandhurst and Military Beagles might not actually be able to make any kills that day, the police sent seven patrol cars, a riot van and a helicopter to protect the hunt. However, the police failed to show the following day when a supporter of the Warwickshire Beagles 'tried to forcibly remove a sab's horn and got a bloody nose for his trouble.' On the Thursday, the only kill (that the saboteurs were aware of) was made before they arrived. The success of the previous four days had infuriated both the beaglers themselves and the police, and as the saboteurs arrived to hit the Malborough College Beagles at their meet at Great

Somerford, they were greeted by a helicopter, a riot van, a police Range Rover, two patrol cars and a police motorbike. Despite this heavy police presence, the saboteurs were able to completely ruin the day's hunting, even calling the beagles and running with them for 200 yards. Such was the impact of concerted saboteur activity, that the festival's final meet was cancelled due to the previous five days of disruption.

Caught in the Brambles

As well as the mass hits of beagling festivals, saboteurs often attended regular meets of beagle packs throughout the season. Many hares' lives have been saved, such as on Boxing Day 1988, when one lucky hare had a narrow escape thanks to Tunbridge Wells HSA and West London HSA:

The Southdown and Eridge Hunt had stopped meeting on Tunbridge Wells Common (they used to do both Lewes and Tunbridge Wells on Boxing Day), so Tunbridge Wells Hunt Sabs went to the Bolbroke Beagles' meet north of Tonbridge. Sabs from West London also came down and at one point I was on my own with Aubrey Thomas. The pack had turned and was coming straight towards a farm house with a large 5ft brick wall that had a thick bramble patch at its base. A hare broke but for some reason rushed into the bramble patch followed by the hounds. We were right on top of this now and thought the hare was done for but I jumped into the brambles and pushed past the hounds who could make no headway due to the very thick brambles. It was chaos with Aubrey blowing his horn and calling the hounds back, hounds barking and yelping from the pain of the thorns and no hunter in sight. I managed to get past the hounds and saw the hare nearly to the wall. There was a gap so I was able to reach in and pick the hare up. The brick wall only ran two thirds the way around the farm house so I could see that the hare could escape from there so I was able to drop it over the wall unharmed (miraculously) where it made its escape.

I waded back out of the brambles with my legs and arms covered in deep scratches and tears to be confronted by the huntsman, Richard, literally red in the face from our sabbing. We just sat down laughing with the adrenaline and sheer joy of what we had achieved. I did have to buy a pair of new sabbing trousers due to the rips though.

Richard hated us because he had been up to the Northumberland Beagling Festival that year and was the opening pack. He turned up on the day only to be confronted by Tunbridge Wells Hunt Sabs who had also travelled to Northumberland!

One fine example (pictured right) of how a very small number of people can achieve amazing results when taking action against beagle packs occurred on 19th October 1999 when the Dunston Harriers met at Hardingham Hall in Norfolk. Three saboteurs were out on the hunt to prevent any kills from being made. At one point during the day, a hare was chased across an open field with the hounds very close behind her. She ran past Mike Huskisson, a monitor from the League Against Cruel Sports, and up a road towards the car of a caring young hunt saboteur, Tim Nickerson. Nickerson crouched behind his car to allow the hare to pass then rushed out onto the road in front of the quickly persuing hounds. By using voice calls and clapping his hands, Nickerson managed to stop the hounds, allowing the hare to make good her escape.

Above: A saboteur saves a hare from the Dunston Harriers near Hardingham Hall, Norfolk, 19th October 1999

National Beagling Day

In an attempt to bolster support of the dying bloodsport, the pro-hunt lobby introduced a 'National Beagling Day'. This event was a futile way of trying to attract more people to this 'sport' which continues to suffer a decline in supporters. National Beagling Day 2000 took place on November 18th and proved to be a complete shambles. Following a tip off from a friendly local, saboteurs had the details of meets of

three packs in the North West. The first hunt was the Cheshire Beagles. A group of saboteurs drove straight into the pub car park where the hunt was meeting and stayed with the hunt until they were forced to return to the meet empty handed a couple of hours later. After lunch, the hunters ventured out again, this time with the Royal Rock Beagles huntsman, Peter Jones, hunting hounds from his own pack as well as the Forest and District Beagles. This second attempt at killing hares was even worse than the first as he gave up after 30 minutes, declaring, "I'm going back. We can't get anything with this bloody lot here!" Only three hours of hunting took place with the huntsman having nothing to show for it other than slightly muddier britches.

Beagle Pack Liberation

Irritated by the then Labour government's procrastination over their pledge to ban hunting, the Animal Liberation Front conducted what would be the second theft of a beagle pack by animal rights activists when in the early hours of 5th January 2001, the Wye Beagles' kennels were raided. 46 of the hunt's 48 beagles were liberated and placed in loving homes, wiping out 53 years of breeding. Only one of the beagles, 'Sexton', was ever recovered by the hunt after a Bristol vet noticed damage to the dog's ear from an attempt at altering his tattoo linking him to the hunt. In a statement claiming responsibility for the raid, the ALF said:

> *As the Government procrastinates on their pledge to ban hunting and hunt sabs continue to risk their lives to protect our wildlife the Animal Liberation Front is taking matters into its own hands. All the dogs will be placed in loving homes.*

The hunt's luck had started to run out in the previous year when Wye College (who the pack was associated with) merged with the University of London's Imperial College. The new establishment banned them from hunting on the college estate's land before publicly denying any association with the hunt, forcing them to change their name from the Wye College Beagles to simply the Wye Beagles. The hunt would later disband in 2014 after 70 years of abusing wildlife around Kent. Quite a few beagle packs have some affiliation with top public schools, such as the Eton College Beagles, the Ampleforth Beagles and the Palmer Marlborough Beagles (who are a merger between the Palmer Beagles and the Marlborough College Beagles). Shockingly, when saboteurs from Berkshire visited a Tuesday meet of the Palmer Marlborough Beagles in March 2018, many of the whipper-ins and supporters were shipped to the meet in a school minibus belonging to Marlborough College, all of whom appeared to be students at the college. The beagles picked up on the scent of a hare in the field next to the meet. Fortunately for the hare, however, a group of saboteurs were hiding in a copse overlooking the farm, watching the whole thing. They immediately made themselves known, taking the huntsman completely unawares and forcing him to simply box up his hounds and head back to the nearby kennels.

Some beagle packs also have a strong military association. Six hunts were members of the Army Beagling Association and many packs including the Wilts and Infantry Beagles, the Catterick Beagles, the Purbeck and Bovington Beagles and the Britannia Beagles actually had their kennels on a military base.

With the exception perhaps for basset packs and minkhound packs, beagle packs are feeling the pressures of a dwindling support base most acutely, with many packs now struggling for survival. Secrecy has become the beagler's biggest ally in avoiding sabotage and the main issue for saboteurs in preventing hares from being killed by these hunts is the challenge of finding their meeting places. This of course has a huge knock-on effect for the long term viability of beagling and is one reason why the bloodsport is in such rapid decline today.

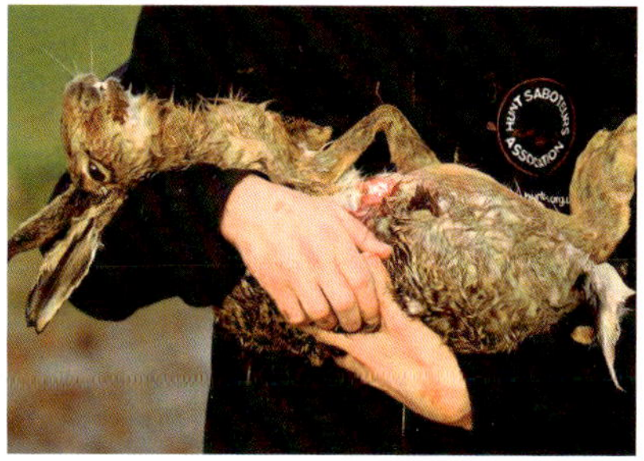

Opposite page: A Kernow saboteur keeps a close eye on the Lambo Beagles, 9th March 2019

Top: Saboteur Joe Hashman takes control of a beagle pack

Middle: A hare is chased by the Easton Harriers, 6th February 2016

Bottom: Norfolk and Suffolk Hunt Saboteurs retrieve the body of a hare killed by the Easton Harriers, 2016

Above: Saboteurs prevent the Westerby Bassets from killing hares, 1990

Opposite page top left: Oxford HSA steal the pack from the Four Shires Bassets, 1992

Opposite page top right: A saboteur pats one of the Leadon Vale Bassets after the hound van was intercepted before even reaching the meet, 10th March 2018

Opposite page bottom: Saboteurs escort the Four Shires Bassets back to the meet, 29th February 1992

Basset Packs

There are currently just seven registered basset packs in the UK, mostly in the Midlands and the South (due to the flatter terrain and lack of dry stone walls) and are governed by Masters of Basset Hounds Association, which was formed in 1912. Despite their rather ungainly appearance and stubby legs, basset hounds can be formidable hunters. The breed originated in medieval France and the first bassets to be imported to England were in 1866 by Lord Galway. The name, Basset, derives from the French word 'bas' meaning 'low'. Although the basset fraternity is regarded as somewhat of an eccentric minority within the world of hare hunting, the breed's exceptional scenting ability is often championed by those engaging in the bloodsport. There are even tales of packs hunting until darkness, then returning the next day to pick up the scent again.

In the winter of 1990, one such pack ended up on the receiving end of an anti-hunt strike when four vans, full of hunt saboteurs, cruised across the countryside of rural Leicestershire towards a meet of the Westerby Bassets. For many of the saboteurs, this was to be their first sight of a basset pack and the reaction on jumping out of the vans for some was simply to laugh. After all, how could an animal with such short legs and huge floppy ears ever hope to catch a hare? However, their amusement was short lived as the pack was soon in full cry and hot on the scent of a hare. Unlike excitable beagles, the bassets didn't check or overrun the line but instead each hound 'owned the line' as they ran across the field, making their characteristic deep cry. The saboteurs tried desperately to call the hounds off using horn and voice calls but to no avail. In the end, they had to resort to simply swamping the hunt staff with people and putting some of the hounds on makeshift leads in order to get them to stop.

In recent years, saboteurs have made an effort to visit basset packs more regularly, although hits on such packs are by no means common. In 2012, the first basset pack to appear again on the radar of the HSA was found quite by chance. Whilst covertly tailing the Eton College Beagle's hound van, saboteurs found themselves being led a great distance into the Essex countryside. The van arrived at what was revealed to be a joint meet at the invitation of the De Burgh and North Essex Harehounds. Having not had the attention of hunt saboteurs for quite some years, the De Burgh had become so complacent that when saboteurs suddenly appeared in the field and challenged them over their illegal hunting, they could not even produce a soiled rag on a length of string (as an alibi for a trail) but instead simply walked back to the meet in awkward, dejected silence.

Basset packs are universally struggling, with most packs having to share kennels with another hunt in order to survive; the Four Shires Bassets with the Old Berkeley Beagles, the East Lincolnshire Bassets with the Southwold Hunt, the Leadon Vale Bassets with the Ross Harriers and so on. Indeed, the Leadon Vale Bassets now typify the struggling bloodsport as the impact of both the Hunting Act and the activities of the Hunt Saboteurs Association have forced them to operate virtually underground and as a result, their following has dwindled to an aging core of supporters. Even the Westerby Bassets who, as stated above, presented problems for saboteurs in the 1990s, packed up almost immediately after two Nottingham saboteurs strolled into their meet in 2013. There has been one newly formed pack, however. The Woolaston Bassets, located in the Forest of Dean, were the first pack of hounds to be formed since the 2004 Hunting Act and had their first visit from saboteurs just a month after their first meet. A joint hit in 2017 proved once again the efficacy of saboteurs' actions against basset packs. Saboteurs from the South Wales, Bristol and Severn Vale groups planned a hit of the Woolaston Bassets' meet just up the road from their kennels in the small Gloucestershire village of Woolaston. The groups decided to meet up beforehand in the car park of a local Tesco superstore. Unbeknownst to them, however, supporters of the basset pack had spotted them and had informed the master, Norman Matthews. On hearing the news and making the obvious connection that the saboteurs were heading his way, Matthews simply left the hounds at the kennels and cancelled the day's hunting.

Top and bottom: Greyhounds course a hare

Opposite page: Dave Wetton and Ronnie Lee at the Oxfordshire Coursing Club, February 2nd 1974

Hare Coursing

Hare coursing is a particularly sinister and calculated bloodsport and dates back to 1776 when Lord Orford set up the first public coursing club, named the Swaffham Club, in Norfolk. Whilst not as popular as many other bloodsports, coursing did have a considerable following, with 23 local clubs registered with the National Coursing Club putting on approximately 100 days coursing each season in the early 1990s. This amounted to around 2200 individual courses run every single year. As well as such organised events, many hare coursers go out in small groups with lurchers and greyhounds (usually without the landowner's permission) in a more clandestine version of the 'sport'. Since the Hunting Act came into force, although the police have been very reluctant to target fox hunting, a concerted effort has been made to track down and arrest coursers, mainly due to the fact that coursing is generally considered a quite working class activity.

In its most famous form, static coursing, hares are scared into an arena by a line of beaters waving flags and shouting. The beaters take care to only push one hare at a time into the open field where a man known as the 'slipper' is waiting with two greyhounds. The 'slipper' then aligns the dogs so as to make sure they have an even sighting of the hare and when the hare is approximately 80 yards away, releases the dogs. As greyhounds would easily catch a hare over a straight sprint, the hare chooses to regularly change direction as the dogs are close, forcing them to overshoot and buying her some time. This is an impressive skill as the hare is able to turn extremely rapidly at full speed. Points are then award by a red coated judge on horseback to whichever greyhound manages to turn the hare. Although killing the hare is not the aim of the bloodsport, coursing supporters do regularly cheer voraciously whenever a hare is caught and disembowelled.

The early days of sabotaging coursing meets involved activists invading the arena during the meet and using a variety of devices such as smoke canisters, fireworks and gas-powered foghorns to frighten the hares in a different direction. This often provoked violence from supporters angry at their cruel pastime being ruined and so tactics later developed to include pre-beating the whole area around the meet a few hours beforehand to drive any nearby hares to safety. However, mobbing the events did have the added bonus that some courses would simply be called off, as was the case at a meeting of the Oxford Coursing Club in 1976 when fifteen out of the 23 courses had to be cancelled due to the 45 saboteurs present. During that same season, a saboteur appeared before a jury for the very first time. Caroline 'Cee' Wetton, was accused of driving at hare coursers Sir Rupert and Lady Mackesson. Fortunately, the jury returned a unanimous verdict of not guilty. The North East group also attended the North Yorkshire Coursing Club meeting at Thirsk. However, before the first smoke bomb hit the ground, a 'cataclysm' of coursers forced the saboteurs to make a hasty retreat.

The Waterloo Cup

The main event in the hare courser's calendar was known as the Waterloo Cup and took place in the village of Great Altcar, just outside of Liverpool in late February or early March each year. Such was the knowledge that the public deemed their 'sport' barbaric and horrifying that the honorary secretary of the Waterloo Cup, Lord Kenyon, was quoted as saying, "we have a rule forbidding photographs of coursing. The ban was imposed to prevent these anti-bloodsports people from getting ammunition to use against us". Of course this annual festival of animal abuse was a very tempting target for activists and in 1975, the Hunt Saboteurs Association paid for a helicopter to circle above the coursing fields for almost an hour scaring the hares away as a peaceful demonstration was taking place below. Hunt saboteurs returned the following year employing more traditional methods of interference. After four hares were killed, saboteurs ran onto the field to stop any further deaths. The group were shortly apprehended by police and later found themselves at Ormskirk Magistrate Court. They were bound over to keep the peace for twelve months.

The Waterloo Cup of 1977 was a particularly horrific affair with 27 hares being killed and one greyhound put down after suffering a broken leg. Determined to put an end to this brutality, on the third day, 130 saboteurs descended on the event. A group, comprised of just over half the activists present, invaded the Withins coursing field (every field at the event had a different name), with the police in hot pursuit. Thirty-eight saboteurs were subsequently arrested and charged with a further two reported for charge. This attracted considerable media attention, perhaps party due to one *Sun* reporter having the golden opportunity to use the headline, 'The Battle of Waterloo' (February 12th 1977). Of those charged, 31 activists were found guilty of an action likely to cause breach of the peace and were handed fines. The HSA appealed the convictions and made an application for legal aid at Preston Crown Court. The applications were all turned down by Judge W.H. Openshaw, a member of the British Fieldsports Society (a fact he failed to mention at the time). The appeal was later heard by Judge Dewhurst at the same court but was upheld without any evidence on the part of the defence being heard.

Another large demonstration was also called against the festival in 1983 but the event organisers managed to get away with the first day unopposed (which saw a total of 66 courses) as they brought the event forward by a day. The hare coursers had no such luck on the second day (March 2nd), however. An impressive total of around 350 hunt saboteurs made their way ahead of the beaters after just five courses that morning and refused to move. The police officers present were reluctant to remove the saboteurs which further infuriated the crowd of coursing supporters already eager to teach the antis a violent lesson. Some ripped up fence posts and moved in on the saboteurs, but were somehow deterred by four police officers at the scene, with one courser goading the saboteurs by holding aloft a hare that had only just been killed. Determined to continue their day, the coursers made it clear to the police that if they were unwilling to remove the antis from the arena then they would do so themselves. Running battles broke out amongst the two sides until eventually the police managed to contain the saboteurs and escort them to the road. Only one hare was left in the field who thankfully managed to escape, although more were coursed in the afternoon as the police kept the saboteurs away. The large group of hunt saboteurs chose not to attend the final day but instead had moved onto a nearby protest against Canadian seal pups being killed for the fur trade.

Sab Almost Killed

The violence escalated the following year when, on his first day out as a hunt saboteur, 34 year old Eddie Coulston had his skull fractured after he was struck on the head with a shooting stick wielded by the Secretary of the Mid-Essex Coursing Club, Paul Willingdale. Coulston had to have a series of operations to remove bone splinters and a blood clot and was left with epileptic fits. Astonishingly, Willingdale was later sentenced to a mere twelve months in prison, six of which were suspended. He was released after serving four months. Coulston remained defiant despite narrowly avoiding death, later saying: "Acts of violence such as the one to which I was subjected to must not deter us from our aims of achieving total freedom from persecution for all the creatures with whom we share this planet."

The event was moved forward by two weeks in an attempt to avoid the massive protests that had been promised by the HSA. Despite this, over 300 people managed to mobilise at extremely short notice and took to the coursing fields. The four day campaign was not altogether successful, however, as both the large crowd of angry spectators and the huge police presence stopped many attempts at disruption. Faced with the extreme violence that led to Coulson's life-threatening injury, the HSA was left no choice than to cancel any further demonstrations that year. The violence was not only between the spectators and the saboteurs, however, as a fight also broke out between two groups of coursers at the Scarisbrick Arms, just down the road from the event in Downholland. One of the coursers suffered a fractured skull in the fracas and a week later died of his injuries at Liverpool Walton Hospital.

Top: Police form a line to keep saboteurs away from the coursing fields of the Waterloo Cup for two hours, 26th February 1985

Bottom: A member of Cotswold HSA stands in front of a Land Rover's megaphones being used to scare hares away from the coursing fields at the Waterloo Cup, 27th February 1985

Opposite page: Activists protest against the Waterloo Cup

During the 1985 Waterloo Cup, a gang of coursing supporters even attacked a line of beaters who were walking back to the event after mistaking them for saboteurs. Despite the difficulties, the saboteurs present did have a positive effect, as one Cotswold saboteur explains:

Around every 15 minutes a hare was coursed. Although they stated the kill was not important, every time a hare was killed there was a huge cheer. At around 1pm we returned to our vehicles and drove round to the other side of the field on the edge of the River Alt. Everyone stood on the river bank and created a wall of noise. This was successful initially but as the number of hares got fewer in the funnel it was decided to stop and stay silent. We withdrew at about 5pm. The police were expected to patrol the major roads for sabs the next morning so 150 of us moved to within 4 miles of the field and stayed in some derelict flats, where food was provided.

The next day we awoke at 5am and departed from the flats for the coursing fields at 5.45am. For 30 minutes we walked along the river bank keeping as silent as possible. However, when we got to the fording place there were about 15 coursing marshals on the other bank armed with sticks. The river smelt of sewage and had a thin covering of ice. At first there was hesitation but then a group jumped in and waded across followed by everyone else. We soon overran the armed marshals and had a beat line strung out over several fields. We pushed hares on to an area of waste land. The line held despite attacks in places from coursing marshals. The police arrived and started arresting people. The arrests had a detrimental effect on the line and it broke up in places. However, we pushed on through and reached some buildings by a road all wet and weary. Vans arrived to take us back to the flats were we ate and dried off. Later we returned to the area, the site had moved from the day before but was still bordered by the river. A Land Rover with loudspeakers was used to scare hares back through the beat line. Fireworks were also launched over the river with some exploding right above the beaters. This did have some effect but when the beat line changed position this tactic was no longer viable. We left the fields and went to Ormskirk magistrates court to watch the hearings of the 20 or so sabs who had been arrested. Most were charged with action likely to cause a breach of the peace and obstructing the police. All cases were adjourned to a later date.

A Bloodsport Pushed Underground...

Although mass strikes against the Waterloo Cup eventually fizzled out, the war was eventually won. After many years of disruption, the Hunting Act was to be the final nail in the coffin for the Waterloo Cup. In no uncertain terms, the act made the coursing of hares illegal. In fact, a whole section of the act was dedicated to outlawing the 'sport'. It reads:

1. A person commits an offence if he -
   a. participates in a hare coursing event,
   b. attends a hare coursing event,
   c. knowingly facilitates a hare coursing event, or
   d. permits land which belongs to him to be used for the purposes of a hare coursing event.

2. Each of the following persons commits an offence if a dog participates in a hare coursing event -
   a. any person who enters the dog for the event,
   b. any person who permits the dog to be entered, and
   c. any person who controls or handles the dog in the course of or for the purposes of the event.

3. A 'hare coursing event' is a competition in which dogs are, by the use of live hares, assessed as to skill in hunting hares.

In 2005, the last ever Waterloo Cup was held, putting an end to 169 years of the sick spectacle. Hare coursing does sadly continue to take place, albeit illegally as clandestine coursing gangs still operate, often under the cover of darkness. However, the sick 'sport' has very much been forced underground and as a result the lives of many hares have been spared.

STOP
LIVE HARE
COURSING

LIVERPOOL
ANARCHIST
GROUP

1980S: THE WAR RAGES ON

Top and bottom: Petersfield saboteurs take the Chiddingfold Hunt's hounds for a run

Opposite page: Dave Wetton addresses the crowd gathered at Trafalgar Square at the end of a joint HSA and LACS march against bloodsports, 25th January 1981

A Burgeoning Movement

After 15 years of solid campaigning with the HSA, Dave Wetton retired as National Secretary in 1980 (although he continued as Membership Secretary for another five years). The HSA was now in a far stronger position than when Wetton first took over the majority of the work of organising nationally in the 1960s. In the early 1980s membership stood at 3,000 and was getting a yearly income of between £10,000 and £15,000. With the rise of unemployment during this period, the HSA also experienced a marked increase in the level of local group activity as people were now able to devote more time to animal rights activism and sabotage more hunts midweek. In 1983 the HSA received its first legacy; £12,000 and a small house. The house was sold and the money from the sale subsequently distributed to local groups.

The start of the main fox hunting season on 3rd November 1984 was christened National Anti-Hunt Day and was marked by the HSA coordinating a day of banner protests and large scale hits. Over 25 fox hunts were hit by a total of well over 1800 saboteurs across the country. Saboteurs on the day also saw the first indications of national police coordination against hunt sabotage. In the South, 100 saboteurs hit the New Forest Foxhounds and prevented the hunt from leaving the meet for two hours. The biggest hit of the day was against the Mendip Farmers Hunt which ended in violence as 25 riders dismounted to attack part of the Bristol group. One saboteur was taken to Wells hospital with a trampled foot whilst another was held down and had anti-mate poured down his throat. The over 100 saboteurs who had gathered at the East Essex Hunt's meet had a better time of it, however, as they continually split the pack and reported no kills. More than 50 saboteurs made it to the Llangibby Hunt to have all their anti-mate confiscated by hunt supporters and a news reporter who was out with the group had his aerial snapped. Despite these difficulties, the day proved very effective and definitely a victory for the HSA. Press coverage of the opening meets was very favourable with most regional TV news programmes showing a sabotage somewhere. In Yorkshire, a particularly good piece of footage was played that showed saboteurs intercepting hounds just behind a fox and ended with the fox escaping from the Badsworth Hunt.

As of November 1985, the list provided by the HSA was able to boast of 91 group contacts, broken up into 15 separate areas across the UK and Ireland.

A Difficult Year

Despite anti-hunt activity steadily increasing with just under 100 active groups, 1985 proved to be one of the most trying years in the Hunt Saboteurs Association's history. Press sympathy was lost almost overnight as it suddenly became fashionable to attack 'animal lib fanatics.' This was coupled with a distinct increase in hunt violence which included an attack on saboteurs by supporters of the Waterloo Cup in which Manchester saboteur Eddie Coulston was nearly killed. A lack of commitment to the vital administration of the HSA began to seep in as some committee members viewed organisational administration as an unnecessary burden far removed from direct action. Some 3,000 members were on the books at the start of 1985 and the salesgoods department was making a healthy profit but within a few months membership plummeted to 1,000 and the salesgoods department was losing thousands of pounds. One positive piece of news that year, however, was that 1985 was to be the final year for the North Warwickshire Hunt as it folded due to financial difficulties. On its last ever meet, around 80 saboteurs along with a TV crew from *NBC News* made a complete mockery of the day's hunting, leaving *Horse and Hound* magazine no option but to just publish a small series of photographs of the day as opposed to a full hunting report. Six van loads of saboteurs from Coventry, Birmingham University, Manchester and others from further afield successfully blocked the hound van's exit from the kennels, meaning that the hounds only managed to get to the meet at 1pm.

SURREY
UNIVERSITY
HUNT SABOTEURS
S.E. ESSEX

Within five minutes of leaving the meet, the saboteurs used horn calls to take the hounds off the line of a suspected bagged fox and that set the precedent for the rest of the day, with different groups of antis frequently calling the hounds.

Regardless of other difficulties, the HSA reported that over 25 fox hunts were hit on the official start of the 1984/85 season, with well over 1800 saboteurs out in the fields. In Wales, the Llangibby Hunt had to contend with over 50 saboteurs; in Scotland, 60 saboteurs took on the Lanarkshire and Renfrewshire Hunt; in England, 100 saboteurs thwarted the efforts of the East Kent Hunt whilst a further hundred visited the New Forest Hunt along with many other hits. Clearly the appetite for direct action was not lost. Over 40 hunt meets were also visited by saboteurs on Boxing Day 1984 in what was probably the largest series of hits for quite some time.

The Western Morning News reported an attack on the kennels of the Dart Vale and Haldon Harriers in Dartington in which the words 'SCUM' and 'KILLERS' were spray-painted in large white letters, the tyres slashed on hunt vehicles and a transporter's windscreen smashed in the early hours of 1st August 1985, causing an estimated £1,000 worth of damage. Twenty-one days later, on 22nd August, the Holcombe Hunt suffered a similar fate as their kennels were damaged in an arson attack, along with a car having paint stripper poured over it and anti-hunt slogans painted on the walls. The Holcombe Hunt's hopes that the attack was a one-off were soon quashed as the following year the hunt secretary, Ray Longster, had his horse box set alight along with sixteen windows of his house smashed and more slogans daubed on its walls.

Shotguns and Tractors

One particularly notable day's sabotage occurred on Saturday 26th October, 1985. Hunt saboteurs from Cannock, Wolverhampton, Rugby, Telford, Birmingham and Warwick universities, Coventry and Leamington Spa met for a joint hit of the Albrighton Hunt in retaliation for an attack by the hunt a few weeks previously. Piled into three vans and two cars, the saboteurs drove to the hunt's kennels at Wiston Green, Shropshire with the intention of blocking in the hound van for as long as possible and therefore preventing the hunt from even starting. Having arrived, one van was positioned straight across the driveway with the others parked up nearby. A burglar alarm was set off and within minutes the huntsman, Nigel Cox, emerged. After seeing the van load of activists, he rushed back to the house and returned wielding a double-barrelled shotgun. Threats were made as the irate huntsman brandished his gun at the group. One saboteur who attempted to photograph the alarming scene narrowly missed a blow to her head as the huntsman took a swipe at her with the weapon. He then proceeded to shoot into the side of one of the vans causing a 3 inch hole in the front grill and a 1½ inch hole through the radiator, making it impossible to drive away. Four people were inside the van as it was shot at with a further four just three feet away from where the blast hit. The huntsman quickly put his shotgun away but was joined by a neighbour, some 60 yards from the kennels, who brought out his pump-action shotgun and began firing over the heads of the activists. The police were quick on the scene and the hunt began about an hour later, with two of the van loads of activists managing to sabotage the rest of the day's hunting. Cox later received a three month suspended prison sentence for firearms offences and was given a conditional discharge for assault and criminal damage.

Yet another serious incident would occur at the Albrighton Hunt some nine years later when a saboteur from Wolverhampton was attacked with a hammer at a cub hunting meet. The six saboteurs present at the meet were attacked when a convoy of hunt supporters' vehicles, led by two tractors, drove towards the group's van. One of the tractor drivers used a fork attachment on the front of his vehicle to lift the van into the air whilst some saboteurs were still inside. A fracas ensued that involved those outside the van, which led to one saboteur needing emergency hospital treatment after being hit with a hammer.

Opposite page: Hunt saboteurs stop a dig-out during the opening meet of the Eridge Foxhounds, 1st November 1980

Top: Huntsman Nigel Cox points his shotgun at saboteurs, 1985

Bottom: A police helicopter attempts to disperse saboteurs on the Albrighton Woodland Hunt near Bridgenorth, 21st November 1987

Top: Hull HSA at the Holderness Hunt, 1989

Bottom: Edinburgh saboteurs use a gizmo to take the Duke of Buccleuch's hounds the wrong way on a fox's scent, 10th November 1993

Opposite page: Saboteurs tussle with police at the Tynedale Foxhounds

Come the 1986/87 season, however, and things were again on the up. The HSA estimated that around 1,000 foxes and 200 hares had been saved that year and an average of 50 hunts were hit each week. At the beginning of the season, the contacts list produced by the HSA listed a total of 102 local groups, but as the season came to an end, this number was up to 124. Nearly 100 Boxing Day meets were visited by saboteurs that year. Many lives were saved that season including West London HSA rescuing six hounds belonging to the Aldershot Beagles from certain death on the M3 and a fox saved by one Liverpool saboteur who leapt on top of the animal as the hounds were about to make their kill. Southern saboteurs even stopped a train to save the entire pack of the Garth and South Berkshire Hunt.

Such was the level of activity during this period that many universities had their own HSA groups. As student activism was so prevalent on campuses all throughout the UK, educational institutions provided a hotbed for animal rights campaigning and fertile recruitment grounds for direct action groups. Amongst the university groups at the time were University of East Anglia HSA, University of Exeter HSA, Brunel University Animal Rights Group, Plymouth Polytechnic HSA, Portsmouth Polytechnic HSA, Manchester University HSA and the University of Surrey Anti-Bloodsports Society, to name but a few. Wolverhampton HSA were even granted the use of Wolverhampton Polytechnic's minibus free of charge each week.

Sabbing in the Land of My Fathers

During the latter half of the 1980s, local groups across the UK were growing considerably in confidence. In 1988, the HSA had nearly 140 local groups across the UK with around 25% managing to go out mid-week as well Saturdays. Things were on the up in Wales as the Swansea group was re-established in 1984 with their first hit being against the Llandeilo Farmers Hunt. It was to be a baptism of fire for the newly-formed group as they were attacked by hunt followers wielding, amongst other things, a pickaxe handle and a shotgun.

Sadly, the hunt managed to kill one fox but packed up early due to the group's presence. The Vale of Glamorgan HSA (later to be renamed Vale and Valleys HSA) was busy making significant strides across South Wales and its concerted efforts forced the South East Wales Minkhounds to cancel their Saturday meets by 1986, instead only venturing out on occasional midweek meets. The hunt folded soon after. Smaller, yet just as dedicated groups, such as Aberystwyth HSA, Clwyd HSA, Lampeter HSA and Llandudno HSA were also filling their time protecting abused wildlife, along with groups from Port Talbot and Cardiff.

Further north, Wrexham, Mold and Bangor University groups were busy taking on Flint and Denbigh Hunt. Bangor HSA often faced tricky times however, as they focused much of their attentions on the United Hunt, about three hours drive to the southeast. Their frustrations came to a head on 8th March 1985 when they were ambushed by supporters of the aforementioned hunt. The hunt supporters let down three tyres of the group's minibus before attempting to hook a tow-chain to it, attached at the other end to a Land Rover and tow the vehicle off the road. According to a report in *HOWL*;

> *The sabs' driver then slammed the vehicle into reverse, knocked over two of the thugs and accelerated forwards through the gap created by the Land Rover. But after a mile of driving on flat tyres, the bus skidded off the road and ploughed into a large bank of earth where it became lodged. A car-load of pursuing psychos double backed to inform their mates of the good news and the sabs had to abandon their vehicle and make off across country. After a three mile walk they found a public phone and called the police who arrived 1 hour and 15 minutes later by which time, naturally, there was not a hunt follower to be found. The minibus had been broken into and ransacked.*

Top: Brighton HSA take control of the Chiddingfold Hunt's hounds

Bottom: Cotswold HSA after a hit of the Old Berkshire Hunt, 15th December 1984

Opposite page: Police forcibly remove a group of saboteurs preventing a dig-out from taking place

Sterling Work in Scotland

In Scotland, the Edinburgh group was continuing to provide a large thorn in the side of the Duke of Buccleuch's Hunt since shifting their focus from the Linlithgow and Stirlingshire Hunt after it folded in 1991. Organised saboteur activity against the Linlithgow and Stirlingshire Hunt began in 1979 when saboteurs from Stirling University and Dundee started visiting the pack towards the end of the 1978/79 season. Following this, a tireless campaign by Central Scotland Hunt Saboteurs was having the rather predicable effect of increasing violence from hunt staff and supporters. The violence reached serious levels during March 1980 where at one particular meet the saboteurs were told, "we're not hunting fox today, we're hunting you." The Stirling University group's minibus was then blocked in and supporters began to dismantle the vehicle by hand. Every window was smashed, every panel dented and every tire slashed. As was becoming a familiar story to those involved in animal rights activity, at the subsequent court case, the majority of charges against the attackers were dropped, but not after seven hunt supporters were fined a total of £2,800 for assaults and breaches of the peace. To save face, the huntsman later invited the saboteurs to an open day at the kennels, 50 of whom duly turned up! The 1981/82 season saw the formation of the Edinburgh group and along with Stirling University, continued the campaign against the Linlithgow and Stirlingshire, with their last meet of the season attracting huge numbers of antis. The hunt began to grow desperate and spent thousands of pounds on civil action to interdict a number of Scottish saboteurs. The numerous court appearances ended in a permanent ban for one of the Edinburgh group's founding members, Les Ward, but the anti-hunt community was galvanised by the verdict and a marked increase in those sabotaging the hunt was noted. After countless incidents of hounds rioting through housing estates, killing cats and attacking dogs, along with the resultant bad press, the hunt was close to collapse in early 1990 when huntsman David Sims and terrierman Ian Marfleet were sacked but, unable to find a replacement for such an unpopular position, the hunt committee was forced to reappoint Sims. It was now becoming apparent that the Linlithgow and Stirlingshire had only a short time left and they made a statement that Saturday 2nd March 1991 was to be their last meet. Over 80 saboteurs turned up to see the end of this calamitous organisation, with one local paper quoted as saying of the event, 'a helluva lot of people for a funeral possession'. A week after the hunt's final ever meet, Edinburgh and Borders HSA received a tip off that a fox shoot was taking place at an RAF base. The hounds used to flush the foxes out, it transpired, were from the Linlithgow and Stirlingshire Hunt. After the hit on the shoot, the saboteurs retired to a pub in Edinburgh and discovered that some of the day's shooters were drinking in there as well. After around ten minutes, the antis left only to find a dead vixen tied to the back of their van. She had been peppered with buckshot on her back right leg, just enough to bring her down. Her head had also been smashed with a spade and her brush had been cut off. Interestingly enough, Robin Cook MP later asked the Secretary of State for Defence, Archie Hamilton over the matter. His reply was, "no organisation or individuals have been authorised to shoot foxes on Ministry of Defence land at Kirknewton Camp."

Scottish Action Against Bloodsports were also very active in stopping the efforts of both the Berwickshire Hunt and the Jedforest Hunt. Other active groups included Fife, Stirling, Aberdeen, Ayrshire and Dumfries. The Clydeside HSA, set up in 1981, was almost a constant sight at any meet of the Lanarkshire and Renfrewshire Hunt. If any further proof was needed of the mentality of hunt followers, at the hunt's game fair in 1990, a supporter of the hunt was charged with behaviour likely to cause breach of the peace after he produced a dead hare and sank his teeth into it, in an effort to persuade the seventy-strong picket by Clydeside HSA that he was biting the animal's head off.

It was not only mammals that the Scottish saboteurs were saving, however. Following a TV appeal for more volunteers, the saboteurs gave up some of their time to aid the Glenburn Toad Rescue Squad during March 1986. A third of the toads, who were trying to cross a busy road to reach their mating ground, had been killed by cars the previous year.

Top: A Tunbridge Wells saboteur on a hit of the Old Surrey and Burstow Hunt

Bottom: Tunbridge Wells Animal Rights' Land Rover after an arson attack by hunt supporters, 1988

Opposite page: Plymouth HSA stop a dig out at the Spooners and West Dartmoor Hunt, 1980

The volunteers waited on stand-by for a wet, mild night when the toads would start their journey to a nearby dam for 'amphibious love-making sessions' and duly carried the toads across the treacherous road.

Further south, Hull HSA were cruising around their local hunts' countries in their infamous green ex-Forestry Commission Sherpa van, a trusty machine that had ferried saboteurs from as far as Portsmouth and Huddersfield in its previous lives. The eight groups in the Yorkshire region (Bradford, Huddersfield, Leeds, Hull, Pocklington, York, Harrogate, and Sheffield) busied themselves against the Holderness Hunt, the York and Ainsty (North) Hunt, the York and Ainsty (South) Hunt and the Middleton Hunt. Many lives were saved including a terrier named Tiny who was rescued by saboteurs at the Middleton after she was buried alive by the terrierman. The Carlisle, Wigan, Kendal and Maryport groups were often joined by the North West group to hit the Conistion, the Lunesdale and the Vale of Lune Harriers.

The Isle of Wight

Although all throughout the 1980s local groups were campaigning against hunts the length and breath of the UK's mainland, the Isle of Wight Foxhounds did also receive saboteur attention. The West London group visited the island twice or three times a year from 1980 onwards and in 1988, the Southern Anti Bloodsports Society (a coalition of hunt saboteur groups in the South) began visiting the island on a regular basis. A local couple, Fred and Amelia Winsor, put up visiting activists at their home in Ventnor and also joined them in the fields. As the pressure mounted on the IOW Hunt, saboteurs' vehicles began to be vandalized and the remains of a dead fox were dumped outside the Winsor's house. In one incident, a police officer witnessed a hunt saboteur being rode down and the huntsman was subsequently charged. The ensuing court case was stalled due to trouble finding a bench that did not personally know the huntsman. After much deliberation a bench was found but they acquitted the huntsman and a reporter with the *Isle of Wight County Times* would later privately state that the chairman of the bench knew the huntsman well.

A few attempts were made at establishing an anti-hunt group on the island and these culminated when over seven million people watched the programme *Out of Order* on ITV in the early 1990s which featured footage of successful sabotage of the IOW Hunt. A group of local hunt saboteurs had taken over from visiting groups by the early 1990s and their legacy runs up until today. In 2008, the Forestry Commission took the unprecedented step of banning the IOW Hunt from its land following evidence by the League Against Cruel Sports of the hunt blatantly ignoring the Hunting Act and digging out a badger sett.

The Isle of Wight is an oft cited example against the hunting lobby's excuse that fox hunting is a form of pest control as foxes are not native to the island. The Isle of Wight Foxhounds introduced foxes to the island in 1845 in order to practise the horrifying 'sport' of fox hunting. Later on, during the 1920s, the hunt records show that an outbreak of mange was taking a heavy toll on the fox population and as a result was limiting hunting. To counter this, John Willis Fleming, the then master of the Isle of Wight Hunt, introduced a dozen badgers to populate the island. The badgers drove foxes away from their diseased earths and cleaned them, forcing the foxes to open fresh earths elsewhere. Badgers have also been persecuted by the hunt, however, and in May 1991, huntsman Steve Clifton and terrierman Jamie Butcher were both convicted of badger digging. Indeed, that same year, badger experts found that most of the setts on the island appeared to have been dug.

Above: A Norwich saboteur has his horn stolen and bent double by a supporter of the Dunston Harriers

Badger Persecution

Badgers have routinely been persecuted by fox hunts. Prior to a meet, an earth-stopper would often block any badger sett entrances in woods that the hunt will draw, thus preventing the fox from taking sanctuary underground, and prolonging the chase. Although this work is kept secret by hunts, due to the fact it is both illegal and extremely cruel, numerous people have been convicted. The South and West Wilts Hunt's earth-stopper, John Rossiter, was fined £160 with £150 costs after he admitted interfering with a badger sett in 1994. In 1992, four members of the Dartmoor Hunt, including a master and a whipper-in were charged under the Badgers Act 1991 with two joining charges of interfering with a badger sett at Little Sherberton. In January 2011, both the huntsman and the terrierman of the Fernie Hunt were found guilty at Harborough Magistrates Court of hunting a wild mammal with dogs and interfering with a badger sett. In 2013, a joint hunt master and the terrierman of the Avon Vale Hunt pleaded guilty to interfering with a badger sett after they were caught waist deep in a sett attempting to locate their terrier in what the RSPCA officer involved described as the 'most severe damage' he had seen. There are also strong links between fox hunts and the underground world of badger baiting. For example, following an undercover operation in 1988, Phillip Willams, one of the terriermen of the Ledbury Hunt, was convicted for badger baiting offences under the Badgers Act 1973.

The South East

The south east of England was (and still is) another hotbed of animal rights activity and supported a large number of local groups. Both Tonbridge and Tunbridge Wells had saboteur groups, so did Brighton, Hastings and Bexhill. The East Sussex and Romney Marsh Hunt bore the brunt of much of the pressure by saboteurs in Sussex and Kent, so much so that on 15th January 1985 they even cancelled their meet due to the threat of a mass hit.

After a very successful hit of the Old Surrey and Burstow towards the beginning of the 1989 season, numerous groups had met up in a lay-by to discuss the day's events before they left. Suddenly six hunt supporters, including the hunt's whipper-in, Mark Bycroft, came through a nearby hedge armed with staves and pickaxe handles. Unfortunately, Tunbridge Wells saboteur Simon Russell happened to be the only saboteur outside of the vehicles at the time. He made a run for it, but was knocked to the ground and beaten, having his right kneecap fractured in the process. The assailants also managed to force open the door of Brighton HSA's van and a tug of war ensued between saboteurs and hunt supporters, with the driver acting as the rope. Being one (or more) of either young, foolish or extremely dedicated, Russell insisted on attending future hits despite wearing a leg plaster and requiring crutches. A mass hit was arranged for the following week in retaliation for the attack which saw 100 activists descend on the meet. The police turned out in force and within an hour arrested all of the saboteurs' drivers along with Russell (who were all later released without charge). Those on foot managed to continue sabotaging the hunt, however, as all the police officers were otherwise engaged.

Some years previously, another serious incident occurred with many of the same people involved, as Simon Russell explains:

> *In the mid-1980s the Crawley and Horsham was known as a very violent hunt and so was only sabbed in numbers. We went along one day with the combined groups of Tunbridge Wells, Tonbridge, Brighton and London in four vehicles (Three Land Rovers and a Sherpa Van). We were driving in convoy with the Tunbridge Wells Land Rover second in line when a horsebox pulled out in front of the lead vehicle. It managed to swerve around it but it was then fully blocking our Land Rover. About 40 hunt supporters, all masked and armed proceeded to attack*

our Land Rover which was a safari model and had windows all down the sides. The windscreen was smashed and the female driver was hit in the head slumping over the middle seat, I was in the passenger seat and managed to grab a large spanner off one of the attackers and used to defend myself until I was also hit and laid across the driver to protect her. In the back sabs were being hit through the broken windows with nowhere to go (it was full) and our attackers were also trying to open the rear door while one sab held onto the handle to prevent this. As I had stopped defending myself I think they thought I was knocked out as they had stopped hitting me and the driver, so I propped her up and shouted at her to drive. She managed to somehow get around the horse box but a supporters' Ford Fiesta car tried again to block us, we kept going and took its whole left side wing with us with only minor damage to our bumper. As we had pulled away so suddenly the back door had finally swung open and a sab fell out. He jumped up and chased after the Land Rover, chased in turn by bumpkins. He managed to jump back in helped by other sabs and it was later found that he had a two inch wound on his leg down to the bone. We stopped at a pub as we had three unconscious sabs and all others were injured in some way. The pub owner refused to let us use his phone even when asked by a bleeding sab and shut the door in our faces so we left a few booted dents in his door and moved on, finally finding a phone box. A single cop turned up and as we were telling him what had happened, a van full of our attackers drove past, he refused to follow it and the owner of course pleaded innocence of anything. No one was ever charged but we continued to sab this hunt.

A few months later, a group of about 10 of us were up on the South Downs on the Southdown and Eridge Hunt when two Land Rovers of terriermen (some were involved in the earlier incident) drove across a field, stopped about 30 feet away and jumped out with spades and staves and started to run at us shouting threats. They had made the mistake of picking a ploughed field thick with flints, so sabs started to pick them up and throw them at the bumpkins before they could get close. They quickly realised their mistake and, cowering behind spades they ran back to their vehicles which by now had smashed wind screens, drove off.

Regionalisation

Due to the number of saboteurs at the time being so great, and to the fact that the lack of communications technology meant that coordination between groups often proved difficult, especially on a national level, some attempts were made of a regionalisation within the HSA. The Southern Anti-Bloodsports Society (SABS) was set up in 1992. Rather than taking members from the HSA and doubling-up on work, its secretary, Linda Blackburn, described how SABS would be a welcome progression in the anti-hunt movement:

> *We aim to work alongside, not against, the HSA as well as working with the League Against Cruel Sports. There should be no need for 'petty bickering' of any kind. Obviously, there are bound to be some differences in opinions between different organisations but we believe that these should not stand in the way of progress. Progress is change and there is a need for another movement which is using direct action campaigns hand in hand with political campaigns. SABS is doing just that.*

Above: Norwich HSA push their van out of the mud

The regionalisation of the HSA was a hotly debated topic and not all agreed that splinter groups were such a good idea. Indeed, whilst some viewed regionalisation as a necessary and beneficial development, the formation of SABS did provoke a hostile response in some quarters. One cause for concern was that if the HSA was to lose members' subscriptions from the affluent South, where approximately one eighth of the membership lived at the time, more pressure would be put upon areas such as the North East as the HSA targeted less active areas like this for development and assistance but depended upon money from the South to put its schemes into action. However, SABS members (including their press officer, Tony Faramus) were adamant that the formation of SABS didn't harm the HSA's membership and that in fact most HSA members in the SABS area were inactive and wealthy enough to be members of both organisations. One vocal critic of the SABS method of regionalisation was Exeter saboteur, Ralph Cook, who foresaw a conflict of loyalty amongst 'potentially good HSA committee members' and that 'in an action-orientated movement with too few capable administrators in its ranks, it is something we can ill-afford'.

It was also around this time that the North West Hunt Saboteurs Association was set up. The formation of the NWHSA, mainly an umbrella organisation for saboteurs in Liverpool and Manchester, was in part a response to a less cohesive national structure. Despite these initial efforts, the concept of regionalisation never truly took off, however.

Hunting with hounds was now taking a severe beating. To curb this rise in direct action and avoid sabotage, many hunts were beginning to choose not to advertise their meets. On Boxing Day 1974, a total of 211 packs advertised their meets in *Horse and Hound*. Ten years on and this number had fallen to 132. During the 1983/4 season around 70-80 packs were advertising their meets in the *Shooting Times* but by mid-October 1984, the magazine had stopped advertising meets altogether. In relation to mink hunts, *Shooting News* confirmed what many were seeing on the ground; "Unfortunately a lot of packs, due to the activities of anti-hunting saboteurs, do not publicise their meets… but it is inevitable under the circumstances". Both the Four Shires Bassets and the Derwent Valley Beagles closed down around this period as a direct result of being forced underground by anti-hunt activity.

Years of saboteur activity against Mr Goschen's Foxhounds, one of a very small number of 'private packs' (that is to say, the whole operation was funded by Mr Goschen himself with no reliance on subscriptions from members), the loss of hunt country, and the death of its owner saw the hunt fold. One notable incident witnessed by antis whilst out on this rather posh pack was the terrierman, when attempting to punch a saboteur, breaking his wife's nose with his elbow as he didn't realise she was standing right behind him!

Anthony Faramus

The story of one saboteur active in the 1980s in particular is a truly remarkable one. Born in 1920 on the island of Jersey, Anthony Faramus worked as an actor and a hairdresser. Having been jailed on charges of fraud, Faramus found himself inside Jersey prison not long after the Nazi occupation of the island. After his release, he began to further actively oppose Jersey's new regime, on one occasion even stealing a Nazi army truck and running over a number of soldiers in his escape attempt. The local authorities considered Faramus an 'undesirable' and deported him to France without proper trial or conviction. After a year in the Parisian concentration camp of Fort de Romainville, he was transported to the Buchenwald concentration camp, a horrific journey on which 55 of the 120 people in his carriage died. He was later moved to Mauthausen concentration camp in Austria, where he stayed until the camp was liberated on 5th May 1945.

By some stroke of luck, Faramus survived the war and later emigrated to the USA, before returning to the UK and, with

Left: Tony Faramus (left) with fellow saboteurs and his wife, Mary (right), out on the Aldershot Beagles, January 1989

an immense empathy for helping those in need and the most vulnerable in society, joined the HSA. Alongside his wife Mary, he was a regular sight at meets of the Aldershot Beagles and lived long enough to celebrate their demise. Faramus was hospitalised after being punched in the head by a police officer whilst being arrested on the Ytene Minkhounds in 1986. He lost consciousness in the back of the police car as a result and during treatment, an ambulance worker from Weymouth was heard to say, "the police have done him over", as though it were an everyday occurrence. The arrest and subsequent conviction was for blockading the hound van at the hunt's meet near Dorchester.

In 1989, being well into his sixties and having lost a lung to tuberculosis during his imprisonment in Mauthausen concentration camp, Faramus was arrested at a hunt in Hampshire. An extremely principled man, he refused to be bound over and subsequently spent a month in prison.
His was a life full of compassion and as an extremely dedicated animal rights activist, he spent much of his time at protests such as the weekly demonstrations against London's notorious Club Row market and was also an active member of the South East Animal Liberation League. Faramus sadly died in August 1990 at the age of 70. Over a hundred people attended his funeral in Farnham at which Dave Wetton read a funeral address. Among mourners were those from within the ranks of Animal Aid, the League Against Cruel Sports and the ALF, and of course the HSA was represented in force with a large contingent of saboteurs arriving fresh back from a hit of the New Forest Foxhounds. Two wreaths were lain, one bearing the motif 'BAN BLOODSPORTS' and the other with the words, 'WEST LONDON HUNT SABOTEURS'.

Top: Essex Hunt chase a vixen, 4th March 1989

Bottom: Nine fox cubs sleep after being rescued by saboteurs from the Essex Hunt, 4th March 1989

With many HSA committee members in Exeter and the South West, a constitution was ratified at the 1986 AGM which stated that the policy of the association shall be:

> **To oppose and undertake to sabotage, where practicable, the pursuit, harassment or killing of any sentient creature for sport or pleasure until such time as these practices cease to exist.**

Exeter HSA was understandably a very active group at the time and even organised a number of national hits that included the 'Devon Sabotage Festival' in 1985 whereby 70 activists from all over the UK travelled to the South West to sabotage the South Devon Foxhounds, the Devon and Somerset Staghounds, the Stoke Hill Beagles as well as a fishing match.

Saboteurs were present at the 1987 opening meet of the York and Ainsty (North) Hunt at Great Ouseburn when two bagged foxes were released. The hunt spent much of the day evading saboteurs along the virtually treeless banks of the River Ouse and failed to find a single worthwhile scent. Eventually they decided to slip a bagged fox but inadvertently let two go at the same time. In the ensuing confusion, saboteurs from Huddersfield and Leeds stepped in and called the hounds to order. Both foxes escaped and the demoralised huntsman blew for home at only 1.30pm.

Another notable day occurred two years later when saboteurs from the Mid-Essex group were visiting the Essex Hunt on March 4th 1989. The hunt had managed to drive a vixen to ground in a small earth. Unfortunately, the terriermen arrived before the saboteurs were able to and quickly dug her out and killed her. They left, not noticing that she was lactating and as such had recently given birth. This was most likely due to the fact that the vixen had tried to protect her young and had fought the terriers just inside the entrance to the earth. Saboteurs later arrived and heard faint 'mewling' sounds from the amongst the wreckage of the earth. On hearing this, they dug and discovered nine newly born and still blind cubs, no more than five days old. Without their mother, the cubs' chances of survival in the wild were extremely low and so the saboteurs drove them to an animal sanctuary south of London, where they were fed puppy food and brought up before being released back into the wild.

Sabotaging the Fell Packs

Although the most common image of fox hunting is of a mounted pack, there are a few packs who hunt on foot. The six packs located in the Lake District, known as the fell packs, are somewhat of an anomaly in terms of the bloodsport. As most hunts aim for as long a chase as possible, the fell packs' stated intention is simply to kill foxes. Started in 1988, a 'Fell Week' was organised annually by the HSA for a number of years that saw saboteurs head to Cumbria as a concerted effort against the fell packs. Sabotage amongst the rugged terrain of the Cumbrian mountains was challenging to say the least, but great success was had by those who did venture there as this story of one saboteur's experience in 1988 testifies:

> *I'd only been out sabbing a few times when people in Leeds Sabs started talking about a 'Fell Week'. I didn't really know what was involved but, as a keen young sab, I knew I wanted to be part of it. In the planning meetings that followed I learnt that the Lake District has six packs of foxhounds - the Blencathra, Coniston, Eskdale & Ennerdale, Lunesdale, Melbreak and Ullswater - who conduct their hunting on foot with light, rangy hounds that can hunt more independently than those of the lowland packs. An experienced Cumbrian sab advised us to forget the word 'fell': this was really 'mountain' hunting and stopping it would not be easy.*

Easter was identified as the best time for a week of action. This was a prestigious time for the fell hunters, their ranks traditionally swollen by visitors whose home packs had finished for the season. We knew we'd need big numbers too: the previous Easter, Tyneside Sabs had been mugged and viciously beaten by thugs from the Ullswater FH.

The first challenge was to raise the necessary funds. The Leeds group reckoned we'd need £600 for the week - a huge sum in the broken Britain of Margaret Thatcher. We hit on the idea of squeegeeing - washing car windscreens when they stopped at traffic lights. It proved remarkably effective: one look at our filthy sponges was usually enough to make the driver cough up, so long as we didn't touch their car. We had the money in a week.

With supplies bought and complex signing-on arrangements made, we headed out to Cumbria to meet up with sabs from all over the country. Our rendezvous point was Cockley Beck, Leeds University's Mountaineering Club hut in the western Lakes, somehow appropriated for our purposes. The drive in was spectacular; the high fells beautiful, intimidating and still dusted with snow. As we approached the hut I realised what a good choice it was: isolated and approached by a sinuous single track road, it would be difficult to launch a surprise attack on us. Leeds got there early and we bagged a decent upstairs room, but any thought of comfort was quickly abandoned as more and more sab groups arrived. The place was soon ridiculously overcrowded, the air heavy with the smell of citronella, cider and damp dreadlocks.

That evening local sabs gave a tactics talk and left us under no illusions about the dangers we faced: the terrain would be craggy, rough and potentially lethal, the hunt support about the same. I found this worrying and my fears only increased when I noticed a fellow Leeds sab rubbing waterproofing-wax into his cheap canvas plimsolls. I thought back to the snow-capped peaks I'd seen on the way in - did we really know what we were getting into?

The plan was to hit the Eskdale & Ennerdale FH who were meeting at the Little Langdale Hotel at 9:30 the following morning. The locals had a good idea of the day's draw so most sabs would aim to get up onto the fell before the hunt had even set off. A smaller group of fast sabs would attempt to intercept the pack as they made their way up the fell. The only downside to this plan was that it involved a 5am start and I awoke to a hive of activity with busy sab caterers dishing out coffee and Sosmix burgers left, right and centre. It was clear that nobody would be going up the fell without first having a decent breakfast and I reflected that these anarchists and crusties were a lot more organised than they looked.

All my fears and doubts from the night before evaporated as we hit the fells and our tactics worked like a dream. I was with the fast group and broke into whoops and holloas as we climbed the fellside and drew parallel with the distant pack. The rarely-sabbed hounds were very responsive and came bounding over. Just as huntsman William Porter was putting his hands on his hips in the classic "bloody antis" position, sab horn calls erupted from the ridgeline far above. The whole pack screamed up the fell towards their new masters, Norwich HSA. We followed in their wake and arrived on the ridge just in time to see the last of them being hunted on into the next valley. The E & E's day just got worse from here and when their supporters resorted to pelting us with rocks we took it as a kind of compliment.

The following morning we awoke to find the fells blanketed in thick fog. A massed convoy of sabs descended on the E & E's kennels whilst others

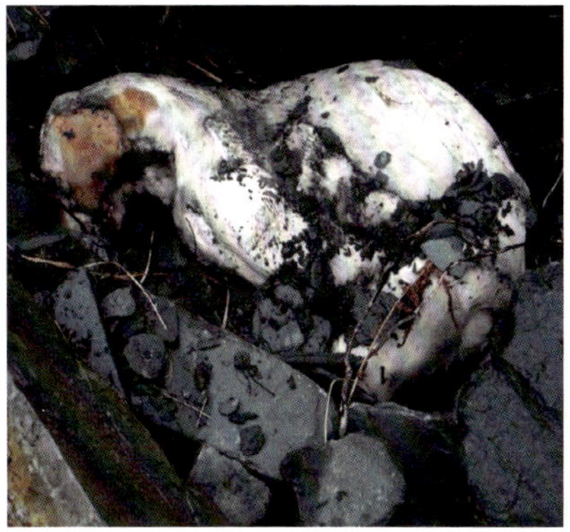

Top: An irate huntsman attacks saboteurs during 'Fell Week', 1991

Above: A Melbreak hound who had fallen to his death from a steep crag near Honister, Cumbria. He was left to decompose where he fell after a hunt official had attempted to hide the body by covering it in rocks, 22nd December 2016

watched roads leading to the supposed meet. There was absolutely no movement at either location: fog, sabs or a combination of the two had dissuaded the hunt from venturing out.

Wednesday saw the premier fell pack, the Blencathra, meet at the Borrowdale Hotel on the shore of Derwent Water. Recently-appointed huntsman Barry Todhunter, resplendent in his new red coat, was parading hounds in front of a large throng of hunt supporters. He might have had less swagger about him if he'd known that two of the keenest supporters were actually sabs, sent in to find out the all-important draw. Without this vital information we might easily climb the wrong fell and be left stranded miles from the action, as we were to find out later in the week. There was no shortage of candidates for the role of infiltrator as, in those days, some sabs chose to dress like hunt supporters. This 'look' could give a tactical advantage but it also meant caution was required, especially on national hits where you didn't necessarily know who was who. This was illustrated during the week when the Leeds van was flagged down by three burly figures in flat caps and wax jackets who were stranded on the roadside. As he rolled down his window the quick-thinking Leeds driver came up with a question to sort the sabs from the scum: "What are Sizzles?" he demanded. "Bacon flavoured Sosmix" came the immediate reply. Their credentials confirmed, the stranded sabs jumped in and we were on our way again.

Thankfully, our moles at the Borrowdale Hotel were subjected to no such questioning and quickly obtained the required information: the hunt would be going straight up Brown Dodd and then along to Watendlath. We headed for the long valley road, while the hardy locals of Carlisle HSA made for the Dodd's summit. Once we were in position it wasn't long before the pack was sighted fanning out across the vast fell and sab horns opened up from all sides. Total chaos ensued with hounds deserting their huntsman and running eagerly from one sab group to another. Todhunter spent the next couple of hours trying to regain his pack but eventually gave up and returned to the meet, having spectacularly failed to live up to the promise of his surname.

Once it became clear to the hunters that we were around for more than a day or so, we fully expected them to launch an attack on our hut. A night-watch rota was therefore established with small groups of sabs assigned to three-hour shifts. It was an unnerving experience sitting in the van staring into blackness of the fells, with only the occasional crackle of the CB to break the silence. It was well into my shift when we picked out several pin-pricks of light winding their way down the valley towards us. We sounded the alarm and almost immediately a large crew of bleary-eyed sabs had spilled out onto the road to protect the building. It was only when the vehicles were upon us that we saw the white and yellow livery of the Cumbria police. A variety of implements - brought out for defensive purposes - were quickly and discreetly dropped behind a drystone wall while the police had a nose around the hut, carried out some petty harassment and then left.

The following morning the Blencathra were back at the Borrowdale Hotel. This time the meet was infiltrated by two Scottish sabs dressed as hikers, one of whom had to conceal a long thin dreadlock down the back of his cagoule in order to look the part. The supporters were less forthcoming this time but only because they didn't know the plan either: the hunt were clearly tightening up their procedures. The police, too, had got their act together and worked in concert with supporters to block our vehicles as the hound van moved off down the valley towards Seathwaite. This action, and our lack of fore-knowledge about their

Above: Saboteurs with the Blencathra Foxhounds during Fell Week, 1990

Opposite: Saboteurs blockade hunt vehicles during Fell Week, 1993

HOWL 50p

Number 36. Magazine of the Hunt Saboteurs Association, PO Box 87, Exeter EX4 3TX Summer 1987

Chris Ogilvie, huntsman with the Coniston FH, realises the awful truth . . .

MURDER IN THE MOUNTAINS!

HSA TARGETS FELL HUNTING

Top: *HOWL* magazine, 1987

Above: Saboteurs with the Blencathra during Fell Week

Opposite page top: Newspaper clipping from the Daily Mail, 26th October 1986

Opposite page middle: Three members of the HRS in Badminton Parish Church, 26th December 1984

Opposite page bottom: Members of the HRS pose for a publicity shot wielding a chainsaw and pickaxe handles

route, meant we never really got to grips with the hunt: the Bradford van was attacked with rocks and later the hunt were able to dig out and kill the only fox of the week.

Back at the hut, nocturnal visits from the police were not the only problems we had to contend with; towards the end of the week we received a deputation from Leeds University who had heard some very unusual reports about their latest mountaineering booking. Thankfully they didn't inspect the hut's septic tank which was by now struggling under the pressure of accommodating one hundred and thirty vegans.

There were no meets for Friday so the day was given over to much-needed rest and relaxation.

We decided to end the week with a bang: two hunts would be targeted. Yet another very early start saw sab convoys staking out the kennels of both the Coniston and Ullswater Foxhounds, with further groups stationed on the Kirkstone Pass roughly between the two. The Coniston unboxed on the pass and were immediately engaged by Tyneside and Sunderland sabs who scattered the pack all over the fell. Inexplicably, the Ullswater's huntsman, who had unboxed a fair way off at Brothers Water, then led his pack onto the same fell and into the chaos. With the two packs hopelessly mixed it was another outstanding day for the local fox population. Unfortunately, this excitement was missed by Leeds sabs as we found ourselves on the snowy summit of Helvelynn, having badly misjudged the Ullswater's route. Our hike back down took us past their kennels and, by the time we got there, the hunt had been abandoned, the hounds were back and Fell Week 1988 was over.

From here on Fell Week became a regular fixture in the sab calendar and brave local sabs have maintained a presence on the fells ever since.

Almost thirty years on from these events, in February 2017, I bumped into the Blencathra Foxhounds while on a winter hike up Skiddaw. They were a sorry sight. Barry Todhunter was still carrying the horn, but his red coat was long gone, re placed by a green jacket to blend into the surroundings. He was accompanied by just five supporters, the massed ranks of hunters that had once dominated the fells having long gone too. We haven't finished off the fell hunters yet, but we're getting there.

Indeed, fell packs continue to become victims of sabotage to this day. Cumbria Hunt Saboteurs almost exclusively sabotaged fells packs during the latter half of the 2000s and into the 2010s whilst Lancashire Hunt Saboteurs later regularly began hitting both the Melbreak and the Blencathra (the hunt of the 'father of fox hunting', John Peel). Both hunts are a shadow of their former selves, often only managing to scrape together a handful of supporters. That being said, they do still hunt and kill foxes and so the HSA's work against the fell packs is not over just yet.

The fell packs would be put under the spotlight again when in 2017 a motion to ban hunting with hounds on National Trust land was narrowly defeated. Fell packs heavily rely on the National Trust with its status as the largest landowner in the Lake District. Despite being smaller in number of participants than other hunts, the fell packs do often cause great havoc in the surrounding villages and intimidate any locals within the small, tight-knit communities who dare to challenge them. One Lake District pony trekking business owner regularly lost up to £800 after having to cancel days of horse riding due to the ponies being terrified of the hunt's chaos before eventually having to abandon her £70,000 per year business altogether.

The Hunt Retribution Squad

With the escalation of hunt violence becoming a distinct phenomenon during the period, some on the anti-hunt side decided that more must be done to stem the tide. The responsibility of the second of the two grave desecrations to have occurred against prominent huntsmen (the first being the disruption to John Peel's grave in 1978) was claimed by a newly formed group known as the Hunt Retribution Squad. On Boxing Day 1984, the grave of the 10th Duke of Beaufort, Hugh Arthur Fitzroy Somerset, was targeted. The Duke was a close personal friend of the Queen and avid fox hunter and had died just some ten months before. According to police, the Duke's grave, situated in the Gloucestershire village of Badminton, had a three foot deep hole dug into it. A wooden cross was also stolen and anti-hunt slogans were painted on nearby walls and gravestones. In a written statement to the Press Association, the HRS claimed:

> *The intention was to remove the remains from the grave and scatter him around Worcester Lodge. We also planned to remove his head and dispatch it to Princess Anne, a fellow blood junkie. It's time the perverted hunters had a taste of their own medicine.*

Numerous suspects were arrested following the stunt but only two were later charged. A jury at Bristol Crown Court later found Terry Helsby and 23 year old John Curtin guilty of conspiring to damage the Duke's grave and coffin, along with stealing the cross from the grave and causing criminal damage to the walls of the churchyard. The pair, including Curtin who was already on police bail for raiding vivisection laboratories, were sentenced to two years imprisonment on the first count and twelve months each on the remaining counts, to run concurrently. In a somewhat unfortunate turn of events, the two had first come to the police's attention after Helsby's mother heard him praise the incident whilst watching television coverage of the raid and had contacted the police.

The raid was big news and although for some the stunt was a step too far, many rallied behind the convicted pair. Paul Weller and his band The Style Council even went so far as to release a benefit EP to raise money for the defence fund.

Bristol HSA, after organising a successful national hit of the Beaufort Hunt which attracted over 150 saboteurs, ended their 1985/6 season by attending the Badminton Horse Trials. Ten saboteurs ran on in front of the Queen and paraded a banner that read, 'DIG DEEP FOR THE DUKE'. Her majesty was reportedly 'not amused' and the ten were arrested and fined £275 each.

The notorious Hunt Retribution Squad first emerged two months previously as a reaction against the escalation of hunt violence against saboteurs and in particular against a vicious attack against saboteur Eddie Coulston at the Waterloo Cup. In October 1984, a London-based magazine called *City Limits* printed a dramatic photograph of the group, consisting of a gang of balaclava-wearing activists wielding axes, clubs, baseball bats and even a chainsaw. To further the impact of the publicity stunt, the HRS threatened serious physical harm to hunters and their supporters as retaliation for their continued violent attacks against saboteurs. This was the first time animal rights activists had advocated physical violence and caused quite a stir in the media. Various threats would also continue to be made over the years under the banner of the HRS against hunt staff and supporters. For example, on 27th February 1989, a 22 year old activist admitted threatening to kill four officials of the Kent and Sussex Minkhounds after Croydon Crown Court heard that his fingerprints were found on sticky tape attached to envelopes containing razor blades that were sent to members of the hunt. Incredulously, the organisers of the 1994 Waterloo Cup were told by the HRS that three stolen land mines had been planted in the fields in which the event was due to take place. On 24th September that same year, nine members of the HRS ambushed the 8th Earl of Yarlborough enroute to a hunt meet and smashed the windows of his Mercedes. In 1995, Barry Turner of the

ARMED TO THE TEETH

THE ANTI-HUNT HIT SQUAD

MENACING: Hooded members of the hit squad pose with their armoury of weapons.

AN EXTREME anti-hunting group is planning a violent war against bloodsports.

Animal lovers condemn 'this sinister group'

By ANGELA PITTS and CHRISTIAN GYSIN

Above: Saboteurs use a gizmo to call hounds out of a wood

Chiddingfold Hunt was attacked and his vehicle trashed in retaliation to an attack on a hunt saboteur the previous week. An anonymous note later stated:

> *[...] for every wild animal killed by a hunt on a chosen day, a hunt rider will be dealt with and/or vehicle trashed. This philosophy has been used on several occasions with satisfying results.*

A pheasant pen in Edenbridge was trashed and the grain store set alight by the HRS in December 1995. A year earlier, a joint master of the Ashford Valley Hunt, Richard Pemble, was branded 'foolhardy' by police after he removed a hoax bomb planted in a toilet near the hunt secretary's tent at their point-to-point meet. According to a phone-in by *Kent Today*, 95% of their readers agreed with the police!

In 2000, following an incident in which a saboteur was run over and almost killed by the hunt, the Old Surrey and Burstow Hunt received a letter from the HRS demanding they stop their activities immediately and informing them that they were now considered 'legitimate targets'. After ignoring the letter two arson attacks destroyed hunt vehicles. The controversial Hunt Retribution Squad continued to take action in retaliation to serious violence dished out towards saboteurs although in recent years the group has since waned from activity. The group would appear again in 2007 when the houses of two members of the Golden Valley Hunt in Wales were spray painted with the initials ALF and HRS.

Suspect Device

Such was the impact of hunt saboteurs and the wider anti-hunt movement throughout the 1980s that the pro-hunt lobby was becoming even more desperate in their attempts to smear the growing animal rights movement. In one such bizarre case, police were called to the remote Somerset village of Seavington St. Mary after a hitherto unheard of group known as the British Animal Rights Society had phoned them claiming responsibility for an explosive device fitted to the underside of a huntsman's Land Rover. Upon closer inspection of the vehicle, however, detectives realised all was not as it seemed. During the forensic search of the Land Rover they found a nail identical to those placed inside the bomb (comprised of petrol and nails inside an HP sauce bottle), only this nail was located underneath a seat cushion. The evidence pointed towards an inside job and the Land Rover's owner, Alan Newberry-Street was arrested. Newberry-Street, a prominent huntsman and director of the British Hunting Exhibition was left no option but to confess that he had planted the device. "I did it to discredit the animal rights and its associations", he admitted during the resulting court case, before being found guilty and jailed for nine months.

The Ecclesfield Beagle Raid

With hunt sabotage revolving around preventing the hunt from killing once they were already out in the fields and woodlands, some were looking at more permanent ways of stopping these cruel organisations. It was August 1985 and a group from the Sheffield ALF was conducting a reconnaissance mission of the Ecclesfield Beagles' kennels in the South Yorkshire village of the same name. Their initial intention was to simply cause damage but upon a more detailed inspection of the premises, a more daring plan was hatched; they were going to liberate the pack of dogs inside. It would be a risky endeavour, not least due to the fact that the kennels were just 400 metres from the police station, but one that would have a huge impact.

During a particularly dark night, twelve activists made their way to the kennels with the main group entering through an adjoining churchyard. Jumping over the wall into the main kennel block, the group was greeted by a crescendo of howling from the beagles, excited as to whom their late night visitors may be. Whilst some of the dogs were quite happy to be led away to freedom, some in one of the kennel sections were slightly less cooperative and the liberators had to leave with a total of 28. They were loaded into the waiting van and with baited breath the group drove down the lane past the police station. Two miles further on, they met another two vehicles in a secluded wood and transferred the beagles. Euphoria set in as they began to take stock of the fact that they had dealt the hunting fraternity the biggest blow yet.

After the raid, one of the group hinted at their motives for taking part:

> *During the raid my mind went back to an incident which occurred 2 years ago when I was among a group of hunt saboteurs at the Ecclesfield Beagles. On this occasion we had not been successful and the huntsman emerged from the wood with the bloodied carcass of a murdered hare. I can still see the look of sadistic pleasure as he wiped his bloody hands on his gleaming white breeches. The look of blankness and death in the eyes of the hare is something I will never forget.*

Years of breeding were lost overnight as the hares of South Yorkshire rested a little safer.

Scarborough HSA formed in August 1984 and along with the Ripon group began sabotaging the York and Ainsty Hunt. In late 1988, having forced the York and Ainsty (North) Hunt to abandon their day's hunting, the Huddersfield, Bradford, and Leeds groups joined 30 of their comrades from Leeds University to pack up the Bramham Moor Hunt after just two hours of being out. After spotting a nearby shoot, the 69 strong crew of saboteurs then proceeded to stop to yet another gang of bloodsports enthusiasts. Having achieved this, 16 assorted beaters and gamekeepers tried to harass the antis and a small scuffle broke out. All 69 saboteurs were arrested under Section 5 of the Public Order Act, putting a slight dampener on an otherwise extremely successful outing. By far the most active group in the North West during this period was the Holcombe Hunt Action Group who coordinated most anti-hunt activity in the area. The Northern Anti-Bloodsports League, who were also based in Manchester, were building strong support bases across the city. Regional hits in the area often included the likes of the Accrington, Leyland, Wigan, Chorley, Merseyside, Burnley and Todmorden groups as well as Fylde Action for Animals. New groups were also establishing themselves in Morecambe, Lancaster University and South Cumbria, whose first hit was against the Bleasdale Beagles. The three groups effectively swamped the hunt, leaving them completely unable to even chase any hares to kill. Cumbria HSA were also active at the time against the Cumberland Farmers Foxhounds. Such was their commitment that three of their members were even jailed for fourteen days in 1987 for non-payment of fines after they were arrested and subsequently convicted of causing a breach of the peace whilst staging a sit-in to prevent the Cumberland Farmers from digging out a fox that had gone to ground. After a three year legal battle, magistrates found them guilty of deliberately refusing to pay around £200 each in fines and court costs because they "didn't commit any crime. I [sic.] was only trying to save an animal's life."

The HSA also continued to promote its invaluable work and placed adverts in various newspapers such as *The Daily Mirror*, *The Times*, *The Guardian* along with smaller publications such as *Spare Rib*, *Peace News* and *City Limits*.

Above: Saboteurs in the Oxfordshire countryside, 1984

The Public Order Act

The establishment was growing scared of the rise of hunt sabotage and of the wider animal rights movement generally and in 1986, the government introduced the Public Order Act. This new law was used with great enthusiasm by law enforcement officials, as in once case in November 1987

when three Portsmouth saboteurs were arrested under the Act whilst they waited for their van to arrive at the start of the day. The police at the time would quite often arrest saboteurs on sight or for the most spurious of reasons and as a result nearly one hundred civil cases had been brought against various police forces by the end of 1989 for wrongful arrests, resulting in over £250,000 being paid out to saboteurs in 1991/92. It was around this time that the Animal Rights National Index was set up. ARNI, as it became known, was a Special Branch initiative that sought to gain as much intelligence as it could on the burgeoning animal rights movement and use that information to curtail action. Being a major part of the movement at the time, the HSA featured quite regularly and the second news bulletin of ARNI, sent out in 1987 to local police forces, went as far as to describe the tactics used by hunt saboteurs, to include advice on how to stop anti-hunt activities and ask the police present on the day to provide details of the saboteurs involved, any new tactics employed, along with any details of upcoming events. Local police forces were advised to;

> **Ensure Hunt Masters are aware of police interest and request they forward any intelligence.**

And;

> **Similarly inform [the] Hunt Master if hunt is likely to be disrupted.**

This collusion between hunts and the police is especially shameful when one takes into account the primary purpose of the whole exercise: to ruthlessly kill a fox just trying to go about their life.

Fractions at the National Level

The situation at the HSA's national committee level was often far from peaceful during this period. For example, the 1987 AGM which took place at the Forest Fields Community Centre in Nottingham proved to be a rather heated affair. After calling Duggs Carre a 'pillock' in front of the membership present, committee member Ralph Cook stormed out of the meeting.

The role of Women's Officer was set up in order to promote equality within the saboteur community. However, some disputed the necessity of this as there was, and still remains, a roughly equal divide of genders within the anti-hunt movement and the HSA was already committed to equality. As a joke, it was subsequently proposed and agreed that the role of Men's Officer be set up in the true interests of equality. No work took place in either role.

An extremely generous donation of £9,500 by an individual saboteur was given to the HSA in 1988, accompanied by a note that requested the money be spent on direct action, particularly helping with van costs for the northern groups. However, at the time some on the committee had hatched a plan to turn the HSA into a Greenpeace-esque organisation, removing the local group structure and having a limited number of large scale direct action events each year to gain maximum publicity. An office in Exeter city centre was rented out and expensive furniture bought with the funds without proper consultation with the entire HSA committee. A meeting was held at the new Exeter offices, complete with hired security guards, such was the nature of the HSA committee's internal relationships at the time. With many committee members not present and one even physically prevented from attending at first, the meeting was not quorate and as such any further plans to change the nature of the organisation were scuppered. Understandably, tensions began to rise and it wasn't long before the situation escalated.

These tensions came to a head at the 1989 AGM. There were also concerns by some that in the run up to the committee election, the coverage in *HOWL* had been biased and questions were raised over whether the subsequent committee election was fair or not. For example, the voting slips had not been numbered in order to prevent fraud taking place. The meeting, held at the London School of Economics,

Opposite page: The Surrey and North Sussex Beagles' staff attack members of North Downs Hunt Saboteurs after they saved a hare from the hunt near Blindley Heath, Kent

Top: Saboteur Colin Skilton (left) on a hit of the Surrey Union Hunt

started 45 minutes behind schedule due to the late arrival of the Chair and the membership records. A vote of no confidence was put forward against the Treasurer after it seemed that much of the £9,500 donation had been spent on office and organisational costs rather than for what the donor had initially asked, however this was denied as it was not on the agenda.

Back from the Brink

Some way through the meeting, a formal proposal was put forward to instate Dave Wetton as Chair after which the incumbent Chair, Dave Weeks, stood down from the position. Just before everyone had departed for the break, Ralph Cook began to pack the membership list into his bag in preparation to leave. Attendees of AGMs were vetted as members on their way into the meeting, hence the HSA's membership list being present. Upon seeing this, Tunbridge Wells saboteur Simon Russell leapt over some of the tables and grasped the membership list. A tug of war ensued as more people entered the melee. Cook lost and the list was handed over to Dave Wetton for safekeeping. Cook and his fiancé, accompanied by Dave Weeks, subsequently left the meeting. The HSA committee effectively ended after this as many of its officers just stopped doing work. However, with the membership list and a £5,000 loan from Aubrey Thomas, a brand new committee (of sorts) was established. A limited company was set up in the name of 'Hunt Saboteurs Association 1989' in order to avoid any legal issues with the old organisation but the change went ahead relatively smoothly with few hitches. The HSA came very close to dying during these incidents but due to the hard work of a few committed individuals, it did not and instead continued to provide a vital support network to thousands of activists across the UK.

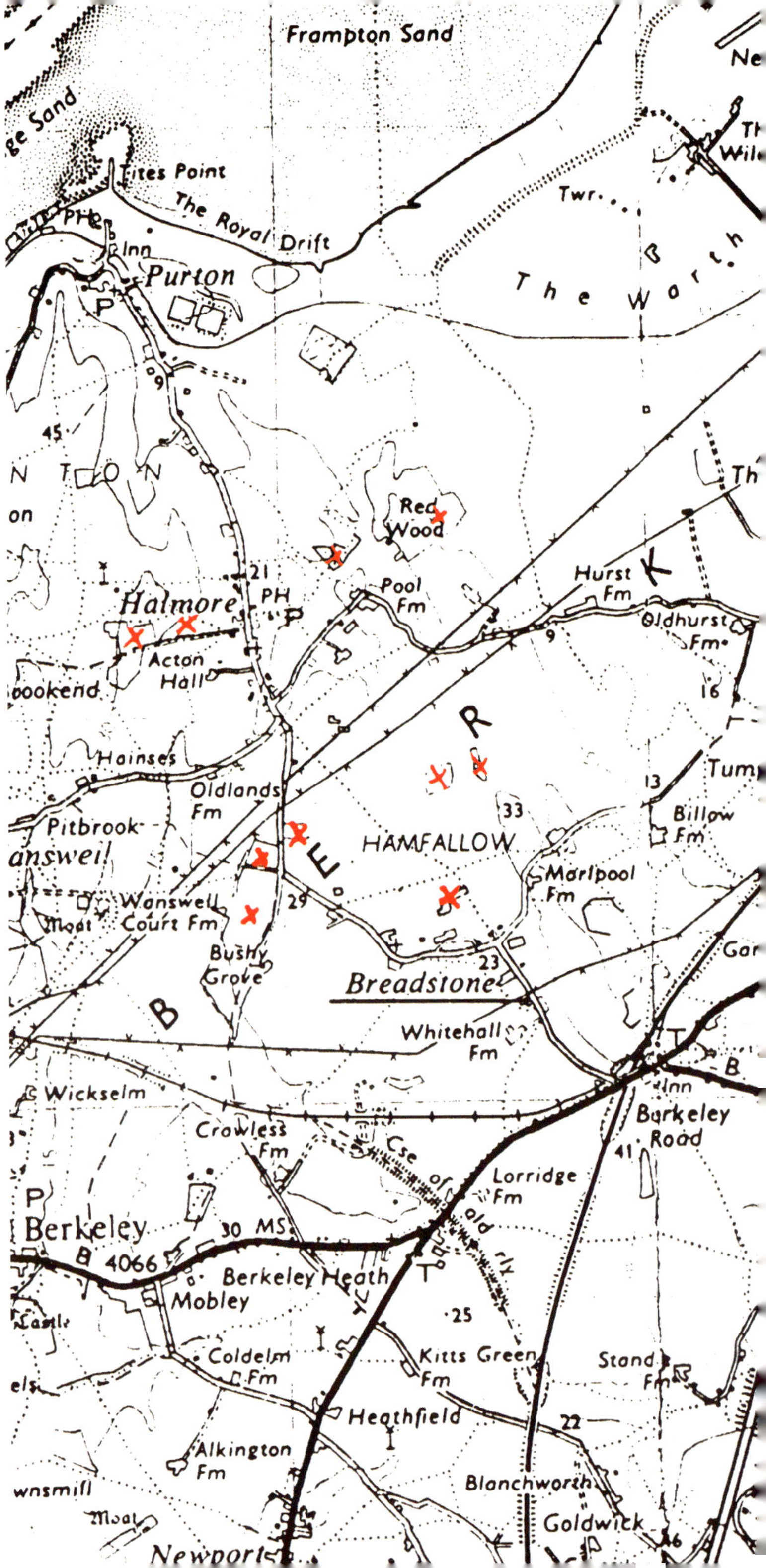

Saturday 18th October, 1986. Hit Report No. 4

The Berkeley Hunt

Location	:	Breadstone, Nr. Berkeley (4km), Stroud (19km).
Time	:	9.00am
Grid References	:	Hunt Meet - Breadstone - Sheet 162 - SO711008
		Coverts (* hunt entered) 708010 Pre-Beat
		701014 -"- -"-
		699012*-"- -"-
		Bushy Grove 697007 -"- -"-
		708017*-"- -"-
		710018*-"- -"-
		703028 -"- -"-
		Red Wood 707030*-"- -"-
		692023*-"- -"-
		695025*-"- -"-
No. of Sabs	:	19 - Cotswold
		65+ - Total (approx) - Bath, Bristol.

Pick-Ups in Gloucester - 6.30am
Cheltenham - 7.00am
Stoud - 7.30am
Dursley - 8.00am

At 8.20am we arrived at Breadstone to find other sabs 'talking' with the 'boys in blue'. We drove past them and continued on until we reached a road junction at 699021.

It was decided that the group would split into 2 - one would walk along the road to make contact with the other sabs, the second would move to Red Wood - 707030 - and a small covert to it's S.W.

Group 1

The van drove back along the road with Cotswold following on foot. We joined the other sabs at 700012, and a stroppy copper with a Welsh accent arrived with threats to arrest sabs if they entered the covert to the west of the road - 699012. A covert with sabs already inside pre-beating.

As the hunt moved off, more police arrived, so we got back in our van to find the group over by Red Wood.

Group 2

We arrived at the small covert - 703028 - and decided to pre-beat it downwind (N.W.) away from the anticipated direction of arrival of the hunt. It was a very small covert with limited undergrowth, and was ∴ useful practice for the new sabs. 1 or 2 hane learnt to wear good coats/jackets. After a period of 10 minutes (and after flushing out a brace of pheasants), we grouped at the N.W. corner and made our way quickly to the S.E. corner of Red Wood.

There was no sight or sound of the hunt.

Red Wood is very large. So large that it was impossible to pre-beat it properly without rookies and only 8 sabs. A decision was made to "block spray" a large quarter of the wood - page 15 of the "HSA Tactics Booklet", however 20 yards into the wood and the undergrowth was impassable. The only alternative we had was to spray just inside the boundary of the wood and along the sides of the main rides within it.

By 9.10am we had finished and regrouped at the western edge of the wood. The walk back to where we were dropped off in the van, involved some good basic sab work - the anticipation of the movements of the hunt, and the actual finding of the hunt.

On the walk back to the road we passed through some open gates. 1 gate open wouldn't attract much attention, but on this occasion 3 gates were open joining consecutive fields. To us this implied, logically, that the hunt would come to this wood, via the road (and the direction of the meet).

Of course, following the 'Country Code', we did securely shut them.

We got back to the road - 704026 - and started our way back to the road junction. After 200yrds we heard a shout (not exactly a holloa) coming from the East. Almost immediatly 2 cars passed us from the direction of the road junction, driven by elderly gentlemen.

3 items of note, made us turn around and head in the direction of Hurst Farm.

1) We were expecting the hunt to come from the S.W. to Red Wood (the open gates in relation to the meet),
2) The shout was probably a distant holloa, and,
3) The drivers were probably supporters.

By turning around and going in the opposite direction, we were moving closer and hopefully onto the path of the hunt as they approached Red Wood.

We ran for ½ mile until we could see the two cars parked by the roadside. Immediatly we saw the hunt to the S.W. at the two coverts in the middle of Hamfallow - 708017 & 710018 - heading towards us. It was 9.25am.

We waited 5 minutes and our van arrived with our other sabs.

The other groups were contacted by C.B.

8 of Cotswold H.S.A. went back onto the land at the corner of Red Wood to await the hunt. Halfway between this wood and the road, ran a hedge with a ditch. It had a few gaps but was otherwise ideal for holding up the pack if they got onto a scent. So this was liberally sprayed in anticipation of the hunts arrival

The other sabs in 2 vans and a Landrover had by now arrived at the road with Cotswold. We waited...

At 10.00am the huntsman had somehow lost control of the hounds - they were "all over the place". He regained control and by 10.10am he took them through the 3 gates we had closed by Pool Farm and had reached the western most point of Red Wood. Unfortunately they went around the sprayed hedge.

The 8 sabs at Red Wood, went in and through to find the hunt entering at the western edge. Within 3 minutes we were surrounded by hunt heavies, numbering about 15, and ordered out. We decided a tactical withdrawal was the wiser move. As we were departing along the main ride, more supporters gathered around us until about 40 yrds from the edge of the wood we all stopped.

It was a marvellous sight. At least 25 sabs were pouring over a gate to join us (mainly Bath). A short debate followed during which time the hunt were not hindered. (10.20am). Why there was no trouble is difficult to say.

Another 25 sabs had arrived by this time, and as we were going around the wood, the hounds found a scent. Fortunately they also lost it within ½ mile after going back by Pool Farm.

We got back in our vans to catch up with the hunt.

In the next 20 minutes the hunt had moved back to the covert at 699012 (10.50am). We arrived and the hunt then departed north, towards 2 woods by Acton Hall.

It was back into the vans and a trip up to Brookend by 11.05am. Here was a bridleway which would take us to the back of these two woods. (683023). All sabs left the vans and made their way along the bridleway. At 11.15am we entered the first of these woods and eventually caught up with the hunt at 11.25am.

The hunt immediately packed in, thoroughly 'pissed off', in a yard at the other end of the footpath - 698025.

11.30am, Halmore.

NO kills.

SHOOTING

Top: West Yorkshire Police inform saboteurs that a 'state of emergency' has been declared, 12th August 1988

Bottom: Saboteur Keith Mann jumps into Nottingham HSA's Land Rover whilst sabotaging the Glorious Twelfth, 1989

Opposite page: Saboteurs occupy a grouse butt during 'Shoots Week', 1993

Grouse Shooting

As well as saving mammals, saboteurs have quite regularly ventured onto shooting estates to hit 'gamebird' shoots. Grouse shooting, which takes place between 12th August and 10th December each year, has been the most high profile form of shooting to suffer sustained saboteur activity. Driven grouse shooting takes places on moorland in the North of England (such as the North York Moors and the Peak District) and Scotland. During a shoot, a line of beaters flush the birds towards a line of around eight to ten shooters (or 'guns' as they are known) who are situated in shooting butts some 20 to 30 metres apart and the grouse are shot as they fly across the path of the 'guns'. Despite the immense cruelty involved in shooting vast numbers of grouse from the sky, the driven grouse shooting industry has also attracted major criticism from conservationists due to the illegal persecution of birds of prey (hen harriers have been pushed almost to extinction as a result) and for harming moorland habitats, both to sustain an unnaturally large population of grouse to shoot. Moves were made to ban the bloodsport in 2016, when ex-RSPB Conservation Director Mark Avery raised a e-petition calling for a ban, which received 123,077 signatures, thus triggering a debate in the House of Commons. Unsurprisingly, however, parliament showed little interest in curbing the bloodsport.

The Inglorious Twelfth

Each year, on the first day of the grouse shooting season, known as the Glorious Twelfth, large numbers of saboteurs take an annual trip up onto the moors to take matters into their own hands and directly stop the shooting of thousands of birds. On August 9th 1978, the HSA's Press Officer, Chris Williamson (who would later go on to become a Labour MP) recorded an interview on Radio Derby about the HSA's plans to sabotage the upcoming grouse shooting season. Fearful that widespread disruption would take place, the Chief Inspector of Buxton Police, Graham Ward, visited Williamson's home the following day and issued him with a summons to Buxton magistrates court for the next morning, although Saturday morning court sessions usually only dealt with remand cases. Williamson was then bound over for six months in an underhand attempt to curtail any saboteur activity on the moors. This tactic by both the police and the courts failed, however, as 90 saboteurs turned up at several shoots across the Peak District on the first day of the grouse shooting season!

The 1984 season was probably the most intensive, successful and widely published campaign against grouse shooting since the HSA first coordinated action against the bloodsport seven years previously. On 13th August, around 200 saboteurs prevented all shooting taking place on the Fitzwilliam-Wentworth Estate on Bradfield Moor, the first time in 40 years the shoot was unable to kill grouse on the opening day of the season. That same day, 30 saboteurs disrupted a press conference held in the village of Hope, Derbyshire, laying a wreath for all the birds killed and commandeering the game cart where they were strung up. The ALF were busy on the day too as five gunshops across the North West had their locks glued and slogans daubed on their windows. Forty shooting butts and a cabin on an estate owned by the Gleneagles Hotel were demolished along with all butts belonging to a grouse moor in Clwyd. On 25th August, 60 saboteurs stopped a large shooting party of 40 assorted gamekeepers, shooters and beaters on the Duke of Devonshire's estate near Skipton.

The following year also proved to be a very successful one, although this time aided by bad weather and low grouse numbers. The media had even announced that very few shoots would be going out in August and the season would not start properly until September. A hit was planned on 17th August and the organisers were worried whether it was actually worth the expense of gathering saboteurs from across the country to attend a shoot which may not even happen. In the end, it was decided that the risk of the shoot occurring was too great and a mobilisation was called. Eighty to a hundred saboteurs from Leeds, Sheffield, Coventry, Cumbria, Manchester and West Midlands met at the Holme Moss TV station car park at 8.30am. The heavy police presence in the area hinted that something was afoot and suspicions that a shoot was due to happen were confirmed when the park

ranger was spotted putting up 'SHOOTING TODAY' signs on the access points to Cowden Moor. Upon news of this, the groups scrambled to cover all of the access points in an attempt to follow any team of shooters onto the moors. As it turned out, this was not necessary as at around 10.30am, a number of Land Rovers appeared at access point 8. They simply swore at the antis and drove away without any further attempt to shoot. The groups returned home joyful in the knowledge that not a shot had been fired on Cowden Moor - but not before 18 shooting butts were demolished.

In August 1988, saboteurs the length and breadth of the UK again took to the moors to disrupt the start of the grouse shooting season. Among the shoots targeted was one on Gunnerside Moor in Upper Swaledale, which was owned by Earl Peel. After a stand-off, at around noon, West Yorkshire Police took the unprecedented step of declaring a 'state of emergency' which gave themselves the powers to (amongst other things) block the roads around the moor. Numerous road blocks were set up to stop the one hundred activists who had gathered and, under police escort, Earl Peel's shooting party was able to travel elsewhere and carry out a walked-up shoot but not before they were denied the use of what they considered to be a prime grouse moor. The HSA's press officer, Angela Majennik, also made the point that the delay caused to the shoot as the eight 'guns' were stranded at Earl Peel's home, Gunnerside Lodge, before the police had arrived, had saved the lives of around 150 grouse. She said:

> *When you consider people are paying more than £1,000 a day to shoot grouse on the so-called Glorious Twelfth, our action today must be of significance. When we moved off after the guns, the police swooped on us immediately, putting one car in front of us and one behind, so we could not go anywhere. The police involved refused to give us their numbers, but we have taken photographs of the officers involved and the registrations of their vehicles and will use them as evidence in a complaint.*

The start of the 1990 grouse shooting season attracted over 100 saboteurs who stopped shoots at four sites: Stanhope, Allenheads, Muggleswick Common, and Gallogill.

On the Glorious Twelfth 1992, Yorkshire Hunt Saboteurs and others sabotaged and immediately packed up two shoots and over the course of the succeeding week of action, over eleven shoots were put to an untimely end. Thirty-five saboteurs were arrested by police officers clearly in the pocket of the powerful estate owners. Indeed in their report, the Yorkshire group noted that "whilst the police task force were busy wasting public money concentrating on us, 200 football fans had a fight at Ripon races – enough said." The *Shooting Times* was also forced to concede that 1992 had:

> *[…] a generally subdued opening to the Glorious Twelfth both in England and in Scotland. Many of our larger moors have chosen not to shoot until this week [the week after] or later to avoid saboteur activity. Several North East moors including Swinton, Ousterbank, Dallowgill and Grinton were assaulted by antis who appeared particularly well organised this year.*

One of the shoots hit that week was one that took place on the infamous Blubberhouses Moor, on the south of the Yorkshire Dales. Blubberhouses Moor was where nineteenth-century bloodsports fanatic Lord Ripon once shot a record number of grouse. This time, however, the Belgian shooting party present only managed to kill less than 30 grouse instead of the possible 200 to 300 birds.
In 1994, one hundred saboteurs completely halted the first drive of a shoot on Harkerside Moor. As 40 officers from North Yorkshire constabulary descended on the area, the group split and went on to stop another shoot on Lofthouses Moor, while decoy vehicles held up the main body of police. The following day, saboteurs met at Castle Bolton before locating a shoot eight miles north on Harkerside Moor and forcing them to take an early lunch as their second drive of

Opposite page: A group of saboteurs during 'Shoots Week' in Yorkshire, 20th August 1992

Top: Saboteurs stop a grouse shoot on the Dallowgill Estate near Ripon, 21st August 1992

Bottom: A shooter tries to confiscate a saboteur's banner near Askrigg, 20th August 1993

the day was called off. After lunch, the shoot was allowed to attempt another drive as saboteurs had already pre-beat the grouse out of the area during the morning. Their final drive of the day was thwarted by a small but bold group of saboteurs who rushed the butts and kept the number of grouse shot at two.

The 1998 event proved to be a massive damp squib for the bloodsport enthusiasts as appalling weather leading up to the day had drastically reduced the stocks of grouse and as a result many shoots were forced to call off in order to 'protect the species'. Indeed, grouse numbers were thought to have halved in the worst affected areas including North Yorkshire, the Pennines and Northumberland. The only large grouse shoot to occur on the prestigious day, on the Duke of Westminster's estate in Lancashire, was stopped after 50 activists from as far afield as Swansea, Croydon and Edinburgh showed up.

Upwards of 50 saboteurs stopped grouse being slaughtered on the Fitzwilliam Estate on 16th August 2003 despite the police scrambling a helicopter and numerous squad cars to stop them. A month later, an estate manager stood on a wasp nest whilst out grouse shooting on the same moor and died within a few hours due to an allergic reaction to the stings he received. In 2004, saboteurs from Manchester, Reading, London, Norfolk, Sheffield, Derby and Leeds headed to Snailsden Moor near Holmfirth following a tip off from a local resident. As the groups found the shoot, they were greeted by employees of Countrywatch who had been called in to protect the shoot against antis. A long stand-off occurred that eventually led to the large convoy of shooters driving off the moor at 2.30pm after miserably failing to shoot any animals.

After a period of relatively little saboteur action against shooting, 2017 saw a resurgence in anti-shooting activity and the Glorious Twelfth that year was no exception. Around one hundred saboteurs descended on the infamous Saddleworth Moor after spotters in the area had passed on the location of a shoot. The shooters immediately broke guns after the beaters spotted the huge long line of people trudging their way through the heather towards them. After much deliberation, the wise decision was made to call it a day and as the large group of saboteurs stood watch over the farm where the shooters had gathered, another phone call came in, this time with the location of another shoot, on the Fitzwilliam Estate in the heart of the Peak District about half an hour's drive to the south. Again, as soon as the mass of saboteurs were spotted appearing over the brow of the hill, shooting quickly ceased for the day and a prolonged yet calm stand-off ensued for the next few hours before the shoot manager told his party to head for home. Interestingly enough, David Dunn was in attendance (looking rather frail from the years that had gone by), yet gone were the days of Countrywatch's thuggery against saboteurs as all he could do was watch the large group of antis from the other side of a dry stone wall, as they vastly outnumbered the bloodsport enthusiasts.

To capitalise on this renewed interest in anti-shooting activity, saboteurs took to the moors again the following year. Instead of heading to the Peak District where shooters may have been warier of sabotage (due to the previous year's hit and its more central location, meaning that it was accessible by more groups), it was arranged that local groups would head to the North York Moors. A shoot was quickly located just north of Helmsley and as one group started to make their way onto the moor to oppose it, news came through that another shoot had been spotted on the Yorkshire Dales. Upon hearing the news, a larger contingent of saboteurs scrambled to Swaledale and rushed down the track that the beaters had been seen taking. As soon as it was obvious what the intention of this crowd of black and camouflage wearing folk was, the shoot manager ordered the shooting to cease and the shooting party made their way back to a hotel in the nearby town of Reeth. No further attempts at shooting were made as a stand-off ensued on the village green outside.

Top and bottom: A gamekeeper threatens North West saboteurs with a pickaxe handle on Stanhope Common, 12th August 1996

Opposite page: Saboteurs look down on the shooting party on the Fitzwilliam Estate, 12th August, 2017

Pheasant and Partridge Shooting

It was not only the grouse shooting industry that had to deal with the problem of sabotage, pheasant and partridge shoots have also been routinely visited by hunt saboteurs throughout the years. As opposed to grouse, pheasants and partridges are not wild birds and the vast majority of the two species are reared in appalling conditions in game farms before being sold onto shoots across the UK. Many pheasants and partridges who are unfortunate enough to have been used for breeding are confined to barren wire cages that have already been made illegal for use with poultry. Neither the common pheasant nor the red-legged partridge are native to the UK.

In most circumstances, simply walking up to a shooting party is enough to stop them killing. This is not always the case however as more gung-ho shooters have been known to carry on regardless. In 1990, for example, nine members of Oxford HSA and Buckingham HSA had come across a shoot in a valley near Wantage whilst looking for the Old Berkshire Hunt. Guided by the gamekeeper onto a public footpath that crossed the valley directly in front of the guns, the saboteurs moved in swiftly and formed a line, one in front of each gun. The landowner quickly appeared and scurried between the bewildered shooters instructing them to ignore the saboteurs and fire anyway. Although most were too confused by what was happening to do anything other than hover uncertainly with guns poised, two shooters suddenly let off four shots directly over the saboteurs' heads, with one shooter firing straight over the left shoulder of a saboteur. Three birds fell to the ground, dead, but no more shooting took place.

Often, campaigning also took place out of the fields. After a 16 week campaign by animal rights groups, disgruntled customers and disillusioned staff, the highstreet store, John Lewis, decided in January 2001 to close its shooting club at its estate in Hampshire. What was perhaps most controversial to the members of staff who made up the partnership of John Lewis was the fact that the club was financed by company profits yet only included 27 members, 22 of whom were senior management.

An inspiring example of an ordinary, compassionate man taking extraordinary action was anti-snare campaigner, John Gill. He made it his mission to campaign against these cruel devices following the death of his collie, Laddie, who was caught in a snare set by a local gamekeeper. Gill worked tirelessly finding and removing snares, using court cases for criminal damage to further the outreach work of his campaign. In November 2001, a charge of criminal damage to 27 snares was even dropped despite Gill admitting on tape that he had done it. Such was the efficacy and high profile nature of his work that two months previously, Gill was hospitalised after three men forced their way into his home and beat him with baseball bats in retribution for his work saving animals.

Factory Farming

Although the shooting industry has worked very hard to promote the shooting of pheasants and partridges as an 'ethical' food source, with shooters just killing a few wild animals to take home for the pot, nothing could be further from the truth. Although other bloodsports have suffered a terminal decline over the years in terms of attendance, public opinion and ultimately viability, the shooting industry has grown significantly recently. Around 61.2 million pheasants and partridges are intensively reared and released to be shot each year. When released, the pheasant becomes the UK's most numerous 'wild' bird with their population eclipsing that of the wren, who has the next largest population of an estimated 8.5 million breeding pairs.

Hundreds of thousands of pheasants and partridges spend the majority of their productive lives in tiny, metal battery cages not dissimilar to those used for egg laying hens. However as opposed to egg laying hens, there are no minimum legal space requirements for caged pheasants and partridges. Each cage typically houses eight to ten females and one male. Females often develop wounds to their backs from repetitive mating from the males.

Opposite page: Saboteurs from East Yorkshire are arrested whilst sabotaging a shoot near East Pocklington.

Top: John Gill, tireless anti-snare campaigner

Bottom: Pigeon shooters pack up after being found by saboteurs at South Warnborough in Hampshire, 1992.

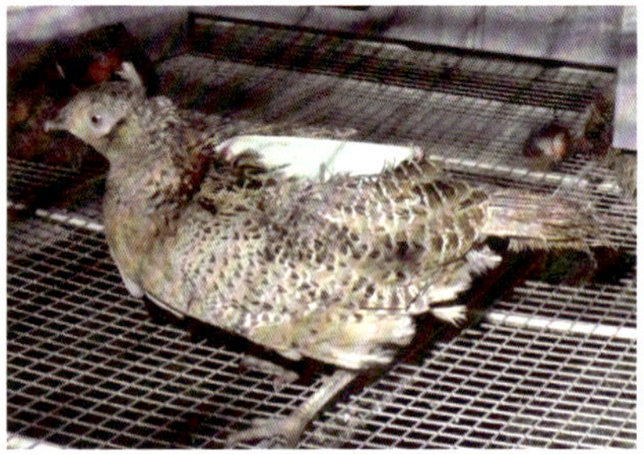

Top: A Nottingham saboteur confronts a pheasant shooter, 2016

Middle: A female pheasant at Knowle Game Farm is fitted with a 'saddle' as her back feathers had been ripped out due to repetitive mating, 2017

Bottom: Pheasant chicks at Knowle Game Farm are crammed into a shed, 2017

Opposite page: Saboteurs put an end to a day's shooting

Stress from a life of incarceration leads to feather pecking, sores on the birds' feet due to the wire mesh flooring and 'scalping'; a term used by the industry to describe the birds' head damage received by repeatedly striking their heads against the top of the cage in futile attempts to escape. The industry's answer to the problem of stress induced aggression and feather pecking is to trim the birds' beaks or to put a 'bit' or a 'mask' onto them. These cruel devices have already been made illegal for use on poultry. Devices known as 'spectacles' are also used which block the forward vision of the birds and are meant to deter feather-pecking and cannibalism. At some farms, bright lamps are positioned above the cages to trick the birds into believing the days are longer, thus making them more productive in terms of egg laying. Many pheasant chicks are crammed into boxes and are sold onto other rearing farms at a day old. Others are reared on site and are sold off to shoots at seven to eight weeks old where they will spend a few months in rearing pens before being released into nearby countryside to be shot.

Exposing the Horror

Numerous exposés have been made to show the systematic cruelty of game farms to the public. Both Animal Aid and the League Against Cruel Sports have documented horrific conditions across a large number of farms and in 2017 the HSA also released an investigation. The investigation centred around Knowle Game Farm near Ulcombe in Kent. Thousands of pheasants were found in barren wire cages, many with severe wounds due to repetitive mating and cannibalism caused by the extreme stress of confinement. Workers at the farm were filmed simply dumping the dead birds in a large pile in a corner of an adjacent field, an illegal act as 'gamebirds' are classified as livestock when in captivity. *The Times* ran the story under the headline 'HORROR AT PHEASANT FARM REVEALED IN SECRET FOOTAGE' and the first paragraph of the article read:

> *Rotting birds lie piled in a heap. There is barely any flesh, only feathers, bones and beaks still fitted with the plastic bits used to stop them pecking each other to death. The bits, which are banned in other EU countries, prevent the birds from closing their beaks.*

Such stark and honest language was a rarity within the newspaper that had quite often ran stories championing game shooting and as such, having the realities of the pheasant rearing industry laid bare to an audience that might not necessarily be on the side of saboteurs certainly provided a boost to the HSA's anti-shooting campaign. Knowledge about the factory farming of game birds was quickly spreading throughout the general public and just a few months later, in April 2018, *The Times* reported that as many as 16,000 partridges, who were being used for breeding, were released by the Animal Liberation Front from Southern Partridges in Devon as well as an unknown number of breeding birds from Knowle Game Farm.

Shipping in Live Targets

As bad as 2018 was for the shooting industry, things were going to get a whole lot worse in the following year. In 2019, the HSA turned its attention to the importation of 'gamebirds' into the UK. DEFRA figures revealed that 15,513,447 pheasant and partridge chicks and ready-to-hatch eggs were imported in 2015 from France alone. A shocking exposé was released showing horrendous conditions at two French game farm cooperatives supplying the UK shooting market. Through research conducted by the HSA and others, it was found that Eurotunnel was the only transporter of these chicks into the UK whilst Brittany Ferries and DFDS Seaways would only transport the hatching eggs. P&O had previously refused to have either on board their ships. A few weeks after the French exposé, saboteurs travelled to Portugal to expose a partridge farm supplying Meadow Game, a hatchery in Northamptonshire. It was found that 25,174,306 live

LAND ROVER

partridges and pheasant chicks and eggs were imported from Europe into the UK between 1st May 2018 and 30th April 2019 (this huge number even excludes partridge egg imports as there are no data). This staggering number means that around half of all partridges and pheasants released each year into the British countryside to be shot originate from overseas game farms. Further analysis of DEFRA figures also revealed that gamebird imports from Poland had increased by 2400% in just four years and so not long after their Portuguese trip, the HSA released footage from a Polish battery farm shipping Bazanty pheasants to the UK to be reared and shot out of the sky. Amongst the backdrop of this continued negative press for the industry, the ALF continued its targeted campaign against game farms. In March 2019, *The Times* reported that 5,000 breeding pheasants were released from a farm in Chilmark, Wiltshire whilst the next month the *BBC* stated that 9,000 pheasants had been freed from Heath Hatcheries in Suffolk over the Easter Weekend. HSA groups were also taking on the shooters as in one highly successful hit by Bath Hunt Saboteurs on a shoot near West Kington Wick in Wiltshire in December 2019. Despite managing to kill around 20 pheasants before the group turned up, the shooting party was stopped in its tracks as high-vis clad saboteurs engaged the shooters, saving the lives of hundreds of birds in the process.

Large numbers of ducks are also intensively reared then shot for 'sport'. Duck shoots have, on occasion, been sabotaged such as when members of the North West Hunt Saboteurs Association came across a shoot at Hoghton Tower, near Blackburn in 2005. They arrived 15 minutes after the start of the shoot, but they put an immediate stop to it as soon as they entered the field. Sadly, a small pile of shot ducks was found in the corner of the field, with some of the birds still alive. One of the saboteurs decided to do the kindest thing and put the dying birds out of their pain as the shooters looked on, totally disinterested in the suffering they had caused. After a long wait in the pouring rain, the shooting party then wisely decided to pack up and no more ducks were killed that day.

Although hunting with hounds has been on the receiving end of the brunt of the HSA's actions, many shoots have experienced saboteur activity (even if this was as a result of saboteurs being in the area due to the fact that they were looking for a hunt). The lack of a sustained campaign against the shooting industry has allowed it to grow to vast proportions, with many estates now offering bag sizes of 200 or 300 birds per day. The industry's cruelty extends further than its stated quarry, however, as not only are gamebirds reared and shot in their millions, but countless numbers of foxes, stoats, weasels, corvids and birds of prey are killed as a matter of routine in order to protect such unnaturally high numbers of non-native birds and therefore, profit.

Opposite page: Members of Bath Hunt Saboteurs hit a pheasant shoot near West Kington Wick, 13th December 2019

Top: A dead pheasant wearing a plastic 'mask' is left on top of a cage in a French game farm, 13th April 2019

Bottom: Two partridges used for breeding are confined in a barren, wire cage at Caçabrava game farm near Tomar, Portugal, 4th May 2019

1990S: A DEFINING DECADE

Top and Bottom: A Petersfield saboteur blocks the entrance to a fox earth from the Chiddingfold's hounds after a fox takes refuge in it. A scuffle with the hunt's terriermen broke out but the saboteurs stood their ground and the dig out was abandoned, 10th Febuary 1990

Opposite page top: A Belfast saboteur calls hounds away from the hunt, November 1997

Opposite page bottom: Belfast HSA, November 1997

Opposite page right: A member of the East Antrim Hunt strikes a hound with his whip

Rising From the Ashes...

The HSA entered what was arguably to be its most defining decade in a rather uncertain state. A caretaking 'holding committee' was running the affairs of the association after the major upheavals and resignations of 1989. Despite some problems on an organisational level, this had little impact on many local groups who were still campaigning with ever increasing vigour. The East Sussex and Romney Marsh Hunt, for example, was visited by the Hastings and Bexhill HSA on 57 of its hunting days, drastically decreasing their annual tally of foxes killed by 75 percent that year.

Public opinion was also continuing to sway against hunting, as there were now more than 120 local authority bans in operation in the UK. Many viewed the late 1980s and early 1990s as the heyday of hunt sabotage. Local groups were regularly getting over 50 saboteurs out on a single day and for many it became a lifestyle. Living on the dole was far easier than it is today and the large number of squats at the time meant that those wishing to devote their time to animal liberation and other social justice struggles could afford to do so on a much more full time basis. Indeed, on Boxing Day 1990, the most prestigious day in the fox hunting calendar, not a single animal was killed at any of the meets attended by hunt saboteurs. The Linlithgow and Stirlingshire Hunt didn't even come out from their kennels to face the antis outside.

In accordance with the mandates set at both the 1989 and 1990 AGMs, the decision was made to make the HSA a limited company and VAT registered, meaning that the organisation would feel the financial benefits of doing so. This also meant that, as a trading company, the HSA's good name and assets were protected from libel, slander and theft of ideas. In true HSA style, during the 1992 AGM, the treasurer, Aubrey Thomas, was actually arrested during the meeting itself over a disagreement about whether the venue allowed saboteurs to bring their dogs inside. Fortunately, West Yorkshire Police allowed him 20 minutes to deliver his speech on the HSA's finances before arresting him! Thomas was released without charge not long after and later received £500 in compensation for the arrest.

North Dorset HSA, Winchester HSA and West Norfolk HSA first sprang into action during the 1990/91 season with the latter's first day out comprising of a successful hit against a pheasant shoot. It was (and still is) the network of local groups that formed the backbone both of the HSA and of the anti-hunt movement as a whole. As money was constantly needed to keep saboteurs out in the fields, a large part of the HSA's remit has always been to financially assist local groups. For example, aside from funding national hits such as the Northumberland Beagling Festival and the Glorious Twelfth, the organisation donated or loaned £2,110 to eleven local groups over the course of the 1992/93 committee. Taking action against hunting was a costly business, with the HSA spending £2,374 on hunting horns alone in 1991.

The Irish Saboteurs

The tide of anti-bloodsports activity had also by this time swept across the Irish Sea. The Ballymena HSA joined forces with the Belfast and North Down group to form one major HSA group covering Northern Ireland and regularly targeted the Iveagh Harriers as well as the East Down Foxhounds and the East Antrim Foxhounds. More challenges presented themselves on the other side of the Irish Sea, however. For example, detention at a routine military checkpoint in October 1990 made the group half an hour late for the Iveagh's Lawrencetown m eet. It proved to be a good day nonetheless as they did manage to intervene to stop the hounds just yards away from a fox. The following week's hunting was cancelled after just two and a half hours as the hunt failed to persuade the police to stop saboteurs from following the hounds. Although being stopped and searched was a regular occurrence for most saboteurs, the situation in Northern Ireland was altogether more challenging. Most groups were well used to having various parts of the Public Order Act read to them by the police but the Royal Ulster Constabulary were stopping the Northern Irish

berghaus

saboteurs every week under the Prevention of Terrorism (Emergency Provisions) Act, which meant that those stopped were legally obliged to provide their name, address, date of birth and details of their recent movements, although in reality the police demanded to know much more. In one incident, the group was surrounded by five bullet-proof police cars whilst a total of 12 officers searched the seven saboteurs and their vehicle. All the hunting horns were confiscated and when asked under what law this was done, the officer responsible simply walked over to his car and took out his sub-machine gun. After 40 minutes the group was free to go but between three and five RUC cars later followed them wherever they went which meant that any intervention in the hunt was impossible.

A Dark Day in Hampshire

The brutality of fox hunting is something that saboteurs, wherever they are active, witness first-hand. The following account from a saboteur at the Hampshire Hunt on 6th November 1993 highlights the compassion of those who attempted to rescue a fox from the hunt and the heartbreak of such an ordeal:

> *It's the worst thing that's ever happened to me while sabbing. An elderly female hunt rider spotted the fox crouching in a hedge. It remained there, obviously terrified, with riders surrounding the area. The huntsman brought the pack onto it, and as it began to run away it was caught by about three hounds. A saboteur ran into the bloodbath and managed to grab the fox and hoist it onto his shoulder. The hounds were snapping at his feet. The huntsman and whipper-in had dismounted and were trying to get through to the fox. I scrambled in, but the hounds had torn the fox away from the sab's arms, and two of them were biting it. As I tried to pull it away from their jaws, the whipper-in leant over me and beat the fox over the head with the bone handle of his whip. He kept striking it, but I couldn't stop him as I was trying to pull the fox away. I suppose he wanted to kill it, so he could pretend it had been a 'clean kill by a bite to the back of the neck.' I really couldn't believe what was happening. I have never seen such cruelty. I was screaming at the huntsman to let go. I was now trying to cradle the fox's head and the huntsman was trying to pull the fox from me with brute strength, as if it were already dead. But it wasn't dead - how could we let go? Eventually one of the police hunt squad arrived. The huntsman relaxed his grip and I gathered the fox into my arms. It struggled and tried to bite my face, so I thought it would survive because it was fighting. Although we had been bitten by the hounds, we took the fox and ran across a field with it. We were jubilant because we thought we'd given the fox another chance. We got to a road, and phoned a mobile saboteur and asked to be picked up. I remember once, while we were in the car, we lifted up the jacket covering the fox to see if it was breathing okay. These two golden eyes stared into our faces. He was beautiful. He was curled up on my friend's lap, nose to brush, staring up. His eyes made me think he understood. We took the fox to woman nearby who looks after wild animals but she took one look at him and said she couldn't treat him. We quickly drove to the town centre and arranged to meet an off-duty vet. We took him into the vet's surgery and laid him on the table. His head and body were covered in puncture wounds from the hounds' teeth and his lips were torn up. We all stood around that table as the vet gently lifted one of his back legs. Part of his intestine snaked out. His belly had been ripped open. The vet put him to sleep.*

It is not only the cruelty of huntsmen that is astonishing but the arrogance too. Following their last meet of the 1992 season, the Vale of Aylesbury Hunt's hound van crashed on the A41 and the road was closed for two and half hours as police rounded up 36 hounds and two horses. Two of the hounds were subsequently put down by a local vet and a

Top: A saboteur cradles an injured fox at the Hampshire Hunt, 6th November 1993

Bottom: Saboteurs from the South East stop a dig out at the Old Surrey and Burstow Hunt, 1991

Opposite page top left: New Forest Hunt riders attack a group of hunt saboteurs

Opposite page bottom left: Jeremy Paxman interviews Sheffield HSA, 1995

Opposite page right: A fox cub introduces themself to Reading HSA at a Chiddingfold cub hunting meet, 1992.

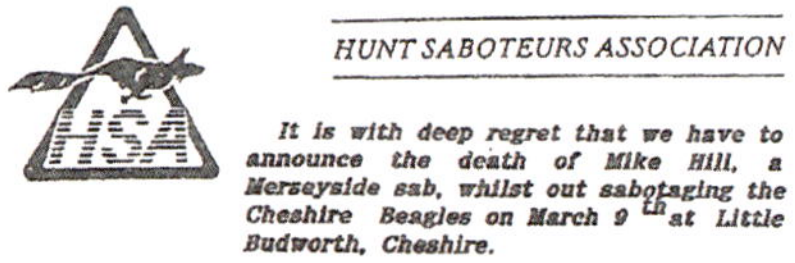

HUNT SABOTEURS ASSOCIATION

It is with deep regret that we have to announce the death of Mike Hill, a Merseyside sab, whilst out sabotaging the Cheshire Beagles on March 9th at Little Budworth, Cheshire.

Top: Mike Hill

Bottom: An extract from a flyer released by the HSA detailing the circumstances of Hill's death

Opposite page: Saboteurs take the body of a freshly-killed fox from a whipper-in of the Puckeridge and Thurlow Hunt, 23rd November 1991

passing motorist's car was written off in the crash. The driver of the van, Mr McCann, was arrested and later pleaded guilty to drink driving and received a one year driving ban along with a £250 fine. Another prime example of the arrogance of huntsmen at the time was when a Land Rover full of saboteurs was present at a meet of the Puckeridge and Thurlow Hunt at Langley Lower Green on 23rd November 1991. A fox was killed on the front lawn of a local opponent to the hunt. Instead of apologising to the homeowner, a red-coated member of the hunt simply walked back to the road, swinging the lifeless body of the fox. Arriving just minutes too late, a group of saboteurs soon turned up and attempted to grab the dead fox from the hunter. A tug-of-war ensued and was only ended by the arrival of a pick up truck full of hunt supporters who managed to take the fox back. Unbeknownst to them, however, Mike Huskisson was undercover within the hunt at the time and managed to take photographs of the fracas as well as witnessing the abuse the local homeowners received for simply being against the hunt.

Mike Hill

On 9th February 1991, Mike Hill became the first saboteur to pay the ultimate price for his involvement in anti-hunt activities. Following the weekly assaults on hunt saboteurs at the hands of hunt staff and supporters, many almost believed it was only a matter of time before someone was killed. Hill was a gentle and compassionate young man who for the two years prior to his death, lived and breathed animal rights. He was vegan and worked at both Heavens Gate Sanctuary and Freshfields Animal Rescue Centre as well as being an active saboteur with both the Yeovil and Merseyside groups. On that morning, animal rights activists from across Liverpool gathered at the city's train station as they had done on many previous Saturday mornings. Hill was among them and had made his way there from Freshfields where he gave a large amount of his time caring for abused and neglected animals.

The Cheshire Beagles held their meet on 9th February at the Red Lion at Little Burworth. Hunt saboteurs had been with them all day since they arrived to find the hunt still at the meet at 1pm. There were repeated scuffles between the two sides throughout the day, which included a wheel brace being used against a Liverpool saboteur at one point. With the later meet time of 1pm, the saboteurs were expecting reinforcements from other groups who were visiting fox hunts nearby but they never materialized as one group was busy saving foxes left, right and centre and the other having never actually made it to their hunt due to their van breaking down.

Despite the numerous fights breaking out throughout the day, the saboteurs managed to keep the hunt on the run for around two hours. Having been unable to kill due to the presence of antis, the huntsman, Alan Summersgill, decided to box up the hounds into his small, blue trailer pulled by an open-top pick-up truck. Summersgill and another man then jumped into the cab of the truck. Impulsively, three nearby saboteurs, Mike Hill, Dave Blenkinsop and Pirrip Spencer, leapt onto the back of the pick-up with the intention of preventing the huntsman from simply driving away and resuming hunting elsewhere. Astonishingly, Summersgill immediately drove off at high speed and erratically travelled along the winding country lanes with a pack of hounds in tow and three saboteurs desperately clinging onto his truck.

The three saboteurs, terrified for their safety and unsure as to where the huntsmen was driving them, took the decision to jump from the vehicle as soon as it slowed down enough to do so or came to a stop at a junction. When Summersgill slowed to around 40mph to take a bend, Hill panicked and took this chance to leap from the truck to the grass verge. He didn't manage to clear the vehicle, however, but instead hit the corner of the trailer and fell beneath its wheels. The trailer, along with its cargo of beagles, bounced straight over Hill's body. Undeterred, yet very aware of what had just happened, Summersgill continued for another mile up the road and only eventually stopped when one of the saboteurs

HUNTING
IS A

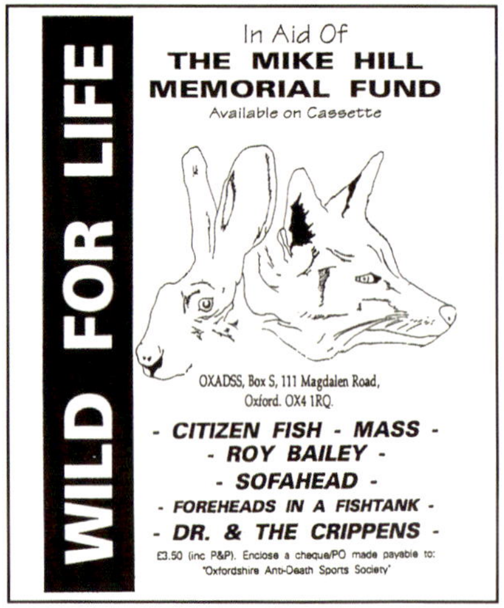

Top: Alan Summersgill

Bottom: An advert for a benefit cassette

Opposite page: Tom Worby

still holding onto the truck managed to smash the back window of the cab. One of the two saboteurs ran back to where Hill had fallen whilst the other rushed to a nearby house to phone for an ambulance. Sadly, it was too late as Hill died not long after as he and Blenkinsop lay on the verge.

Summersgill simply preceded to continue driving and only later that afternoon handed himself into a police station. He spent a few hours in the cells before being released without charge, his solicitor being the chairman of the Cheshire Beagles' neighbouring pack, the Royal Rock Beagles. To this day, Alan Summersgill has not been brought to justice after killing a compassionate eighteen year old boy.

The following morning, phones were ringing constantly as the nation's press tried to ascertain what had actually taken place on that fateful day. They were told that a silent vigil was to be held the following Monday (the next scheduled hunt meet) outside the home of Alan Summersgill. On the day, 150 protesters were joined by Granada TV and a host of national and local newspapers, along with just a handful of officers from Cheshire Police. For around half an hour, the demonstrators stood in silence with just a gate separating them from both the pick-up truck and its trailer that had killed Hill just two days previous. Before long, however, a small group made their way around the back of the kennels and with the ineptitude of the police presence and furious at the loss of a friend, the crowd lurched forward. Windows of the house were smashed, so too were those of the truck. The eight police officers at the scene were completely overwhelmed as they attempted to make arrests but were constantly stopped from doing so. In fact, only one person was arrested at the kennels, after having been handcuffed to a drainpipe running down the side of the house. One clever police officer managed to take some footage of the early stages of the incident before stashing the camera underneath a marked car. This sneaky act was spotted, however, and one of the protesters quickly took the camera, never to be seen again. Police reinforcements quickly came and as the crowd rapidly dispersed across the neighbouring fields, a group was arrested a few miles away at Chester train station. Three others were also arrested when they went to visit their detained friends at the police station and all were charged under Section 1 of the Public Order Act. This included Hill's girlfriend, Julie Burgess. The protesters were remanded in custody and a huge police operation was set up to track down as many of those present at the demonstration as possible. Many were arrested by police forces across the UK and eventually 41 people were charged with rioting.

By this time, Summersgill had reportedly gone into hiding as his bungalow was gutted by a fire started by the Animal Liberation Front a week after Hill's death. The hunt was on its last legs as it desperately looked for a new place to kennel its beagles, and locals wanted nothing to do with them due to the increasing pressure by animal rights activists.

Some 14 months later, 17 of the 41 people arrested went on trial at Mold County Court. Among those in the dock was Keith Mann, who had been singled out as an organiser just for stating to the press that it was their intention that the hunt would cease to exist. The CPS offered the defendants a deal that if they pleaded guilty to violent disorder then the more serious charge of riot would be dropped. Six took the deal due to being clearly identified at the kennels but the rest declined. The prosecution's case centred around a piece of video footage taken by one of the protesters, found on his person when he was arrested at the scene. After two weeks of the trial, five of the defendants were found guilty of threatening behaviour and given three months suspended prison sentences along with court costs of £250. Those who had pleaded guilty of violent disorder were imprisoned for twelve months. Keith Mann was found not guilty, whereas Dave Blenkinsop was sent to prison for 15 months. Sometime afterwards, and in order to bring about some kind of justice, a private prosecution was brought against Summersgill accusing him of failing to stop at the scene of an accident along with reckless driving. The prosecution's evidence even contained an independent witness who lived close to the scene and saw the truck speed past her but

Summersgill once again escaped conviction. In a further cruel twist, the inquest into Hill's death later returned a verdict of accidental death. Despite this, the pressure was too much for Summersgill who later emigrated to America.

The anniversary of Hill's death would continue to spark mass hits across Cheshire. On the sixth anniversary, a weekend of action saw the arrests of 86 saboteurs, around 60 of whom were arrested on a visit to the Cheshire Foxhounds and a further four the same day for robbery after it was alleged that gun cartridges were stolen from a couple of nearby pigeon shooters. Protests that were organised at the homes of the masters of both the Cheshire Foxhounds and the Cheshire Beagles led to the arrests of another 23 protesters. Cheshire's Chief Constable estimated that in the 1992/93 season, 8,800 hours were spent policing hunts in Cheshire at a cost to the taxpayer of £119,850.

The death of this courageous young man, who chose to spend his life campaigning to end the suffering of animals, truly shocked not only the anti-hunt community but the wider animal rights movement as a whole.

Tom Worby

Two years after the tragic death of Mike Hill, the anti-hunt movement was to suffer another great loss in an incident all too reminiscent of the previous. It was early 1993 and Tom Worby's girlfriend had seen an HSA information stall in his hometown of Milton Keynes and had expressed an interest in joining the group out in the field. On their first day out with the group, fifteen year old Worby and his girlfriend accompanied around 40 saboteurs on a hit of the Cambridgeshire Foxhounds at their closing meet at Low Farm near Gravesley, Cambridgeshire. As soon as they found the hunt drawing a wood next to the meet, the group called some of the hounds out of the wood with the use of a horn. With them, came a furious joint master, Geoffrey Fox, who shouted abuse at the saboteurs before disappearing back into the trees. Shortly after, the whole field came out from the woods, including huntsman Anthony Ball and his hounds. The police were called and the hunt waited for their arrival. After a while, a lone policeman turned up who instructed that the saboteurs were trespassing and should leave the area. With trespass not being a criminal offence, the group declined and after much deliberating and with the realisation that the police were not going to put any further resources into removing the saboteurs, the hunt headed back to the meet. Whilst the rest of the riders were drinking and chatting at the farm, Ball loaded the hounds into the hound van and together with his son Christopher and the kennel groom, drove up the farm track towards the road. Unsure as to whether this meant that the hunt were calling it a day or whether they intended to drive the hounds elsewhere to hunt, the saboteurs headed up the track as well. At this point the group had been split into a main group farthest behind, a smaller group a little way up the track and two saboteurs almost at the meeting of the track and the road. When the van reached the first group, the saboteurs did not move from the road and some even sat down in case Ball was indeed attempting to resume hunting elsewhere. The van, however, nudged its way through the group and continued at a steady, slow pace. Realising that it wasn't about to stop, those who were sitting quickly removed themselves from its path.

After passing the first group of saboteurs, the hound van rapidly gathered speed. It was fast approaching the second group, stood at a portion of the track sandwiched between a steep ditch on one side and a small, one foot high verge with a dense hedgerow on the other. Ball continued to accelerate and drove straight towards the group. To avoid being hit, most of them hurled themselves into the ditch beside the track. Unfortunately, Worby, who was more towards the other side of the track, could only step onto the tiny verge but there was virtually no room whatsoever due to the width of the hound van. He was caught on the passenger-side wing mirror and was dragged along with the vehicle for a good 50 yards, all the while screaming at the top of his voice,

Top: Wolverhampton HSA during a 'Shires Week'

Bottom: 1990's HSA logo

Opposite page: A saboteur holds up a hare klled by the Quorn Hunt, (visble in the background) during a 'Shires Week', 1994

banging against the side of the van and against the door. He then lost his grip and slipped down, bounced back against the hedge and fell forward again underneath the left back wheel. The van drove straight over his head.

The other saboteurs ran over to Worby and tried to comfort him. He was bleeding out of his ears and nose but was still conscious. As they screamed for help, some nearby hunters laughed and announced the whole thing as a victory for them, even threatening those expressing the urgency to get an ambulance. Finally, the lone policeman on the day was informed and he called for an ambulance. Before the ambulance arrived, Tom died in the arms of his girlfriend.

Anthony Ball was later questioned by the police over his actions on the day of Worby's death but the Crown Prosecution Service decided to take no further action against him. However, in June that same year, Ball announced to the press that he was to retire permanently from hunting and on 10th June the hunt's joint master, 'Gurney' Sheppard, stated that the hunt was unlikely to continue but cited 'creeping urbanisation' as the primary factor to save face. Unfortunately, at a general meeting of the hunt a month later, the membership outvoted the committee on their proposal to cease hunting.

The press coverage of the tragic incident was hugely biased as the mainstream media simply swallowed up the BFSS's blatant propaganda. Worby was portrayed as a 'problem child in council care' and 'involved in drugs misuse' whilst other hunt saboteurs were depicted as 'neo-Nazis cynically recruiting children in schools'. In the week following Worby's death, a memorial rally was held in Cambridge at which over 500 hunt saboteurs were present. Hunt supporters showed their true colours as a Fitzwilliam Hunt supporter shouted abuse at the crowd in a vain attempt to provoke a reaction and David Dunn of Countrywatch was spotted videoing those present at the rally as intel for his security company.

Following Worby's death, Cambridgeshire HSA, along with Peterborough HSA, waged a tireless campaign against the Cambridgeshire Foxhounds. The hunt was taking a severe beating and was only kept going with help from the nearby Oakley Hunt, who hosted more joint meets and often provided a contingent of supporters in order to save face for the national hunting community. The hunt employed 386 stewards over the course of the season and, at a cost of £30 each per day, a total of £11,580 was spent that year on security alone.

Hitting the Shire Packs

During this period, a number of 'Shires Weeks' were organised which saw multiple HSA groups join up and hit what are known as the shire packs; the Quorn Hunt, the Belvoir Hunt, the Fernie Hunt and Cottesmore Hunt. These hunts are centred around the traditional hunting county of Leicestershire and as such are regarded as some of the premier packs of the UK. A 'Shires Week' consisted of a week of action sabotaging these particular hunts. At Shires Week 1992, it was decided that although these hunts would remain the focus of attention, the saboteurs would split into smaller groups and so cover more hunts. The first day saw a hit of the Blankney Hunt in Lincolnshire where sadly two fox cubs were killed, the second of whom being only about six inches long. Before the saboteurs were able to get a photograph of the incident, the huntsman shoved the cub into his coat before passing it to another rider. At least one hunt was hit every day that week. A bizarre form of policing would also take place on the Friday which saw Leicestershire Police turn up to the Quorn Hunt in seven vehicles and issue leaflets to the saboteurs entitled *Advice to Hunt Protestors*. An extract of the leaflet read as follows:

> **Those who wish to protest against fox hunting can help the police greatly to ensure that the peace is kept. There are five DOs and five DON'Ts to remember.**

Among the 'dos' were:

1. Do keep your temper.
2. Do comply with any lawful request by a landowner, or his agent, to leave PRIVATE land.
3. Do respond positively to a request to move away if it is made by a police officer who reasonably fears a Breach of the Peace may occur.
4. Do give a statement to the police if asked to do so and be prepared to attend court if necessary.

The 'don'ts' were just as biased:

1. Don't threaten or assault members of the hunt or spectators.
2. Don't put yourself in danger by attempting to prevent horses or hounds following a particular route.
3. Don't blow horns or create loud noise in an attempt to distract horses or hounds - it may result in injury being caused.
4. Don't use bad language or other abusive behaviour.
5. Don't expect that the police can act in every case in the way you would wish. They are bound by law and the strict rules of evidence.

Curiously, the leaflet didn't explain what trespass had to do with the police, with it being a civil matter, nor did it mention anything about a suspect's right to remain silent during police interviews. In essence the leaflet was simply asking the saboteurs not to intervene at all. It was officers from the same police station (Melton Mowbray) as those handing out the leaflets who had even tried to implement a 200 metre 'exclusion zone' around the Cottesmore's huntsman, Captain Brian Fanshawe the season before!

At this point in time, the anti-hunting movement was thriving. The governing body of fox hunts in the UK, the Master of Foxhounds Association (MFHA), was extremely worried about the movement's expansion and launched a recording system whereby hunts were asked to record and report back the number of saboteurs at each meet. In one edition of *Hunting* magazine, much of this information was collated and came to the conclusion that between January 1993 and July 1994 (the date of the publication), a total of 802 meets had been disrupted with an aggregate of 11,131 protesters counted in that period (this number is, of course, the number of appearances and not individual persons). More than 50 saboteurs were present on 31 occasions. On 20th March 1993, 400 saboteurs were counted at a meet of the New Forest Foxhounds and a meet of the Essex Foxhounds on 23rd January 1993 saw 250 saboteurs turn up.

The Brixton Mob

Perhaps the most infamous group in the HSA's history was the Brixton group of the late 1980s and early 1990s. The 'Brixton Mob', as they were often affectionately known, had less of the nuanced tactics skilfully employed by some smaller groups but instead often opted to simply swamp hunts with saboteurs and as such cause as much chaos as possible. This tactic proved to be very effective as many hunts were stopped this way either by the fact it was impossible to actually do any hunting or sometimes even on the advice of the police. Black bomber jackets and balaclavas were the fashion of choice as the group's reputation more often than not proceeded them. On numerous occasions they would be called in by other groups across the country on joint hits in retaliation for hunt violence the previous week.

A New Era of Violence

Due to the movement's growing efficacy and expansion, many hunts began to turn more and more towards violence to deal with antis. This was nothing new, as those who inflict extreme violence upon animals often think nothing of doing the same to those who oppose them, but hunt violence was on the rise again throughout the early 1990s. Indeed, Tim Asplin, the then joint master of the Essex Union Hunt summed up the twisted ideology of many animal abusers when he outrageously stated in 1976, "horse-whipping a hunt saboteur is rather like beating a wife – they're both private matters". The wife of a joint master of the Wheatland Foxhounds, Richard Milner, even approached the HSA in 1991 with revelations that she was the victim of domestic violence that culminated in an attack in which she was so badly beaten by her husband she required medical treatment. She contacted her former opponents so that her allegations were more widely publicised and to make people realise that "it's not just hunt saboteurs who are beaten up by the hunt."

Between 1990 and 1995, over 60 hunt staff and supporters were convicted of violent crimes towards anti-hunt activists. One Bramham Moor Hunt supporter even attacked saboteurs with a scythe, leaving two with head wounds. In January 1994, three saboteurs spotted an official of the Old Surrey and Burstow Hunt thrashing a horse to force it into his horsebox whilst they were driving home. The three stopped to take photographs of the cruelty but the huntsman turned and attacked them with a hammer. This terrified his horse, who was only prevented from bolting when one saboteur held and calmed the petrified animal. Her compassion was rewarded when the huntsman turned on her too, inflicting similar serious head wounds to those of her friends. In March that same year, a whipper-in of the Four Burrows Hunt rode his horse over hunt saboteur John Prescott, causing him massive internal injuries that included three fractured ribs and serious internal bleeding. An attack by hunt members followed during which the saboteurs defended themselves. Unsurprisingly, only saboteurs were arrested including Prescott who was forced to spend several hours in police custody vomiting blood before being allowed to go to a hospital. He remained in hospital for five days, much of that time on a drip feed.

Opposite page top: Brixton HSA face off with police

Opposite page bottom: The 'Brixton Mob' and friends overwhelm the Surrey Union Hunt, 1993

Top: Bramham Moor Hunt supporter, 9th January 1993

Bottom: Part of Brixton HSA's fleet of Land Rovers, 1995

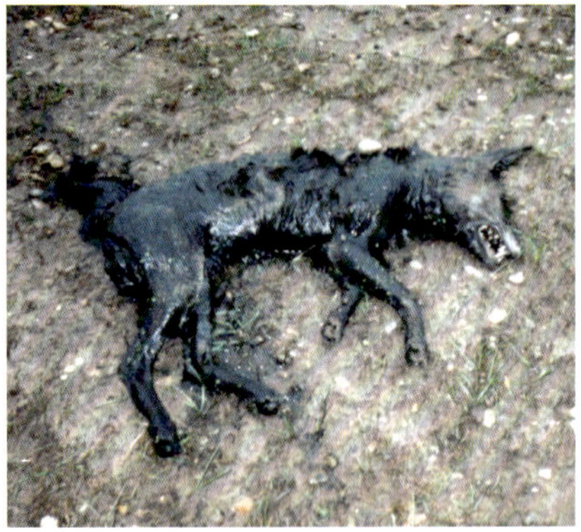

Top and bottom: A fox is killed by the East Sussex and Romney Marsh hounds after becoming stuck in a drainage ditch

Opposite page: Saboteurs from the New Forest and Winchester occupy an earth after a fox is chased underground by the New Forest Foxhounds

Arrest was viewed by saboteurs as an occupational hazard as many police forces used a strategy of indiscriminate arrest in order to protect the hunt, consistently overstepping their powers and often arresting saboteurs for simply being near a hunt and detaining them all day so that the hunt could continue unopposed. This tactic often backfired, however, as many of those arrested would sue the police. In the eighteen months prior to February 1993, for example, more than 80 saboteurs won damages from the police after bringing claims for wrongful arrest and imprisonment. These damages totalled a staggering £80,150 and according to figures compiled by John Mackenzie (a solicitor who represented many of the saboteurs) the police were forced to pay legal bills of more than £250,000 over these cases. Police bias was always hugely in favour of the hunt, with very few hunt supporters facing any kind of legal consequences for their violent outbursts. To evidence this fact, the HSA documented the number of saboteurs and the number of hunt supporters, members and officials arrested between 2nd January 1988 and 2nd April 1988. Only thirteen hunt supporters were arrested during this period, all for violent offences. On the other hand, a total of 95 saboteurs were arrested, the vast majority for breaches of the peace for such actions as spraying scent duller on the ground, trespassing and horn blowing.

These incidents are the tip of the iceberg when it comes to hunt violence, but the attacks upon saboteurs have never deterred them from taking action against animal abusers. One southern saboteur recounts a violent yet particularly successful day out in Surrey:

> *Possibly the best day but most continually violent day I have endured as a sab took place at a children's meet of the Surrey Union at Farley heath in the early 90s. The hunt was sick of being sabbed every day they were out and had just abandoned Saturday hunting altogether after a national hit.*
>
> *We stopped them getting one fox right at the start which continued to run in between the pony club kid's horses and their proud parents. About 10 sabs were out but I got knocked out with a riding crop to the head and carted off to hospital for stitches. Although I was seen really quickly at the A and E I was treated but still concussed, which might explain why I thought it was a good idea to go back to the hunt as it was not yet 1 o'clock. I got a taxi back to the hunt and was met by some fairly shocked looking cops who were just helping another sab into an ambulance after the huntsman had ridden his horse over the sab's head as he sat in an earth protecting another fox.*
>
> *When we got back with the hunt the riders, young and old, were lined up happily watching a group of terriermen digging down to a fox in some trampled bracken. As the terrierman dug he was getting showered with earth from our boots so much so that he kept having to stop to spit out and swing a few punches. After about 10 minutes of struggling, he had managed to grip the fox with his left hand and was trying to shoot it with a small pistol. He was waving the gun around and actually pointed it straight in the face of one young female sab – at this point all hell broke loose as we dived on him to get the gun pointing away from anyone. The fox also chose this moment to sink its teeth right into the fleshy part of his hand between the thumb and forefinger, which made him scream even more! A quick thinking sab then somehow managed to grab the fox by the scruff of its neck and its tail and launched it into mid-air away from the terriermen and the riders. The huntsman saw this and sheered the hounds straight onto it, but luckily we managed to spray down and stop them dead with whips and shouts.*
>
> *The fighting continued from this dig all the way back to the meet which was about ½ a mile away and strangely (as so often seems to happen in situations*

POLICE

POLICE

where the hunt think they have the upper hand) the police were nowhere to be seen. That day we stopped them killing at 3 different dig outs (at a children's meet!). My over-riding memory is of that lucky fox, with its legs running in mid-air and hitting the ground at full pelt, knowing that we had directly stopped them killing it. A bit of an extreme example of sabbing, but when hunters say we never have any effect, I can think of a few in Surrey from that day who should not deny it!

The Battle of Holmbury Hill

The Surrey Union Hunt were at this time one of the most powerful and influential hunts in the country, yet suffered continued sabotage from the 1980s right up until the present day. It was estimated that in the 1990s, around 80% of their meets were hit. The large number of animal rights activists situated in the South East, along with the formation of the South East Animal Liberation League (SEALL) meant that the hunt often had to contend with huge numbers of saboteurs, with several mass hits that saw over two hundred activists turn out. On such occasions, hunting was often abandoned at a very early stage of the day. These mass hits were usually orchestrated as a response to violent ambushes carried out by hunt supporters. For example, in January 1991, after having endured sabotage at almost every meet that season, the hunt organised an ambush on the Lukyns Estate near Ewhurst which led to five saboteurs being hospitalised with fractured skulls, broken wrists and broken noses. As a result, three hundred saboteurs turned out in retaliation at a later meet on 12th January near Forest Green and a huge fight broke out in the woods above the meet that became known as the 'Battle of Holmbury Hill'. The antis won the day and many were arrested on violent disorder charges in the days that followed but all charges were eventually dropped.

The effects of the 'Battle of Holmbury Hill' were long lasting, as veteran saboteur Colin Skilton recounts:

The Surrey Union met at The Parrot pub in Forest Green. The sabs' plan was tactically good, with only the local groups at the meet so as not to give the game away to the hunt and the police. The rest of the hundreds of sabs met away from the hunt meet and at a later time so they wouldn't be detected by incoming hunt supporters.

The local sabs radioed through the hunt's movements and the hunt ran into the hundreds of waiting sabs, achieving complete surprise at Holmbury Hill. The rest, as they say, is history. The Surrey Union didn't meet on a Saturday again for the next ten years and never again launched any large scale attacks on sabs. The number of riders also dropped dramatically causing the hunt to almost fold through lack of support and money.

SEALL provided a large and well organised group of people who helped enormously in the fight against fox hunting in Surrey, Kent and Sussex. Other similar groups such as the Northern Animal Liberation League were already in existence at the time of SEALL's formation and aided the structure of the group. The fledgling organisation's first hit was against a battery chicken farm where faults in the group's coordination and discipline became apparent and the mass hits on fox hunts came about as a method of training to rectify these issues.

SEALL went on to successfully raid Wellcome Research Laboratories in Beckenham and the Royal College of Surgeons in the Kent village of Downe, releasing photographs and horrific details of experiments on animals which gained national publicity.

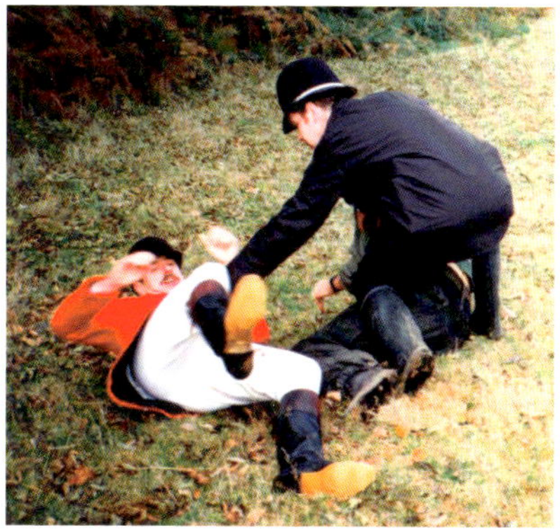

Opposite Page: Saboteurs protect a fox who has gone to ground from the Surrey Union Hunt

Top: A saboteur takes a tumble with a Surrey Union redcoat.

Bottom: Saboteurs wrestle with the Surrey Union Hunt's whipper-in over a roe deer that the hounds had just killed

Top: Extract from *Hounds* magazine, early 1990s

Bottom: Employees of RKR security arm themselves with pickaxe handles

Opposite page: A group of saboteurs is ambushed by members of the Crawley and Horsham Hunt

Hunts Turn to Security Firms

A worrying development was starting to take place when on 24th August 1992, Yorkshire saboteurs went to the Dallowgill Moor Estate in North Yorkshire as part of their ongoing campaign against grouse shooting. Around ten men set about violently ejecting them from the land. This was perhaps nothing new and is something that saboteurs are very used to dealing with. What makes this particular incident significant, however, was the fact that the men were not just supporters of the shoot, but in fact belonged to a countryside-based security firm known as Olympic International. As opposed to fox hunting, where masters are expected to financially prop up the hunt, grouse shooting (along with most other forms of shooting) is a business venture and successful sabotage of a day's shooting can cost the estate upwards of £10,000. Keen to protect their business interests, the estate saw it fit to employ a private security company that was in reality nothing more than a rural rent-a-mob.

A similar incident would also occur just four weeks later. The Northumberland Beagling Festival was on its last legs due to continued sabotage and its organisers, the Newcastle and District Beagles, knew that the 1992 festival had to run smoothly in order to ensure the event's continuity. In previous years the hunt had designated various whipper-ins and supporters to specifically deal with saboteurs, even dressing them in yellow armbands emblazoned with the word 'Agent'. Despite this, their effect was minimal in deterring activists. Most probably with the advice of the British Field Sports Society, the hunt decided to employ Estate Management Services to provide security for the festival at an estimated cost of £15,000 over the whole five days. Estate Management Services had very close links with Olympic International as both were based at the same location just outside of Barnsley and were both run by Brian Pursglove. A team of ten men from EMS, described by one saboteur as 'intellectually-challenged flesh mountains', were transported to and from each day's meet in a cattle truck and ordered to drag any saboteur in the fields back to the road. The hired thugs were far from professional and, when the police were elsewhere, resorted to brutally attacking saboteurs, abetted by local farmhands.

Nick Herbert of the BFSS was busy promoting the concept of hired security as an answer to the increasing pressure by anti-hunt activists and declared, "from now on we are going to start hunting the saboteurs". To try and counter claims of over the top vigilantism, the BFSS went into full propaganda mode, trying their hardest to blame the increase in violence on hunt saboteurs. Despite their campaign being based on a pack of lies, so much mud was thrown at the HSA that eventually some stuck and even the League Against Cruel Sports felt moved to wade in and wrote a full page article in their journal, *Wildlife Guardian*, on hunt violence.

Buoyed up by the championing of violent mercenaries by the BFSS, many fox hunts were now considering the option of hired help. The BFSS even went as far as to produce a 23 page, 'strictly confidential' booklet entitled *Hunt Stewarding: A Manual for Masters of Foxhounds* that advised hunts on how to train and employ their own stewards. As Brian Toon of the Masters of Foxhounds Association announced, "Of the 193 packs recognised by our association, seven or eight have said they are training their own marshals – or stewards – or are intending to do so. I am not prepared to name them but they are in the counties of Gloucestershire, Essex, Cambridgeshire, Hampshire and Dorset". Indeed, after this statement, seven of the UK's then most violent hunts (the Bicester with Waddon Chase, the Essex, the Chiddingfold, Leconfield and Cowdray, the Hampshire, the Hursley Hambledon, the Surrey Union and the Warwickshire) employed private security firms.

The security firms offered two primary services; the provision of their employees to act as stewards for removing saboteurs from private land and/or the training of local hunt supporters to do the same. Estate Management Services even went as far as to place adverts in the *Shooting Gazette* and *Hounds* magazine to promote themselves as a solution to the problem

of hunt saboteurs. A Norwich-based firm called Milton Security were also mentioned in the *Shooting Times* as offering a service to shooters which even included the deployment of light aircraft! Unsurprisingly, this offer was never taken up.

Countrywatch

The Warwickshire Hunt stated publicly that they were using the services of another security firm, Countrywatch, to deal with saboteurs. Such was the level of violence used by employees of the firm that when three of Countrywatch's staff were found by police to have armed themselves with staves and baseball bats, even the company's boss, David Dunn (a former New Zealand soldier), was moved to state he had dismissed the offenders. This was only a token gesture, however, as during the beginning of a Surrey Union meet in 1993, Dorking Police confiscated a minor arsenal of weapons from a Countrywatch vehicle that included iron bars and billiard cues along with high-powered catapults and a stun gun. Later on, the police ordered the hunt to abandon the day's hunting due to the violence of their stewards. Just a month before, a gang of around 20 Countrywatch employees brutally attacked a group of saboteurs at a meet of the Old Surrey and Burstow, even punching one in the face while he was being held by a police officer. Perhaps the most outrageous incident, however, was on 5th February 1994. Just as the South Dorset Hunt was packing up, Countrywatch employees broke into the garden of a local woman well known for her anti-hunt beliefs and attacked her. David Dunn, fearful that news of this would severely damage his company's reputation, posed as a police officer to try and gain entry to the woman's house and persuade her to not take the matter further. When she refused, rightly being suspicious that he was in fact linked with her attackers, Dunn proceeded to intimidate and threaten the woman to not make any further complaints about the assault.

Employing professional security firms was a costly business and it was estimated that each Countrywatch employee received around £85 per day. With rising costs of the actual day to day running of hunts, many began to prime their own homegrown gangs of local lads to 'sort the antis out'. In January 1992, Robin Ryland-Smith, a master of the Warwickshire Hunt, gave fellow hunters some rather extraordinary advice in the form of a thinly veiled threat when he was quoted, "masters who consider they need help should find half a dozen fit and sensible men and invite Countrywatch to spend a day teaching them procedures for containing those who are out to disrupt hunting". Although this was clearly just training up hardened hunt followers with scores to settle to fight, the police were only too keen that the buck of responsibility of dealing with saboteurs was passed on. In fact, supporters of the Essex Farmers Hunt were even treated to a weekend of training by the local police force. This came to light in an issue of *Police Review* in which Inspector Martin Reed told the journal that, "a comprehensive training course for the stewards, run by a representative of the British Field Sports Association, was held recently under police supervision." The thuggery of the stewards used by hunts to deter saboteurs was by no means something confined to the fringes of such organisations but instead was actively encouraged by hunts' masterships. For example, Stephen Wilson, a steward who was found guilty of attacking a television cameraman filming at the Middleton Hunt was later promoted as terrierman for the neighbouring Sinnington Hunt.

The Battle of Stagden Cross

Essex Farmer thugs trained by Estate Management Services later hospitalized a young saboteur which lead to a mass hit that same month during which a saboteur's head was split open causing an alleged riot. National hits in retaliation were commonplace, as they served as a deterrent against further hunt violence due to the fact that if any saboteur suffered serious injury, the hunt could expect even more disruption at future meets. For example, in response to the appalling violence dished out by stewards from the Essex Foxhounds, a national hit was called against the hunt on 23rd January 1993.

Top: Kent police turn out in force at a joint hit against the Ashford Valley Hunt

Middle: Surrey Union Hunt joint master, Mark Sprake, is arrested under Section 5 of the Public Order Act

Bottom: Saboteurs prevent the Essex Hunt from hunting at Stagden Cross, 1993

Opposite page: Countrywatch on patrol at the Surrey Union Hunt, 1993

Top: Southampton HSA's vehicle attacked at a meet of the Crawley and Horsham hunt on 9th March 1996

Bottom: Thugs from the Portman Hunt near Guys Marsh, 29th November, 1997

Opposite page top: Supporters of the Cumberland Farmers Hunt attack saboteurs with a hammer, early 1990s

Opposite page middle and bottom: New Forest Hunt terriermen threaten saboteurs with a pickaxe handle and axe, 1996

The hit proved to be an interruption to the status quo in Essex, one that the hunt, along with their friends in the police, didn't appreciate. On the day, the police had no idea how to control the vast number of saboteurs and started to arrest people on a totally random basis, ending up with a total of 27 arrests. Many saboteurs were arrested for one offence before later being charged with another. However, whilst in custody, all were re-arrested and charged with conspiracy to cause violent disorder. The charges were farcical and a number of those arrested successfully sued Essex Constabulary to the tune of £30,000 over what was later dubbed the 'Battle of Stagden Cross'.

The Bicester with Whaddon Chase Hunt had no qualms about promoting follower Richard Cheshire to the position of hunt steward despite (or most probably because of) his conviction of ABH on two hunt monitors. Cheshire would later go on to push a saboteur under a moving vehicle driven by the hunt's terrierman, Michael Smith, earning both himself and Smith a jail time of two months each. Far from distancing themselves from this unpleasant individual, the hunt kept Smith's job and tied house open for him on his return.

The West Sussex Badger Patrol Group even had to resort to hiring their own uniformed security guards to protect them from the Chiddingfold Hunt's stewards along with RKR Security thugs. RKR Security had at least three employees with criminal records for violence, two of whom had convictions for assaulting police officers and another who served a three year prison sentence for wounding with intent. The Chiddingfold's stewards were powerless however to prevent other activists visiting huntsman Jeremy Whaley's home and damaging his Range Rover to the tune of £1,300 with the words 'HUNT SCUM' painted on the side in August 1993. Desperate to stop the constant hits against their hunt, two months later the hunt's committee voted to dismiss Whaley for attracting too many saboteurs. According to journalist Alec Smart, "a primary reason for his dismissal is his high profile in hunting and his frequent confrontations with 'antis'. This has attracted hunt saboteurs, badger protection groups and environmentalists from a wide area keen to disrupt his perceived arrogance." Whaley himself was far from squeaky clean as he was caught by an undercover investigation by the League Against Cruel Sports dealing in undeclared animal skins, an illegal money earner commonplace among hunts.

Standing up to the Hursley Hambledon

Another extreme incident of hunt violence that season was at the Hursley Hambledon's closing meet. The local group's van had been deliberately cut off from the other groups' vehicles by hunt supporters (some of whom had been called in for the day from the New Forest) who proceeded to ambush its occupants. Fence posts were hurled through the windscreen and every window and panel of the vehicle was smashed causing over £2,500 worth of damage. The van's nine occupants were dragged out and beaten, leaving six of them requiring hospital treatment, including one saboteur who suffered two cracked ribs and head injuries after being repeatedly struck with a fence post. One of the victims described the attackers as "like a lynch mob, howling for blood". At the Garth & South Berks Hunt, a woman was beaten unconscious by a nightclub bouncer acting as a hunt steward and another bouncer at the Oakley Hunt threatened saboteurs with a flick-knife.

The violence dished out by the Hursley Hambledon Hunt continued to escalate as many saboteurs tooks pacifist stances and Hampshire Police remained uninterested. This all changed however on 13th December 1997, when a mass hit of the hunt took place in retaliation for a previous attack. A large contingent of saboteurs from across Southern England arrived at the meet around 40 minutes after the hunt had set off and damaged every single vehicle that they could find that belonged to the hunt and their supporters. Forty-two hunt saboteurs were indiscriminately arrested on the day. Just three were later charged with conspiracy to commit violent disorder as the police believed that they had organised the mass sabotage. As a result of the huge extent of the damage, violence from the Hursley Hambledon (and other surrounding hunts) waned and Hampshire Police were forced into a position of much more impartial policing.

In Dorset, the Portman Hunt could only be sabotaged with large numbers of people and only then if they stuck together in one large group for safety. Although fights were commonplace with this hunt, on 29th November 1997, a new level of violence was reached. The hunt had managed to kill close to their meet at Guys Marsh near Shaftesbury shortly after 60 saboteurs had arrived. Almost immediately, the hunt had clearly telephoned other locals to inform them that they had company. According to the HSA's press release of the ensuing incident:

> *When hunt supporters from the surrounding hunts arrived after about one hour, they wasted no time in attacking the saboteurs. Wearing balaclavas and wielding pick axe handles, the hunt thugs went on a rampage, battering any saboteur they could find. At one point, two hunt followers pulled out shotguns to threaten the saboteurs.*

It is worth mentioning the significant number of military personnel acting as hunt security. Serving personnel from Catterick Garrison near Richmond were deployed at hunts throughout Yorkshire during the 1993 season and employees of Estate Management Services deployed at the Surrey Union boasted about being in the army. This was later confirmed by police officers who stated that they were indeed serving members of the Grenadier Guards. From November 1991 until at least February 1994, Irish Guards were present at meets of the Chiddingfold alongside stewards. The leader of the gang of squadies was even heard to have told a saboteur; "I can tell you people are going to get murdered in their beds, tracer bullets through the window, Belfast rules OK, enough said?"

Thugs, Wreckers and Bullies

A well known Brighton saboteur, Phil DeSouza, was sentenced to nine months imprisonment for assault and affray charges following a fracas with two joint masters of the Southdown and Eridge Hunt in September 1996. The Countryside Alliance wallowed in the verdict and used it once again to smear anti -hunt activists as violent thugs. The reality was, however, that DeSouza's was the only conviction for anything remotely confrontational that year, whereas convictions against violent hunt staff and supporters had already reached double figures. The countless incidents of extreme hunt violence during this period forced the HSA to enter the political arena as they used a press conference at the House of Commons to launch an eight page booklet entitled *Thugs, Wreckers and Bullies*, that detailed the seriousness of the issue and did much to counteract tabloid sensationalism and smear campaigns from the BFSS. The title of the document came from a speech in Didcot in which Michael Howard MP described hunt saboteurs as 'thugs, wreckers and bullies' to a crowd of Conservative Party supporters. Ironically, on the same day as his speech, three saboteurs were admitted to Lancaster Royal Infirmary following an attack by supporters of the notorious Vale of Lune Harriers. The press conference was hosted by the Labour MP for Nottingham, Alan Simpson, who even joined Nottingham HSA when they hit the Quorn Hunt in March 1993. At the conference he stated that from his experience, he believed that saboteurs were overwhelmingly decent people just trying to save animals from a brutal death and that the only threats of intimidation he could perceive were from various hunt supporters. He also took the opportunity to reiterate the fears of many at the time who viewed that the Criminal Justice Bill was being used to suppress legitimate protest as a part of a general crackdown on dissent rather than being any sort of attempt to tackle crime. Also present at the conference was Jo Harris of Portsmouth HSA who told of her experiences of a year-long campaign of violence and sexual harassment from supporters of the Hursley Hambledon Hunt. Former hunt supporter and BFSS worker Lynn Sawyer, along with the HSA's Press Officer, Campaigns Officer and Chair were also in attendance.

Top: Clive Richardson's car after an arson attack by hunt supporters, 1995

Middle: Tyneside HSA after a nerve-wracking day on the rarely hit Haydon Hunt, 17th November, 1990

Bottom: Merseyside saboteurs are stopped and searched by police, 1994

Opposite page: A Nottingham saboteur cradles an injured fox

Soon after, evidence was submitted to the Home Affairs Select Committee investigating the use of private security companies present at hunt meets and examining whether there was a need for regulation of the private security industry. The report, named *Public Order, Private Armies*, covered a wide range of issues from the use of indiscriminate violence, the employment of convicted criminals as security, the illegal abuse of the law of trespass by hunt security and the way in which the police ignored criminal offences committed by members of the security firms. It also detailed 20 specific cases of brutal assaults by hunt stewards and called upon the police to act against these vicious vigilantes.

Despite bias from the police, many charges against saboteurs failed to lead to convictions. For example, that same year, Cornwall saboteur Mary Lynch had her charge of aggravated trespass dropped after her bail conditions banned her from the whole of West Cornwall for five weeks. She was caught allegedly 'luring hounds with chocolate biscuits!'

Home Visits From the Hunt

Not only were saboteurs often the victims of serious violence during the day of hunting itself, some also suffered reprisals in their own homes. On 12th October 1995, Clive Richardson, a dedicated hunt saboteur and a leading figure in East Northants Against Bloodsports, was alerted by a passer-by that his Land Rover trailer had been set alight following a two year campaign against him by the Woodland Pytchley Hunt. Prior to this, in November 1994, the brake lines and electrical lines were cut on Richardson's car in an attempt to cause a very serious accident. In April 1995, animal entrails were dumped on Richardson's doorstep and smeared across the front of his house after he and colleagues had photographed carcasses at the Woodland Pytchley's kennels. Shockingly, just eleven days after Richardson's trailer was set on fire, a second arson attack took place in which his garage was burnt down, causing an estimated £5,000 to £10,000 of damage. Fortunately, the fire services managed to contain the blaze (despite the attackers dragging a neighbour's car onto the road to prevent the emergency services from gaining access) before it engulfed the house, where Richardson along with his wife and ten year old son were sat watching television.

The campaign waged against Richardson wasn't the only case in which hunt supporters had tampered with a saboteur's vehicle in order to cause a serious accident. During the night of 13th November 1992, both the front and rear brake pipes of Liverpool HSA's vehicle were cut and one of the tyres punctured. Luckily, the damage was discovered by the group as they attempted to head out early the next morning. The following week, a freshly severed head of a fox was also dumped on the doorstep, clearly showing the depravity of those who abuse wildlife.

Raiding the BFSS

Anti-hunt activists were also stepping up their resistance to animal abuse outside of the killing fields too. On 22nd November 1993, thirteen anti-bloodsports campaigners launched a surprise daylight raid of the BFSS's London HQ. As John Roll-Pickering, the BFSS's Director of Recruiting arrived at work, the thirteen barged past him and barricaded themselves into the first floor suite of offices, emptying filing cabinets as they went. The police shortly arrived (having only come from the police station next door) with the aid of a sledgehammer and arrested the occupiers on suspicion of false imprisonment and criminal damage. According to the ALF Supporters Group's newsletter, 'two officers leapt into the room, knocking their third colleague over and causing him to cut the top off one of his fingers. The first one into the room maintained his balance, if not his dignity, and shouted, "right, you're all going away for a long time for this."' The original charges were dropped (Roll-Pickering even admitted that he hadn't been held against his will) and the thirteen were later charged with Section 5 of the Public Order Act.

SchNEWS

'BREAK THE LAW...'

CJA ARRESTOMETER

7 AGGRAVATIONS

RAMBLING ON..

photocopy! distribute! contribute!

Top: A saboteur rescues a wounded fox

Bottom: *Schnews* issue 42, 28th September 1995

The Criminal Justice Act

Such was the impact of hunt saboteurs on the sordid activities of those whose lives revolved around inflicting unimaginable suffering to animals, that those in power felt that something needed to be done to curtail this growing compassionate movement. The 1990s is generally thought of as a period of a multitude of radical cultures, with whole communities being formed, based around strong ecological and anti-capitalist ethics. For many during this period, direct action and campaigning was a way of life. The free party scene was in full swing as ravers organised free festivals all across the UK's countryside. One such festival was to play a large part in urging the then Conservative government to push ahead with legislation that was to have a wide ranging impact on a variety of counter-cultures including those taking part in hunt sabotage. It was May 1992 and 40,000 people had made their way to the Malvern Hills for the Castlemorton Free Festival to enjoy the biggest unlicensed gathering of its kind since the Stonehenge Festival in the mid-1980s. The police were unable to prevent the vast crowd from partying as numerous sound systems including Bedlam, Circus Warp, Spiral Tribe and DiY blasted out music across the West Midlands countryside. The festival sparked calls for new police powers to deal with such events as Michael Spicer, the local Conservative MP, rather embellished what he saw as a growing problem in a parliamentary debate in June that year: "on that day, new age ravers and drugs racketeers arrived at a strength of two army divisions, complete with several massed bands and, above all, a highly sophisticated command and signals system". He continued; "the problem of mass gatherings must be dealt with before they take place. [...] Chief constables should be given discretionary powers to ban such gatherings altogether if they decide that they are a threat to public order". Sure enough, in March 1993, the government signalled its intention to bring about new powers against such gatherings and later stated that this would be included in a new Criminal Justice Bill in November that same year.

Michael Howard put the Criminal Justice and Public Order Bill before Parliament in January 1994. The bill set out to introduce a sweeping array of new police powers that included increased stop and search powers and the infamous 'powers in relation to raves'. However, the bill also set about introducing a new offence designed specifically to deal with hunt saboteurs, that of aggravated trespass. The bill gained Royal Assent on 3rd November 1994, now meaning that:

> **A person commits the offence of aggravated trespass if he trespasses on land and, in relation to any lawful activity which persons are engaging in or are about to engage in on that or adjoining land, does there anything which is intended by him to have the effect –**
>
> **(a) of intimidating those persons or any of them so as to deter them or any of them from engaging in that activity,**
>
> **(b) of obstructing that activity, or**
>
> **(c) of disrupting that activity.**

This new offence carried with it a maximum of 3 months imprisonment or a £2,500 fine and was intended to criminalise the very act of sabotaging a hunt, as obviously the vast majority of hunting with hounds takes place on private land and therefore saboteurs must trespass in order to successfully stop it.

Failure of the Act

The Brighton-based alternative news collective, SchNEWS was born out of the movement against the Criminal Justice Act and monitored the impact the new law was having on protestors campaigning on a whole number of issues. Its 1995 'CJA Arrestometer', revealed that hunt saboteurs were the group facing most repression from the act, having had 170 arrests in relation to the CJA in the year since it was passed. The second largest group were football fans who were arrested 116 times, with road protestors suffering 88 arrests and ravers just 10. Over 500 people were arrested in the first year of the CJA, yet around 90% of cases were either dropped or the defendants acquitted. Rather than aiming for convictions, the police were simply using the act to intimidate and deter protesters, arresting them then handing out lengthy bail conditions that prevented them from participating in such actions for months at a time.

Despite the increase in arrests, the Criminal Justice Act failed to have the impact on hunt sabotage it was intended to. For example, in the 1994/5 season alone, 127 different packs of hounds were sabotaged; 88 of which were fox hunts, 27 beagle packs, 9 harrier packs, 2 buckhound packs and 1 basset pack. Many arrests under the act were also successfully challenged. For instance, the first hunt related arrest made under the act in Cornwall occurred on 13th December 1994 when Penwith Fox Protection Group member, Philip Elston, was arrested at a meet of the Western Hunt near Penzance. Elson was later awarded £500 plus costs for an unlawful arrest. Completely undeterred, he stated:

> *Now that this matter has been resolved I intend to continue with the job in question, namely to prevent the untimely and cruel deaths of wild animals. There have been several attempts to stop law-abiding people like myself from protecting wild creatures. The CJA has been the most recent change in the law. Until a ban on hunting with hounds has been imposed, activists will continue in their efforts to help the hunted animal.*

A Step Forward in Parliament

Campaigners had for a long while fought for legislation outlawing the sick practice of hunting with hounds and in 1996, were offered a glimmer of hope. The 1996 Wild Animals (Protection) Bill was intended to finally put an end to hunting with hounds and give wild mammals some legal protection against specific acts of cruelty. This hope was short lived however as the clause banning the use of packs of dogs to kill wildlife was removed in order to prevent pro-hunt MPs from voting against the entire bill. The act defined what it was to be a wild mammal (one that is neither domestic nor captive) and made it an offence to 'mutilate, kick, beat, nail, or otherwise impale, stab, burn, stone, crush, drown, drag or asphyxiate any wild mammal with intent to inflict unnecessary suffering.' Anyone convicted of doing so now faced the prospect of a twelve week prison sentence and/or a fine of up to £5,000. Although the act was a step in the right direction, it had minimal impact in stopping the suffering of wild mammals as exceptions were made if one could show that the killing happened in a 'reasonably swift and humane manner [...] in the course of either lawful shooting, hunting, coursing or lawful pest control activity.' Indeed, the first person to be convicted under the Wild Mammals (Protection) Act, a youth from Great Yarmouth, was given just 120 hours community service and ordered to pay £50 in costs for kicking, beating and stabbing a hedgehog. Such lenient sentences were hardly deterrents for those who got their kicks from abusing animals.

Digging Out

The 1996 cub hunting season got off to a very successful start for the HSA as soon as the South Shropshire Hunt were joined by saboteurs at the top of Oak Hill, near Minsterley, they simply rode back to the meet. After some deliberating, the huntsman chose to have a second attempt at finding some fox cubs to kill. However, after only 30 minutes he again made his way back to the meet, this time to box up and head for home.

Top: Hastings HSA stop the Southdown and Eridge terrie men digging out a fox, 1999

Bottom: Saboteurs prevent a dig out form taking place

Above: Terriermen of the East Sussex and Romney Marsh Hunt dig out a fox and throw the live animal in front of the hounds, 1996

On the South Coast, one fox had an extremely lucky escape after the East Sussex and Romney Marsh Hunt had chased the animal to ground in a drainage ditch near Walland Marsh. The terriermen were quick on the scene and after blocking the field end of the drain with a spade, they entered a terrier and in the ensuing 20 minute underground battle between the two captive animals, the terrier managed to drag the fox into the waiting net that had been strung over the entrance. The terrierman, holding the terrified creature by the scruff of the neck, then threw the fox into an open field to run for dear life as the huntsman encouraged the hounds on. The fox, muddy, bloodied and emitting a strong scent perfect for hounds to follow, had an amazing escape as the nearby group of saboteurs stepped in and called the hounds away from the line of the fox using voice calls and whip cracks.

The practice of digging out foxes and releasing them to be hunted again was frowned upon (officially, but not in practice) by the hunting fraternity themselves. Following an incident in which the Quorn Hunt were filmed releasing a live fox cub in front of the waiting pack, the MFHA produced a code of conduct which stated that:

> **If the fox is handled, under no circumstances may it be released and hunted again.**

Although publicly these practices are condemned by the hunting community, in reality such incidents are not infrequent, with many foxes having not been blessed with the luck that saboteurs were close by. Codes of conduct and statements to the press rarely bear any resemblance to what actually takes place on a hunting day.

By 1996, the HSA's offices were in Nottingham, but moved to Brighton during the year. As of March that year, the organisation's membership stood at around 5,000. At this time, there were also some 130 local active groups. The Hunt Saboteurs Association was clearly an organisation going from strength to strength. With the invention of the Internet in 1989, the HSA didn't take too long in exploiting this new technology in the name of animal rights. In 1995, the HSA set up its first website to more easily distribute news and advice to both local groups and members of the public with the rather clunky (by today's standards) address of http://envirolink.org/arrs/HSA/hsa.html.

The Countryside Alliance

Repeated attempts to bring about a ban on hunting with hounds urged the formation of the Countryside Alliance. The CA, although it likes to promote itself as campaigning for a wide variety of countryside issues such as poor rural mobile phone signal and the closure of rural post offices, is in reality a lobby group created solely to promote the interests of bloodsports enthusiasts. It was formed in 1997 as an amalgamation of three organisations: the Countryside Business Group, the Countryside Movement and the British Field Sports Society (who featured most prominently in the new organisation) and was a reaction to the newly elected Labour Party's promises for a better deal for animals. The CA launched themselves onto the scene in the summer of 1997 when they organised a mass mobilisation in Hyde Park named the Countryside Rally. The huge demonstration was to show their grievance at the Mike Foster Bill, a private members bill with the intention to ban hunting with hounds. Around 100,000 bloodsports supporters attended as the CA used its vast inherited wealth to charter planes, coaches and trains to get people to London. Supporters of the Oakley Hunt were even told by the hunt committee that they 'should arrange to take a day off work, or pretend to be sick, or whatever'. Furthermore, hunt members were instructed to 'keep the children back from school and be there! If you simply cannot be bothered then please do not bother to come hunting with the Oakley next season'. In a press release, the HSA even advised its members to 'steer clear of the pro-bloodsports Countryside Rally' after it became obvious that a huge turnout was to be expected and that the hunters were collectively getting themselves into a rage.

A letter to the *Countryman's Weekly* the month before hinted at the frustrations of many on the pro-hunt side:

> *The time for gentlemanly conduct has long passed, a change to stronger tactics is now needed. Some risks must be taken.*

Even the then editor of *Horse and Hound,* Arnold Garvey, publicly stated that he was prepared to go to prison if need be!

A Heartbreaking Loss

Although, during the vast majority of times when saboteurs were present, hunts found it impossible to kill, the occasions when they did manage to kill in front of saboteurs were particularly heartbreaking. For example, during November 1998, as saboteurs were on the Old Surrey and Burstow Hunt not far from Edenbridge, an extraordinary set of events took place. The group suspected that a bagged fox had just been released (due to the fact that the hounds suddenly went into full cry, with no chase beforehand and that the terriermen were lurking very close at hand) and not long after one saboteur found himself literally lying down using his whole body to protect the fox from the entire pack of hounds, all the while the huntsman and terriermen were attacking him. Miraculously, he managed to scoop the fox up into his coat and dive into the back of Brixton HSA's Land Rover which was waiting nearby. As the vehicle sped towards Last Chance Animal Rescue, which was not too far away, the terrified animal was turning blue and gasping for air, forcing one of the passengers to attempt to blow air into his nose. By some stroke of luck the group spotted a queue of people with cat baskets waiting for a local veterinary surgery to open whilst travelling along Edenbridge high street. Unfotunately, the surgery was not yet open and it was at this moment that the fox died on the lap of one of the saboteurs still in the back of the Land Rover. A vet came running out as soon as she heard that there was an emergency but sadly it was too late. She checked the fox over to find that he was a big, otherwise healthy dog fox, save for a small puncture wound on one side of his chest. The group then carried on sabotaging the hunt with the body wrapped up underneath a seat in their vehicle, whilst taunting the hunt that he was still alive and that they would be footing the medical costs. His body was later buried among brambles in Streatham.

Boxing Day 1998 passed without any major incidents, except that one beagle from the Forest and District Beagles, near Maccesfield, died after being caught in a snare.

Bringing Down the Buckhounds

The 1990s was also to be a very bad decade for members of one particular hunt located in the South; the New Forest Buckhounds. The New Forest gets its name from William the Conqueror who established the area as his first hunting forest in England and as such it became known as the 'new hunting forest'. Historically, the term 'forest' referred to a royal hunting area in which certain animals such as deer were protected by law against poachers, so that the king and the aristocracy could kill them themselves. There are numerous sources that state that it was the Normans who reintroduced fallow deer into the forests of England, having become extinct in Britain during the last Ice Age.

The New Forest Buckhounds were a particularly vile and merciless organisation that chased and killed fallow buck throughout the New Forest and saboteurs were determined to put an end to it.

During the summer of 1991, hunt saboteurs in the South were busy thwarting the efforts of the Ytene Mink Hunt (previously known as the Courtenay Tracy Otterhounds, after its founder). The hunt was being hit week after week and mass hits were commonplace. As a result of large numbers of anti-hunt activists coming together and a run of successful

Top: A Croydon saboteur cradles a dead fox killed by the Old Surrey and Burstow Hunt, November 1998

Bottom: A fox runs away from the Cottesmore Hunt, 1993

BAN THE HUNT
RITUAL MURDER
C739 DKN

direct actions, friendships were formed and solidified and the group became inspired to take on the Buckhounds that winter. Tactics against this peculiar form of hunting were quickly learnt both through the study of old hunting literature and from experience in the field, and practically every single meet from 1991 to 1997 was sabotaged. Due to the nature of the terrain of the New Forest, specifically the lack of roads and the fact that the vast majority is open access land, the hunt was followed by saboteurs working entirely on foot. CB radios were vital in communicating between groups, with secret codes being used to stop pro-hunt earwiggers using radio scanners. The classic tactics employed against fox hunts such as covering the quarry's scent with anti-mate spray and using the hunting horn to call the hounds away were used to great effect and saved many a buck's life. When their numbers were great enough, saboteurs would also on occasion simply block the hunt's kennels (located in Brockenhurst) and prevent the hunt from even starting.

At the opening meet of 1992, the hound van was again blockaded and as a result, over two hours of hunting were lost and the hunt once again failed to kill. Five saboteurs received criminal convictions for the day's actions but the blockade proved a great success. Due to the efficacy of the antis' efforts, however, arrests became more and more frequent as obscure by-laws were employed which often prevented anyone from interfering with the hunt. Both police officers and Forestry Commission staff were very quick to report people acting against the hunt. The criminal justice system wasn't entirely one-sided, however, as the huntsman, John Stride, was convicted of assaulting a saboteur. As is often the trend when saboteurs become increasingly effective in their efforts against a particular hunt, the Buckhounds started bringing in thugs from elsewhere and violence against the antis rapidly increased. With this increase in violence came an increase in numbers of bucks killed due in part to the fact that it was becoming more difficult to bypass the heavies and actually interfere with the hunt. After constant sabotage at nearly every meet, the New Forest Buckhounds were getting more determined than ever.

By 1994, numbers of hunt saboteurs had dramatically dwindled and those remaining desperately needed a new strategy in shutting down the New Forest Buckhounds for good. The tactics used by other groups monitoring the hunt were noted and the remaining saboteurs set about fundraising for video equipment. Having rebranded themselves as Wildlife Action, the saboteurs no longer interfered with the hunt's activities but instead followed on foot and filmed its atrocities. This stark change of strategy attracted a considerable amount of criticism as the hunt was allowed to continue unabated and many buck lost their lives over this period. It was an extremely difficult decision that went against the intuition of many involved, including stalwarts of the campaign, Peter White and Joe Hashman, but ultimately proved effective. For four years, the group filmed chases of five hours or more and hounds savaging buck as the huntsmen tried to catch up. As yet unseen, horrifying scenes were recorded that included three hunt followers standing on an exhausted buck just before its death, a buck being held underwater before being shot and hunt supporters paying money for parts of the dead animals as trophies. The public were appalled at what they saw as the footage found its way onto local television news. Pressure was now mounting against the Buckhounds and the Forestry Commission was forced to suspend the hunt twice after their hounds were filmed savaging deer. The offices of the commission were even occupied by anti-hunt campaigners. The pressure eventually came to a head when on 28th July 1997, after a landslide Labour victory, the New Forest Buckhounds disbanded. This was particularly poignant as up until then, the New Forest Buckhounds had been the only registered pack hunting roe deer in England, Scotland and Wales and the only one hunting deer outside of the West Country. As a final death knell to 900 years of hunting in the New Forest, the Forestry Commission decided four months later to never again issue deer hunting licences on its land.

Opposite page: Saboteurs bloackade the entrance to the New Forest Buckhounds' kennels in Brockenhurst

Top: An HSA recruitment poster

Bottom: Saboteurs cover the scent of a fox with citronella oil at a meet of the New Forest Hunt

Top: West Sussex Wildlife Protection

Bottom: Simon Wild and a lost hound from the Hursley Hambledon Hunt, 1993

Opposite page: The rescue of Copper the fox

Copper the Fox

Over the years, countless animals have been saved every week by the actions of those willing to put their bodies on the line and directly intervene. Every now and then, certain incidents of animals being saved take on a distinct importance within the overall narrative of the anti-hunt movement. One particular fox, obviously totally unbeknownst to him, was to have a very significant role in the fight against bloodsports after his lucky escape from a hunt in Sussex. Simon Wild, a prominent wildlife campaigner, takes up the story:

On 6th February 1999, the West Sussex Wildlife Protection hunt sab group had gone to the Chiddingfold, Leconfield and Cowdray Hunt at Petworth, West Sussex. We received a call from one of the sabs to say that when he tried to rescue a fox from the hounds, he was bitten, and it had gone down a rabbit hole. The sabs had made some heroic efforts to sit on the hole until the hunt and terriermen had gone away, and then a policeman had volunteered his helmet to prevent anyone being bitten. At the time, Sussex had the highest number of police in the country (over 80) attending hunts on a Saturday, and our sab group regularly attracted 20 officers. We raced over to Upperton Common where the sabs and police were surrounding the rabbit hole. We could see the fox tail, but how could we get it out? My wife Jaine, as an experienced wildlife rescuer decided everyone should move away, and with half an hour's patience the fox moved far enough backwards to be caught, then placed in a cage and taken to Richard Edwards, a specialist wildlife vet at Bognor Regis. Here the vet found the fox was under a year old and had a comatose appearance and little pulse. It had several bite wounds, blood in the urine and was placed on a drip. To the vet's great surprise, the next morning the fox was lively and had removed the drip. I tried to develop some media interest with my local BBC South, but was told it would 'cost a licence fee' if they came and collected the video from me, so I rather gave up. The fox was later transferred to Hydestile Wildlife Hospital in Surrey for recuperation and all I got was a short piece in a local paper. However, on returning from a brief holiday, we got the vet's report and we mentioned the incident to a lady who had offered her services in promoting stories in the media. Before I knew it there was a media storm on two fronts: as before the Hunting Act, Professor Bateson had exposed 'stress myopathy' in deer that were chased for hunting, and by contacting Professor Bateson with the vet report he had said this was the first indication of similar myopathy occurring in hunted foxes. The conclusion brought about a media frenzy, coming as it did when hunting was under threat of legislation and I soon found myself being interviewed for a live broadcast for BBC national news on Upperton Common and Hydestile. Further, the policeman's helmet had aroused the interest of the Daily Mail and while I gave an accurate account to the Mail journalist, they decided to spin it so that a policeman had saved the fox in its final seconds, by placing his helmet over the hole it was in. Together, with the image of the helmet and recovering fox it made half a page. The Mail on Sunday then rang me, and decided to run a counter story claiming 'the truth had gone to ground' as the police officer had admitted arriving just after the incident. However, the double dose of media brought further attention in an unexpected way: the story was seen as so compelling, that with some artistic licence, it formed the main storyline of police dramas A Touch of Frost and Dalziel and Pascoe, and children's programme Nature Boy, and featured in news stories worldwide. There was a final irony as Pearson's publishing firm paid our sab group for a video grab of the policeman's helmet to use in a children's educational publication; the irony being that Upperton Common where the fox was saved, was owned by Viscount Cowdray, of which Pearson's publishing is the family business! Copper was later released to a non-hunting area, never aware of the far-reaching effects his tumultuous rescue had created.

13:43

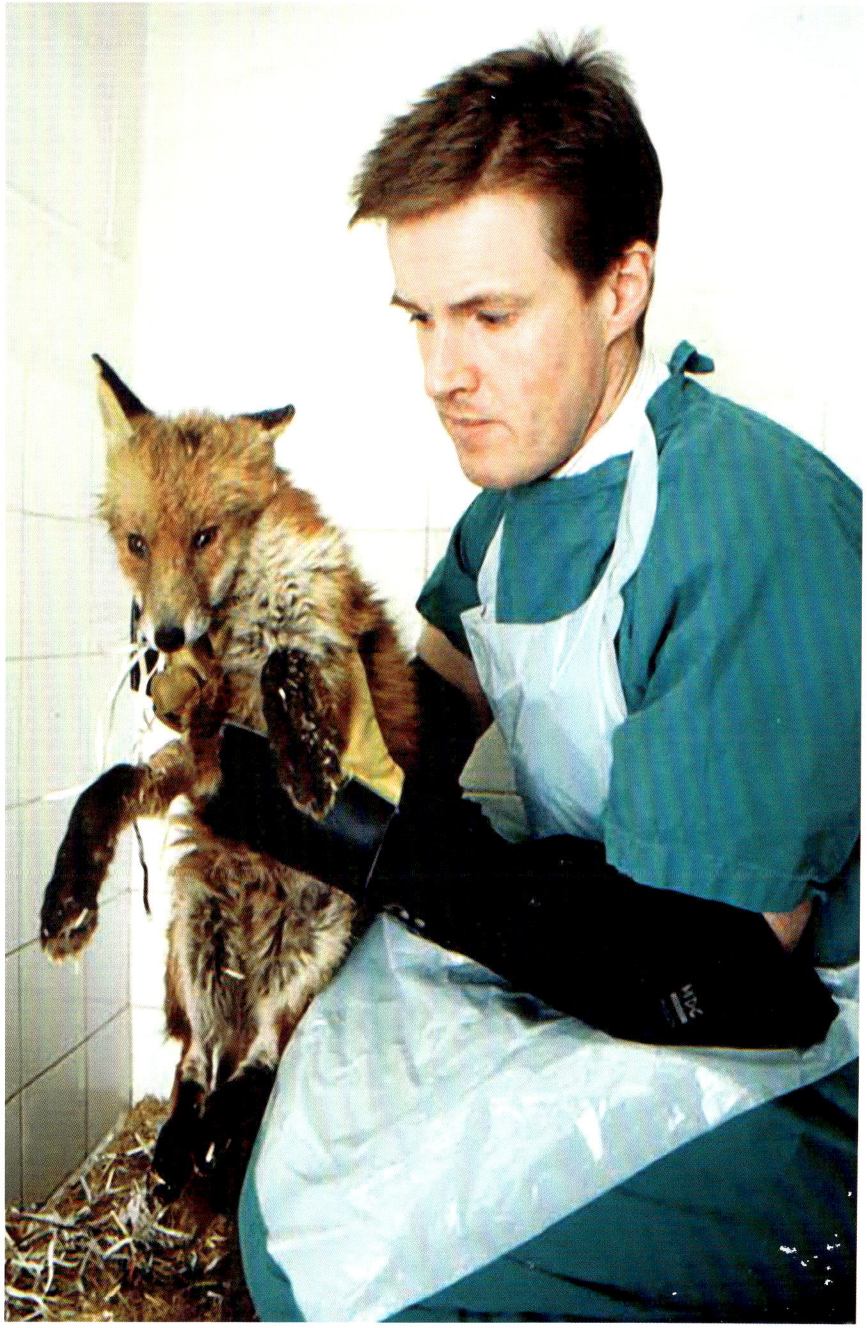

IF THE FOX
DIDN'T ENJOY IT
HE WOULDN'T
JOIN IN.
JRA
547D

The Burns Inquiry

In December 1999, Home Secretary Jack Straw MP set up an inquiry into hunting with hounds. Named the Burns Inquiry after Lord Burns who chaired the inquiry, it set out to explore the 'practical aspects of different types of hunting with dogs and its impact on the rural economy, agriculture and pest control, the social and cultural life of the countryside, the management and conservation of wildlife, and animal welfare in particular areas of England and Wales' along with the consequences any ban would entail. The inquiry turned out to be quite farcical and was seen by the HSA and most in the anti-hunt movement as a cover-up. Despite this, the inquiry did find:

> There is a lack of firm scientific evidence about the effect on the welfare of a fox being closely pursued, caught and killed above ground by hounds. We are satisfied, nevertheless, that this experience seriously compromises the welfare of the fox.

In regards to hare hunting the inquiry found:

> There is a lack of firm scientific evidence about the effect on the welfare of a hare being closely pursued, caught and killed by hounds during hunting. We are satisfied, nevertheless, that although death and insensibility will normally follow within a matter of seconds, this experience seriously compromises the welfare of the hare.

The conclusion with regards to deer hunting was even more pointless:

> Most scientists agree that deer are likely to suffer in the final stages of hunting. The available evidence does not enable us to resolve the disagreement about the point at which, during the hunt, the welfare of the deer becomes seriously compromised.

Needless to say, it is blaringly obvious that hunting causes horrific suffering to the quarry, a day out with an HSA group could have easily ascertained that!

Opposite page: Quorn Hunt supporters on Boxing Day, 1993

Above: A fox killed by the Cheshire Forest Hunt

Right: A fox killed by the Old Surrey and Burstow Hunt is hung onto the door of the BFSS offices in Camberwell, London, 1995

Below: Old Surrey & Burstow hounds disembowel a live fox, 2001

ANGLING

Steadfast HSA

Angling has always been towards the back of the agenda in regards to the anti-hunting movement. Perhaps this is due to the fact that angling remains a far more popular bloodsport than say, fox or stag hunting, with an estimated 4 million participants. Perhaps it is due in part to the fact that for many, it is much easier to empathise with other mammals and as a result putting an end to angling is a far greater task for animal liberationists. Whatever the reason, this is not to say that angling has never been sabotaged as over the years there have been numerous hits against both fishing competitions and fish farms. Indeed, such was the nature of this particular issue that the HSA's stance on angling even led to a bitter dispute with the League Against Cruel Sports. At its 1983 AGM, the HSA decided to employ direct action against angling and subsequently published an article in *HOWL* outlining the case against angling and offering advice on how to sabotage it. Following this, at a committee meeting on 15th January 1984, committee members remained steadfast in their position and published the following points about the cruel sport of angling and their decision to combat it:

1. **Fishing is a bloodsport.**
2. **Discarded fishing line, lead weights and hooks cause the deaths of many waterside animals and birds. The RSPB estimates that some 4,000 to 5,000 swans die each year through lead poisoning alone.**
3. **Anglers pollute the environment and destroy habitats.**
4. **More fish are killed in one year's angling than all other hunted creatures put together.**
5. **Abolition of hunting with dogs is not near at hand.**
6. **The Labour Party will probably drop its manifesto commitment to abolish bloodsports with or without the HSA's campaign against angling.**
7. **The HSA is not a political organisation and is committed to opposing all cruelty in the field.**
8. **All HSA members were aware of the 1983 AGM discussion programme, of which angling was a part, in keeping with the constitution. The AGM was attended by over one hundred members. The angling question was agreed by a large majority vote.**

The League, fearing that their relationship with the Labour Party would be soured by any assault on angling, asked the HSA to remove the article. The answer was a polite yet uncompromising, no. The League then went on to publicly disassociate itself from the HSA with its Executive Director, Richard Course (who later joined the pro-hunt lobby), describing the HSA as a "bunch of lunatics". A policy of non-cooperation was adopted by the League and it cancelled its annual goodwill £1,000 donation to the HSA. All references to hunt saboteurs were cut from its magazine and on some occasions the League would not appear on television debates unless certain HSA representatives were excluded from the programme. The two organisations have since become closer and the relationship between them has warmed, in part due to Course's resignation in 1988. It is interesting to note that in 1989, the League awarded one of its prized silver medals (only 12 had been given out in its then 64 year history) to a Mrs Walters for sabotaging a hunt. Walters had rightly gained widespread praise from the media after she had sat on a fox earth and refused to move. Prior to this, she had heard a horn near her garden and then had seen the fox dive underground. She sat in the middle of the pack and refused to move for 20 minutes until the North Ledbury joint master, Christopher Tolley, agreed to leave the fox alone. Whilst recognising the bravery of Mrs Walters, the HSA did note that it was a little odd how thousands of saboteurs from all walks of life had been taking similar action for 25 years and had generally received hostile reactions from the media and, until the two organisations had grown closer, the League.

Above: Saboteurs protest at the International Whaling Commission in Brighton, 19th July 1980

Opposite page: A saboteur disrupts a lone fisherman

Above: CAA's logo

Opposite page: Saboteurs put an early end to some anglers' activites

Angling has always been closely tied to other bloodsports and is often championed in magazines such as *Countryman's Weekly* which openly supports other cruel hobbies such as hare coursing, fox hunting, deer stalking, etc. Indeed, to view angling as somehow less cruel than other bloodsports is quite nonsensical. Angling's governing body, the National Anglers Council even joined with the British Field Sports Society and the British Association for Shooting and Conservation to launch the Campaign for Country Sports to lobby for the interests of bloodsports in the run up to the 1983 General Election.

The Campaign for the Abolition of Angling

Brought about to put the plight of fish back on the animal liberation agenda, the Campaign for the Abolition of Angling was formed in 1981. The group, based in Romsey before relocating to Sevenoaks, very much advocated direct action and formulated the most effective ways of putting an end to a day's fishing. Some of these were outlined in *HOWL* No. 49:

1. *One of the best ways has got to be the use of a canoe or rowing boat to make the anglers pull their lines in and disturb the fish. They may not even realise you're sabbing them, unless you've got a purple Mohican.*

2. *The fish can be disturbed by throwing medium-sized stones in the water – not huge rocks as they may stun the fish through vibrations in the water.*

3. *Standing behind anglers, having a noisy chat about how many they've caught, can cause a shadow, disturbing the fish.*

The CAA was born out of the increased public awareness of the cruelty of angling that had come about by the *Medway Report*. The independent report, commissioned by the RSPCA, came to a conclusion that was blaringly obvious to all but the most close-minded; fish feel pain. Through its newsletter, *PISCES*, the organisation sought to provide its members with updates from the world of angling as well as reports of actions taken against it. Many issues of the publication even included a list of reports taken from the ALF Supporters Group's diary of actions that mostly consisted of fishmongers' windows being smashed but did also include a report of incendiary devices having been left in the offices of a fishing club in Dormansland, Surrey in January 1987. The office was reportedly totally destroyed but not before a number of useful tools were stolen. Much of the campaigning of the CAA was also aimed at banning the use of lead by the industry that perversely advertises itself as a 'harmless pastime'.

In 1984, ten saboteurs from Cannock Chase HSA staged a banner demonstration at Calf Heath Reservoir at an all night angling match after discarding the contestant's pegs and directional signs. In 1986, trout fishing along the River Kennet and the River Lambourn in Berkshire was successfully disrupted by Oxford HSA who disturbed the water surface and kept the fish away from baited hooks. On 29th June, nine saboteurs from Oxford, Leamington, Coventry and Bath sabotaged fishing matches in Wiltshire and on the River Thames at Cassington. Furious at being prevented from killing any fish the anglers responded by hurling their lead weights across the river towards the antis.

Disruption on the Riverbanks

On various years the CAA launched a national day of action against angling that was timed to coincide with the start of the season. 1988 was to be a very successful year with 26 groups taking action against the bloodsport. Among those out that day were Norwich HSA and along with other

members of the CAA, they easily prevented four fishermen from killing anything on the River Yore. The eight saboteurs pre-fed the waters around Norwich between 4am and 6.30am on the opening day of the season (16th June). Two days later, West Kent Animal Rights took two rowing boats onto the Medway near Tonbridge, announced their intentions by loud-hailer, and proceeded to row backwards and forwards thus disturbing the water whilst more saboteurs on the banks threw handfuls of light gravel around the angler's floats. A similar tactic was employed by saboteurs from Bristol and Bath on the River Avon near Bathampton. West Wiltshire HSA also used two boats and a canoe to create water disturbance and cause anglers to reel in along a three mile stretch of river. A different approach was utilised by eight members of Cambridge HSA who did TV and radio interviews before sabotaging 20 anglers on the River Cam. That year's Anti-Angling Day proved a massive success and gained the anti-angling movement more press coverage than it had ever generated before.

Fish Freed

The HSA launched a mini-campaign against a trout pool in Thorpe Park (an amusement park in Surrey) in 1984. The park sold visitors the opportunity to catch trout in a small, overcrowded pond for £1 each. Saboteurs attended the park to see for themselves what this entailed and ended up stopping the fishing. The police were called but no charges were brought because the park's management didn't want any publicity over their cruel fishing pool. Their hopes were dashed, however, as two blockades of the main entrance to the park were organised. In a night-time raid on 4th June 1984, saboteurs released 30,000 rainbow trout from the fish farm at the park. The fish, who were worth over £8,000, were kept in 20ft square breeding nets attached to floating collars. In order to free them, the saboteurs unhooked the nets, which then sank to the bottom of the lake, allowing the fish to swim to freedom. One local hunt saboteur, who was not personally involved in the raid, said in a statement to the local paper:

> *In one area of the park, trout are being hooked out of the lake by visitors and, in many cases, thrown back again badly injured. It's a cruel sport and the fish are suffering.*

The HSA had forced the company responsible for the trout pool (Kingsmead Fisheries) to cancel their contract with the pleasure park in December 1984. However, this was not before saboteurs again freed thousands of rainbow trout from nets floating in the middle of a fourteen acre lake in Horton (also owned by Kingsmead Fisheries). That same year, the HSA donated £1,000 to Sea Shepherd, enabling them to purchase the island of Little Greenholm in the Orkneys. The island had previously been the site for many confrontations between Sea Shepherd activists and hunt saboteurs on the one side and seal cullers and the police on the other.

In 1985, Bickleigh Mill fish farm was raided. Fishing rods and nets were broken and rainbow trout worth £1,500 were released into the nearby River Exe. The Western Times allegedly received a phone call from hunt saboteurs claiming responsibility. Five years later, in 1990, Wessex Fly Fishing School near Tolpuddle was burnt down using an incendiary device along with two anglers' cabins on the river Frome by the ALF. One angling match in West London was duly stopped for an hour and a half before the Metropolitan Police overreacted in classic style causing the saboteurs to scatter throughout Hayes, with one escaping the law by hiding in a wheelie bin on a nearby industrial estate. The event ended with six arrests for threatening behaviour but all were eventually found not guilty.

Above: A demo outside an angling shop, Mevagissey, Cornwall, 1994

Opposite page: Brighton-based Sea Sabs protest against a shark fishing festival, Looe, Cornwall, 1994

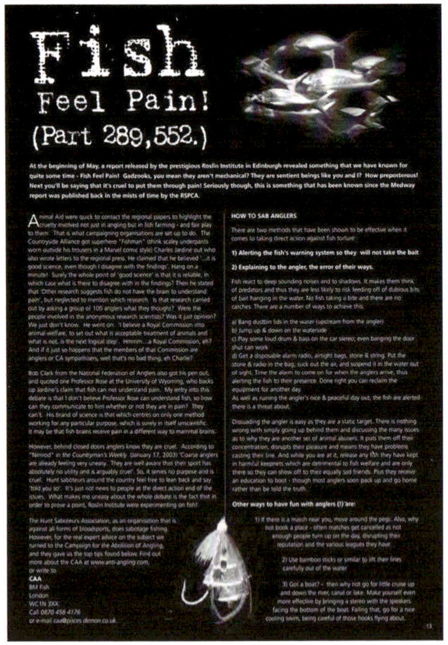

Fish Feel Pain! (Part 289,552.)

At the beginning of May, a report released by the prestigious Roslin Institute in Edinburgh revealed something that we have known for quite some time - Fish Feel Pain! Gadzooks, you mean they aren't mechanical? They are sentient beings like you and I? How preposterous! Next you'll be saying that it's cruel to put them through pain! Seriously though, this is something that has been known since the Medway report was published back in the mists of time by the RSPCA.

Animal Aid were quick to contact the regional papers to highlight the cruelty involved not just in angling but in fish farming - and fair play to them. That is what campaigning organisations are set up to do. The Countryside Alliance got superhero "Fishman" (think scaley underpants worn outside his trousers in a Marvel comic style) Charles Jardine out who also wrote letters to the regional press. He claimed that he believed '...it is good science, even though I disagree with the findings'. Hang on a minute! Surely the whole point of 'good science' is that it is reliable, in which case what is there to disagree with in the findings? Then he stated that 'Other research suggests fish do not have the brain to understand pain', but neglected to mention which research. Is that research carried out by asking a group of 100 anglers what they thought? Were the people involved in the anonymous research scientists? Was it just opinion? We just don't know. He went on: 'I believe a Royal Commission into animal welfare, to set out what is acceptable treatment of animals and what is not, is the next logical step'. Hmmm...a Royal Commission, eh? And if it just so happens that the members of that Commission are anglers or CA sympathisers, well that's no bad thing, eh Charlie?

Bob Clark from the National Federation of Anglers also got his pen out, and quoted one Professor Rose at the University of Wyoming, who backs up Jardine's claim that fish can not understand pain. My entry into this debate is that I don't believe Professor Rose can understand fish, so how can they communicate to him whether or not they are in pain? They can't. His brand of science is that which centres on only one method working for any particular purpose, which is surely in itself unscientific. It may be that fish brains receive pain in a different way to mammal brains.

However, behind closed doors anglers know they are cruel. According to "Nimrod" in the Countryman's Weekly (January 17, 2003) 'Coarse anglers are already feeling very uneasy. They are well aware that their sport has absolutely no utility and is arguably cruel'. So, it serves no purpose and is cruel. Hunt saboteurs around the country feel free to lean back and say 'told you so'. It's just not news to people at the direct action end of the issues. What makes me uneasy about the whole debate is the fact that in order to prove a point, Roslin Institute were experimenting on fish!

The Hunt Saboteurs Association, as an organisation that is against all forms of bloodsports, does sabotage fishing. However, for the real expert advice on the subject we turned to the Campaign for the Abolition of Angling, and they gave us the top tips found below. Find out more about the CAA at www.anti-angling.com, or write to:
CAA
BM Fish
London
WC1N 3XX
Call 0870 458 4176
or e-mail caa@pisces.demon.co.uk

HOW TO SAB ANGLERS

There are two methods that have been shown to be effective when it comes to taking direct action against fish torture:

1) Alerting the fish's warning system so they will not take the bait

2) Explaining to the angler, the error of their ways.

Fish react to deep sounding noises and to shadows. It makes them think of predators and thus they are less likely to risk feeding off of dubious bits of bait hanging in the water. No fish taking a bite and there are no catches. There are a number of ways to achieve this.

a) Bang dustbin lids in the water (upstream from the angler)
b) Jump up & down on the waterside
c) Play some loud drum & bass on the car stereo; even banging the door shut can work
d) Get a disposable alarm radio, airtight bags, stone & string. Put the stone & radio in the bag, suck out the air, and suspend it in the water out of sight. Time the alarm to come on for when the anglers arrive, thus alerting the fish to their presence. Done right you can reclaim the equipment for another day.
As well as ruining the angler's nice & peaceful day out, the fish are alerted there is a threat about.

Dissuading the angler is easy as they are a static target. There is nothing wrong with simply going up behind them and discussing the many issues as to why they are another set of animal abusers. It puts them off their concentration, disrupts their pleasure and means they have problems casting their line. And while you are at it, release any fish they have kept in harmful keepnets which are detrimental to fish welfare and are only there so they can show off to their equally sad friends. Plus they receive an education to boot - though most anglers soon pack up and go home rather than be told the truth.

Other ways to have fun with anglers (!) are:

1) If there is a match near you, move around the pegs. Also, why not book a place - often matches get cancelled as not enough people turn up on the day, disrupting their reputation and the various leagues they have.

2) Use bamboo sticks or similar to lift their lines carefully out of the water.

3) Got a boat? - then why not go for little cruise up and down the river, canal or lake. Make yourself even more effective by bringing a stereo with the speakers facing the bottom of the boat. Failing that, go for a nice cooling swim, being careful of those hooks flying about.

13

Above: 'Fish feel pain' article from *HOWL* No.79, 2003

Opposite page top: A seal safe from shooters during 'Operation Seal Guard'

Opposite page bottom: Sheffield Hunt Saboteurs confront Usan seal killers, 22nd April 2014

Disorder

The first ever charges against saboteurs under Section 2 of the Public Order Act (violent disorder) were for an incident involving fishermen. Saboteurs from Hastings, Croydon and Tunbridge Wells had failed to locate the Old Surrey and Burstow Hunt but had found a group of anglers whilst out looking and instead decided to stop them. After the saboteurs had remonstrated with the anglers, the majority packed up straight away. However, one particularly macho fisherman squared up to one of the Croydon saboteurs and pushed him in the chest, forcing him to fall into the river. The fisherman then found himself the victim of a shove into the river, after which the saboteurs made a hasty retreat from the area. Unbeknownst to them, however, one car was followed back to Tunbridge Wells by the anglers and all five of the car's occupants were arrested in the town centre. Rather unluckily, another saboteur who had returned in a separate car and happened to be walking by was recognised by the police and also arrested. Foolishly, the fisherman's court statement focused solely on one saboteur who had been wearing a rugby shirt and who was not even the one who had been involved (as well as omitting the fact that he had pushed the saboteur into the river first) and the charges were dismissed as violent disorder requires three or more participants.

Over 15 HSA groups were also involved in the CAA's 1998 week of action making it one of the most successful to date. In North London, activists sabotaged fishermen on the Walthamstow reservoir, with some taking to the water in canoes whilst others stayed on foot. The press were very keen to report on the week's events with numerous articles appearing in the *Independent on Sunday* and the *Daily Express* and even an interview on Radio 4's *Today* programme.

Another water inhabitant, the whale, also received a little aid from the HSA after it had joined forces with members of Friends of the Earth, the Vegetarian Society, Compassion in World Farming and Animal Aid to form the Brighton Anti-Whaling Coordinating Committee as the International Whaling Commission was due to meet in the city in 1980. Despite dozens of animal welfare organisations being asked to help finance the campaign, in the end the only response came from the HSA and Friends of the Earth. With numbers of demonstrators ranging from just 30 up to 1,000, a protest was present outside the Metropole Hotel on every night of the meeting. Despite the protests, the commission agreed on its quotas to kill thousands of whales across the globe.

In January 2007, around 30 hunt saboteurs smashed up fishing equipment and confronted anglers at the Bank House Fly Fishery in Lancashire. In a letter to the *Manchester Evening News*, the HSA wrote:

> *There is no `new campaign' against angling - it remains an abhorrent and cruel activity, and as such will continue to be included within our remit as an organisation against all bloodsports. It's not about `people-hating', it's not about `class hatred' and it's not about 'terrorism'. It's about cruelty - plain and simple. If you want to spend an afternoon by the river bank then by all means do, just take a good book, or maybe a bin bag and gloves so you can clean a bit of our countryside up for others to enjoy. Leave the hooking of a fish out of the equation, and we'll gladly leave you alone.*

Seal Culling

In Scotland, numerous seal culls have taken place with up to 4,000 of the animals shot each year. The reasoning behind the culls is that seals and sea lions damage commercial fish stocks and so dent fishing companies' profits. Sea Shepherd had wanted to disrupt the 2013 cull but due to various factors hadn't managed to. During the following year, however, they instigated a meeting with the HSA and both organisations set about organising a joint action against the

Scottish Wild Salmon Company (also known as Usan) in 2014. As part of what was named Operation Seal Guard, hunt saboteurs and Sea Shepherd volunteers were in the area for quite some time, stopping Usan killing seals over the Easter period. After an aggressive outburst by the seal killers towards a Sea Shepherd volunteer on 21st April, Sea Shepherd 'asked the Hunt Saboteurs Association to reactivate their undercover teams as well as introduce new covert operatives to the area'. In solidarity, saboteurs from Sheffield and further afield headed up to Gardenstown in Aberdeenshire to lend their assistance and on 22nd April, confronted the seal killers. An extensive clean up of Crovie Beach took place on 25th April, the same day that Sea Shepherd met with the local police, the council and Usan and made it clear that they would not be leaving the area until Usan handed in their seal shooting licences. However, it was agreed that the hunt saboteurs present would leave the area on the understanding that Usan would not kill seals in the five days that they were given to consider handing in their licences. The saboteurs headed home but not long after, on 2nd May, the HSA announced that rather than giving up their licences, Usan had in fact taken in their salmon nets and had appeared to have closed down their operations in Gardenstown. Unfortunately, Usan did return to catch salmon in Gardenstown and Crovie on 10th May, but thankfully did not resume seal shooting.

2000S: HOPE FOR ABOLITION

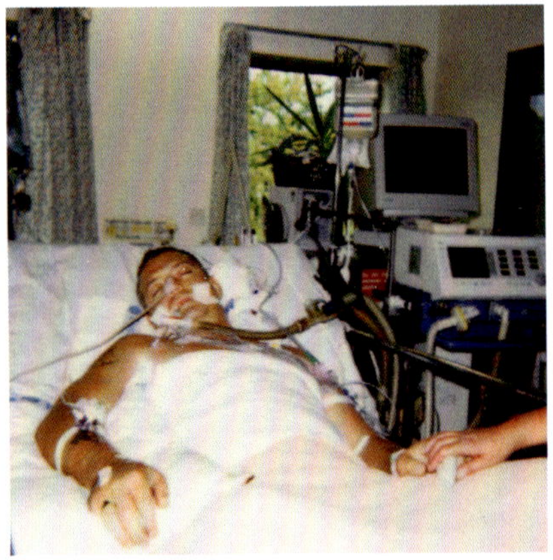

Top: Steve Christmas in the intensive care unit of Princess Royal Hospital, Haywards Heath

Opposite page: Huntsman Mark Bycroft is surrounded by saboteurs

Pushed Close to Death

The year 2000 was almost witness to the third death of a saboteur at the hands of the hunt. On 1st September, Steve Christmas, a 34 year old saboteur from the Croydon group, was airlifted to the Princess Royal Hospital in Haywards Heath after being deliberately run over by a 4x4 vehicle at a meet of the Old Surrey and Burstow with West Kent Hunt. Two wheels of the vehicle, driven by gamekeeper and hunt supporter Martin Maynard, drove over Christmas' body, leaving him with a crushed pelvis, four broken ribs and internal bleeding. This was not the first incident of the day as a mere 20 minutes before this attack, three hunt thugs jumped from Maynard's Land Rover and, aided by huntsman Mark Bycroft, attacked the group of activists, with the vehicle knocking one saboteur to the ground. During his four week stint in intensive care, Christmas underwent a tracheotomy as well as two major operations; one to fit a metal plate to his pelvis and the other to remove two feet of bowel. Dawn Preston, a spokesperson for the HSA at the time, stated:

> *This incident shows both the hunters' and hunt supporters' total disregard for life – whether it be human or animal. It must be a sick and twisted individual indeed who is so fearful of his favourite 'sport' being banned that he tries to kill those who seek to prevent him from torturing our wildlife. Do not forget that two hunt saboteurs have already been killed in the last ten years – and at one stage today I was terrified that another name could be added to that list. How many lives have to be lost before we see an end to this abhorrent sport and those that partake of it?*

Immediately after the incident, Maynard returned to the spot where he had almost killed Christmas to taunt the group of saboteurs desperately trying to help their friend. Christmas was left unable to work again due to the severity of his injuries, which included an inoperable double groin hernia. After four years and £22,000 in legal fees, an appeal overturned an initial decision not to award compensation and Christmas was awarded £18,500 in criminal injuries compensation.

The day after the assault, around 40 saboteurs descended upon the hunt's kennels in Felbridge, Surrey to protest against the horrific attack. Emotions were high and the situation inevitably escalated as the three police officers stationed at the kennels were overwhelmed. Seventeen windows of the three-house complex were smashed although Bycroft and his family had been forewarned by police and had fled prior to the saboteurs' arrival. The police subsequently conducted a number of dawn raids of local anti-hunt activists' houses in which 26 people were arrested for violent disorder. The charge was later changed to conspiracy to commit violent disorder. Despite the wide reaching investigation, only five saboteurs were convicted, mainly due to CCTV images of them having met at East Grinstead train station. The five luckily escaped prison sentences with community service orders being given out instead. The CPS, on the other hand, chose to drop Maynard's charge of 'causing grievous bodily harm with intent' due to a key witness serving an unrelated prison sentence despite there being three witnesses, a vehicle description and number plate, the name of the driver and tyre tracks running across the ground and over the victim. The hunting community tried desperately to paint a portrait of Bycroft as a decent, innocent victim trying to make a living whilst being continually harassed by animal rights fanatics. Nothing could be further from the truth, however. Bycroft himself had a long history of violence including a conviction of assault in 1991 when he was a whipper-in of the Old Surrey and Burstow.

Maynard was instead only charged with driving offences that included driving without a licence and insurance, and received a paltry fine of just £75. This verdict was only after a two year delay and increasing pressure on the police to act. After finding Maynard not guilty of almost killing Christmas, Judge Thorpe made the outrageous statement that, "the only thing I will say to the defendant is this was a regrettable accident because he has a slightly unfortunate antecedent history [in other words, Maynard had a record of violence] so he is going to have to be fairly careful in support of the hunts and I say that because I have just seen the press have come into court".

Top: A dead fox dumped on the front seat of Christopher Black's car, 2004

Bottom: The Avon Vale Hunt's hounds with saboteurs

Opposite page top: Saboteurs take the Cotley Harriers' hounds away from their huntsman at Coney's Castle, Marshwood Vale, Dorset, 2005

Opposite page bottom: A supporter of the Cotley Harriers squares up to a saboteur, 2005

Despite the numerous incidents of assaults by hunt supporters occurring at hunts in the South East, namely the Surrey Union and the Old Surrey and Burstow, local police forces were continuing to show extreme bias in their policing of meets and spent a considerable amount of time and money to ensure hunts were able to kill as they pleased. It was a common sight to see mounted police officers riding alongside the field, no doubt pleased to have a jolly out with their friends. Over the course of ten meets of the two hunts in late 2002 and early 2003, a total of over 263 police officers were deployed and on one occasion officers were paid triple wage to police a kennel meet of the Surrey Union. Although in other cases of potential public order disturbances, such as football matches, the club in question would be charged by the police force, the huge bill for policing hunts was entirely footed by the taxpayer.

One major deterrent for police officers to so blatantly side with those killing wildlife, and since the Hunting Act doing so illegally, has been the large sums of money dished out to saboteurs in compensation for wrongful arrests. A group of seven saboteurs from South Wales were granted £21,000 in compensation by Dyfed Powys Police for wrongful arrest at a meet of the Sennybridge Farmers Hunt near Brecon as well as trespassing on their property when searching the activists' homes. At the time of their arrest, the group were simply sitting in their minibus eating lunch. In what proved to be a rather lucrative outing, eleven saboteurs were handcuffed and arrested at a meet of the Meynell and South Staffordshire Hunt in January 2008 under the Trade Union Regulations Act for disrupting a lawful activity. Derbyshire Police were later sued by the eleven and subsequently settled out of court, paying a whopping £38,300 in compensation to the activists. In 2006, a Hastings saboteur received £6,000 in an out of court settlement with Surrey Police after the story of one of their officers was found to be completely false due to contrary video evidence of the arrest. These pay-outs were not a new phenomenon, however, as it was not uncommon for saboteurs to receive compensation. For example, nine saboteurs received substantial compensation after they, and many others, were arrested during a hit of the Old Berkshire Beagles in November 1989. On the day in question, around 50 police officers, including a helicopter, were in attendance. The only saboteur to evade arrest was Aubrey Thomas, who was pursued by the police for over 15 miles. This included running underneath a line of electricity pylons for around five miles to avoid the helicopter overhead before eventually mingling into the crowd at an Aylesbury United football match. This particular case cost the police over £250,000 and was key in forcing not only Thames Valley Police, but police forces across the country to overhaul their strategy of policing hunts. However, these handful of cases barely scratch the surface of compensation paid out by the police to saboteurs and, more pertinently, only a very small number of wrongful arrests and illegal police behaviour towards anti-bloodsports campaigners end up with compensation being awarded.

More Hunt Home Visits

The pro-hunt community once again showed their complete lack of concern for inflicting violence on others when in the early hours of 5th November 2002, a gang of hunt supporters fired a burning firework through the letterbox of the Dorchester house of a well known saboteur. The firework hit the inside wall with such force that it created a large dent and filled the whole house with smoke. Luckily the saboteur's 18 month old son, who was asleep at the time, escaped injury. The saboteur was under no illusions as to the reasons for the attack:

> *Some hunt supporter has done this because we had such a great day on Saturday at the South Dorset Hunt. They were hunting on the outskirts of town and we stopped them chasing a fox that lives round the back of some people's houses. The huntsman was so angry he lost it completely. He was even swearing at his own supporters.*

This was not the first attack that this saboteur had received because of his actions as an animal rights activist. On a previous occasion, another group of hunters had visited his house armed with pickaxe handles and other weapons with the intention of causing serious (and quite possibly deadly) injury. He was at home at the time and was extremely thankful when the attackers eventually left after having failed to gain entrance to the property. His relief was heightened by the fact that the front door had been left unlocked and had the attackers tried the door the incident would have had a quite horrific ending. Indeed, that same Saturday, a hunt saboteur at the Essex and Suffolk Hunt was driven into by a hunt supporter armed with an iron bar. He was forced to cling onto the vehicle for half a mile as it drove at speeds of up to 50mph before stopping at a crossroads where the saboteur had a chance to jump off.

In 2005, prominent anti-hunt campaigner Simon Wild, was awoken at 4am by an explosion at the garage of his house in Pulborough, West Sussex. He raced outside to find his almost new Citroën diesel van engulfed in 20ft high flames. The arson attack was almost certainly carried out by supporters of the Crawley and Horsham Hunt, outraged by the recent hunting ban and a hunt that Wild regularly attended. Just a month before, another compassionate Pulborough resident, 17 year old Christopher Black, found a disembowelled fox dumped in his car after he had gone with his mother to sabotage the Chiddingfold, Leconfield and Cowdray Hunt.

Karma was to have its way at a different violent incident in February 2003, however, as members of the Oakley Hunt, joined by Bicester with Waddon Chase supporters, launched a serious attack on the saboteurs' vehicle. Just minutes after the assault, one hunt supporter who was particularly aggressive towards a saboteur, threatening home visits and the like, keeled over and died of a heart attack.

Disease Vectors

At this point in time, the Albrighton Hunt was one of the most consistently sabotaged hunts in the country with unrelenting pressure from the Wolverhampton, Stoke and Birmingham groups. All fox hunting was suspended from February 2001 until the end of the season due to the horrific outbreak of foot and mouth disease sweeping the country. That year's Waterloo Cup hare coursing event was even cancelled as well. Indeed, it was acknowledged that hunting played a major role in spreading the disease and contributed to the scale of the outbreak until it was suspended. The Animal Welfare Information Service explained:

> *As a vector for the spread of disease there is little to beat hunting. The meets are often at farms. The horseboxes are parked in and around farm buildings. The hounds and followers tramp all over the farm. They have their meet. Rampage over the nearby fields, in amongst the stock. They torment and probably kill some wildlife, for fun. Then they return to the meet, pack up, and disperse to various locations all over the hunt country and beyond. Then a few days later they meet up at another farm on the other side of the hunt country and repeat the performance. This is an excellent way of spreading any disease, let alone one as infectious as foot and mouth. No wonder they are keen to get in quick and woo our ever gullible media into believing that it was the government, animal rights fanatics, indeed anyone but themselves who spread this disease!*

The Dumfriesshire Hunt had been badly hit by the foot and mouth outbreak and with dwindling subscribers, the Protection of Wild Mammals (Scotland) Act proved to be the final straw. It was disbanded in 2002 and its distinct black and tan hounds were drafted to hunts in France, leaving its 30,000 acre country free from fox hunting.

Top: A Hastings saboteur puts a video camera to good use, 2005

Bottom: Brighton HSA keeping tabs on the Chiddingfold, Cowdray & Leconfield Hunt, 2005

Opposite page: A south-east sab helps remove some illegal fly-posting, 2005

The same year was also to be the last for the Garth and South Berks Hunt after 211 years of wildlife abuse. Despite the usual claim that urbanisation was the main factor in the decision to close, local saboteurs believed the real reason was a waning of popularity. "I've been demonstrating against the Garth Hunt for 25 years," one said, "when I first started there used to be more than 100 riders and around 200 foot followers. Last year, before foot and mouth, there were just six riders and four followers."

Three in a Row...

The Reading, West London and Southampton groups were hugely active around this time. In 2000, they had the good fortune and tenacity to hit three different types of hunts in one day and save the lives of three species; fox, hare and rabbit. The morning saw the three groups strike the Hampshire Hunt whereby four foxes were seen and kept alive including one who had been marked to ground. The groups also had inside information that the Sandhurst and Aldershot Beagles were meeting close by at Preston Candover. On the way, Southampton HSA found and packed up two ferreters who were hunting rabbits at Cheesefoot Head. Once all the saboteurs had arrived at the beagle pack's meet, the huntsman was left no option but to cancel the day's hunting. A stalemate ensued and with just under an hour left before darkness, the huntsman asked the saboteurs present if he could let the beagles out of their trailer to let them have a wee. This request was granted (he had even offered to hand over his horn as proof he would not go back on his word and take them out to hunt) and as soon as the dogs had relieved themselves they were driven home.

A Legislative Victory

The 2000s was to see perhaps the most significant milestone in the fight to end hunting with hounds. After almost a century of political campaigning by the likes of the League Against Cruel Sports, the International Fund for Animal Welfare and the RSPCA, and around 40 years of direct action by the HSA, the Hunting Act was passed on 18th November 2004. Scotland was already ahead of the times having previously passed the Protection of Wild Mammals (Scotland) Act in 2002 that outlawed traditional fox hunting and hare coursing. At that year's AGM there was even talk of changing the name of the HSA to the Hunt Monitors Association! Indeed, the year after the Hunting Act came into force, the HSA's Press Officer, Dawn Preston, explained:

> *The traditional primary tool of a hunt saboteur in the past was always the hunting horn, so we could gain control of the hounds and seek to prevent them successfully hunting the fox, hare, mink or stag. Today our main tool is the video camera, as the very last thing the hunts that are arrogantly breaking the law want is to be caught in the act. The appalling thing is that it is we who are consistently keeping the hunts under surveillance rather than the police.*

In the run up to the passing of the act, there were numerous large demonstrations by hunt supporters who were furious that their bloodsport was being banned. The Countryside Alliance organised a huge demonstration against New Labour's plans to ban hunting with hounds under the banner 'Liberty and Livelihood' which saw 400,000 protesters take to the streets of London in 2002. Images of bloody scenes appeared in the national press as riot police and hunt supporters fought pitched battles in the street. Another protest was organised at the Labour Party conference in Brighton that took place just a month before the act was passed and attracted around 8,000 bloodsport enthusiasts. A horse carcass was dumped outside Brighton Train Station with a sign pushed into the stomach that read, 'IF YOU BAN HUNTING, THERE WILL BE LOTS OF THESE.' Two dead calves were also left on the Old Steine, one of the main roads in the town centre. These sick stunts achieved little more than show the public that pro-hunt people viewed animals as mere tools to be used. However, keen not to miss an opportunity, members of Brighton Hunt Saboteurs printed a batch of t-shirts with the slogan, 'TONY BLAIR LYING BASTARD' on the front (a hint to the Iraq War) and made a fair sum of money selling them to the crowds of hunters; money that would be put back into sabotaging the very 'sport' that they had come to support!

As confirmed by Avon and Somerset Police, the first huntsmen to be prosecuted under the Hunting Act were Maurice Scott, a master of the Devon and Somerset Staghounds and hunt servant Peter Heard for an incident on Exmoor on 25th April 2006. They were later joined by huntsman Donald Summersgill. A later landmark case for the act was to take place in December 2012 at Oxford Magistrates Court. The RSPCA took out a private prosecution against Heythrop Hunt Limited, the first time a hunt had been prosecuted as a corporate body rather than as individuals. The Heythrop Hunt Limited, its huntsman, Julian Barnfield, and its master, Richard Sumner, all pleaded guilty to four charges of unlawfully hunting a wild fox with dogs. What was to make this case even more significant was that it was the hunt of the then prime minister David Cameron who is thought to have ridden with the hunt on at least six occasions. The RSPCA spent a huge £327,000 on court costs which led to many within the pro-hunt lobby claiming that the prosecution was purely politically motivated. The head of the RSPCA, Gavin Grant, robustly defended the prosecution stating:

> *Questions have been raised over the amount of money it has cost the RSPCA to bring this case. I understand and sympathise. I would have liked to have saved that money and could have done so if these huntsmen and the Heythrop had obeyed the law. They did not, and you cannot put a price on justice. After all, the animals cannot bring the case or speak for themselves.*

On 21st February 2005, just three days after the Hunting Act came into force, saboteurs from the South East hit the East Sussex and Romney Marsh Hunt just to the north of Hastings. After the terrierman's assistant, Timothy Skinner (who had attacked saboteurs the week before), taunted the group with a dead fox on the front of his quad bike following a dig out, he was allegedly assaulted and suffered quite serious injuries. Some of the saboteurs' vehicles were able to escape but the police managed to smash the driver's side window and the windscreen of one stationary vehicle before arresting its seven occupants. They were originally arrested on suspicion of causing ABH but were later woken in the middle of the night in their police cells to be re-arrested for causing GBH with intent. After 32 hours in custody and seven 'no comment' interviews, the seven were released minus all their possessions, clothes, their Land Rover and its contents and were charged with violent disorder. However, these charges were later dropped to aggravated trespass. The subsequent ten day hearing, which had a total of 36 prosecution witnesses, proved to be a complete shambles. The huntsman and his terrierman, John Bartley (who had six previous convictions, most for violence), were unable to prove that they were hunting legally and Bartley's stories over their use of a trail (or lack of) varied as proceedings went on. The police were extremely keen to get a conviction and try to curtail animal rights activity in the South East but made a number of errors in their handling of the case which led to the judge dismissing the case and allowing the saboteurs to go free.

Despite being an important milestone towards the eventual total abolition of hunting with hounds, the Hunting Act is openly flouted by the UK's approximately 200 packs of hounds at least twice a week. Some claim, when challenged, to be following a 'trail', that is to say that the hounds follow an animal based scent (from the species of the hunt's normal quarry), that has been laid across the countryside as opposed to chasing live quarry, and when foxes or other animals are killed it is merely an 'accident'. The reality is that this is rarely the case, with only a few hunts even bothering to produce a token rag tied to a length of string as an alibi. There have been positive changes, however, in that the number of dig outs has decreased dramatically and when they do occur, the terriermen are much more likely to abandon them when

NEW HUNT QUARRY
LABOUR MPs
KEEP
HUNTING

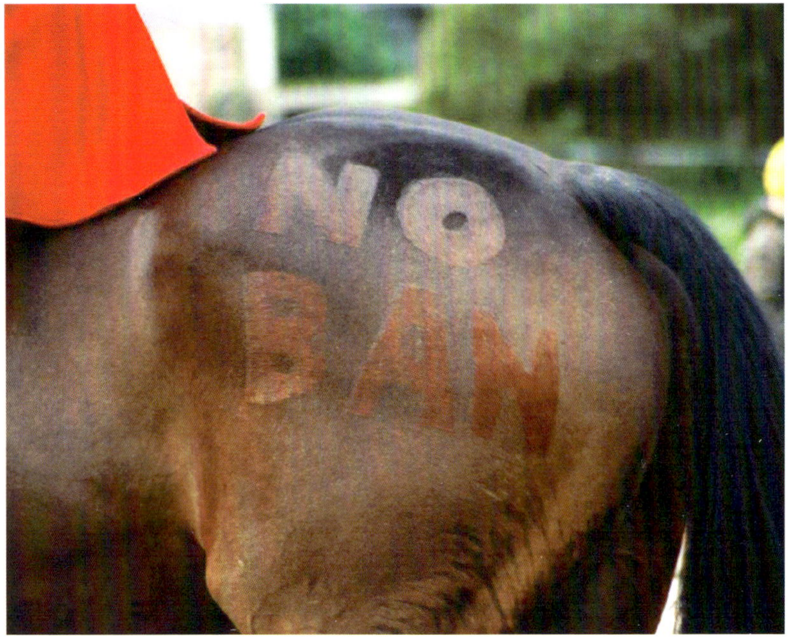
NO
BAN

IT'S
OVER

saboteurs are present to avoid prosecution. Also, the camera has become an invaluable tool for many anti-hunting campaigners as often simply the knowledge that they are being filmed is enough of a deterrent to stop hunts openly chasing wildlife.

Despite this, much remained the same, as one South London saboteur recounts his experience of when the ban came into force, police bias and one courageous yet simple act of sabotage:

I started hunt sabbing in 2003 when I was seventeen years old. This was two years before the Hunting Act 2004, that largely made traditional fox hunting illegal, came into effect. At this time, I was active against hunts in the South East and the group I had joined was a strong group, of generally older, more experienced sabs. Most had been at it since the mid-1990s, with some starting as far back as the early 1980s.

Looking back, I can now see that it was a funny time to be a hunt sab as after over a century of struggle and 50 years of sabotage, hunting was now getting the official recognition of its criminal nature. In those immediate pre-ban years, we were still properly disrupting a 'lawful activity', but everyone on all sides at the time, except for some particularly romantic bumpkins who'd watched Braveheart once too many times, knew the ban was imminent. However, as sabs we never really knew what was going to happen once the ban was implemented. In one mood you would naively believe, that despite the absolute criminal corruption and collusion of the police that was (and still is) a regular occurrence, that once fox hunting was illegal the police would be honour bound to uphold the law and would take action against the criminal behaviour of the countryside killers. In more sober moods you knew that nothing was really going to change and that the scum would still go on murdering wildlife and you would still go out trying to disrupt that. I remember one particular AGM of the HSA around those years where people spent a good amount of time debating whether, due to the law changing, the Hunt Saboteurs Association should change its name to the Hunt Monitoring Association or some similar bollocks. But I think in some ways, despite the actual failure of the ban to help wildlife in an immediate and absolute sense, the ban was welcomed by a lot of people, sabs and non-sabs alike, as it gave the appearance of closure to the long fought struggle against fox hunting. Some of the older sabs had grown tired and worn out and lost that energy, drive and determination that youngsters in all social struggles possessed, and I would regularly encounter people within subcultures and networks naturally aligned with wildlife defence who would express with an apparent seriousness that I found hard to believe; "they're still out hunting? I thought they banned that!"

Two instances from that time stick in my mind in particular. Once we were sabbing the Southdown & Eridge on the hills of the South Downs. This is always a treacherous territory to sab on as it is open countryside, lacking vehicular access and has the many peaks and dips of a small mountain range – once the hunt set off on a gallop it's hard to keep up with them. This time we were there when the pack of hounds had got onto a fox, flushing it out from one of the Downs' scrubby bits of bush. The whipper-in saw the fox go, but between him, the hounds and the huntsman was a post and barbed wire fence that at one section had been knocked to the ground to allow the hunt to access the adjacent land. As the huntsman went red faced and blew his horn to encourage his hounds on and began to chase his innocent victim, one of our sabs managed to get up to the fence line and literally pull up the damaged bit of fencing, standing his ground and blocking the huntsman from proceeding. This huntsman, who was a particular coward who regularly tried to upset sabs but lacked

Top: A Croydon saboteur cradles an injured fox

Bottom: A young saboteur with the body of a fox ravaged by hounds

Opposite page: Croydon, Hastings and Brighton saboteurs attend a meet of the Old Surrey and Burstow at Woldingham the day after the ban came into force, 19th Febuary 2005

Top and bottom: Saboteurs block the path of the Southdown and Eridge huntsman

Opposite page: Saboteurs prevent the Surrey Union terrier men from digging out a badger sett

the actual spine to get his hands dirty and attack us, rode his horse up to the fence and cracked his whip once or twice before backing down. With no control and encouragement, the pack disintegrated with disinterest and the fox was able to escape. This incident always stood in my mind because not only was I inspired by the quick thinking of this sab but also his very simple but deadly effective act of direct action. It was literal sabotage – instead of the traditional tactics of whip, gizmo or citronella bottle he had used his body and the environment to block the passage of the hunt and save the animal. It was a great episode in civil disobedience – that the hunt with all its pompous self-claimed prestige, and the freaks on horseback, and vehicles and ugly thugs on quad bikes were stopped from tormenting a little fox by the lone, defiant sab who showed that 'they shall not pass!'

Another incident around this time was on the Surrey Union. Now, hunts in Surrey always received protection from a particular bunch of aggravated coppers who with absolute open hostility and paramilitary seriousness effectively acted as private security for the hunt. This weekend they were excelling at being twats and had stopped a large group of us, between 15 and 20, as we followed the hunt along a public footpath. Despite us being quite within our legal rights to transverse a public footpath, the police were determined to have their own way and prevent our passage in an effort to allow the hunt to get away from us. So after a short argument with the police, off we went, directed by them, the long way around, hoping we could flank the hunt or something. As we walked the edge of a field we came across the Union's bulbous-headed terrierman and his sidekick in a little woodland around a badger sett. They had their shovels out and nets stretched over the holes to catch any terrified animal that tried to escape their terrier, who was waiting in a cage on top of their nearby quad bike. Straight away one of our women sabs went in first (as is usually the case) and the bumpkin's shovels and nets went flying. As my mate made light work of the equipment, I stood in the way of the police and acted all awkward: "Am I in your way? Sorry, I'll move, shall I move here or there?" etc. Essentially, the police had, from a public-order point of view, done something that would see them repeating the year had they still been at Hendon: they had left four dayglow clad clowns alone with a couple of bumpkin scumbags and fifteen-odd, now irritated sabs, all because they wanted to protect the hunt. A short stand-off developed with one officer getting particularly nervous. "Shall I get the tasers!? I'll get the tasers!?" he kept saying in jumpy tones to his colleague, who thankfully recognised he was being ridiculous and ignored him. I informed the panicked officer quite calmly and in a matter of fact manner, that if he got the tasers it would not be a good idea as it would escalate the situation. Anyway, the stand-off quickly de-escalated as with all the sabs present the police knew they could not allow the bumpkins to continue to interfere with a badger sett. The bumpkins retreated from the wood and started to pack their equipment away to the amused jeers and mockery of the sabs. However, as the two bumpkins mounted their quad bike the police decided it was an appropriate time to start gassing people with their pepper spray. They managed to spray a couple of sabs for no reason, but failed to take into consideration wind direction and two of their own got a strong dose of pepper spray! I couldn't stop laughing as I saw them bent double, red-faced with eyes steaming! Rather than 'keeping the peace' the police had gone out of their way to initiate a confrontation and then incapacitated half of their present officers! Far from the professional and authoritative image the police like to put across, this incident made me realise that they are prone to panic and adept at responding in an incompetent manner. It's a good thing they don't carry guns!

Police Collusion

The fact that the police have been turning a blind eye towards hunts all across the UK openly breaking the law at least twice a week every season was summed up in a statement by North Wales police chief Richard Burnstrom when he said in no uncertain terms, "hunting is definitely not a policing priority. Don't let me give you the impression it is." To further compound the fact, the Hunting Act was even removed from the 2008 edition of *Blackstone's Police Manual*, the required reading for police officers taking exams for promotion to sergeant and inspector.

The police's record in dealing with blatant breaches of the Hunting Act has been nothing short of shameful. Week in, week out hunts ride out fully equipped and with the intention to break the law as police officers simply look on (that is, if they are in attendance at all). With the criminal justice system disinterested in prosecuting hunting offenders, those that do find themselves convicted under the act receive such paltry fines that any deterrence is pretty much non-existent. In January 2008, the huntsman and whipper-in of the Minehead Harriers pleaded guilty of illegal hunting and were fined £300 with £500 costs each. In September 2013, Nick Bycroft, the huntsman of the Crawley and Horsham Hunt, was given a 12 month conditional discharge and ordered to pay £150 costs with a £15 victim surcharge after illegally hunting in Angmering Park near Arundel. Four members of the Middleton Hunt pleaded guilty to breaking Section 1 of the Hunting Act. The huntsman, Tom Holt, was fined £200 with a £20 victim surcharge with £85 costs whilst his whipper-in was fined £100 and ordered to pay a £20 victim surcharge. Further similar convictions have occurred but these examples demonstrate the fact that there is no real deterrent to huntsmen to not chase and kill foxes.

Even when hunters are convicted of violent crimes, their punishments are almost laughable and extremely low compared to if the violence had been dealt the other way around. For example, South Lakeland Magistrates Court decided to give the huntsman of the Coniston Foxhounds a conditional discharge (along with an order to pay £150 in compensation and £58 in costs) after smashing the driver's side window of a saboteur's car.

A Gruesome Accident

An accident was to occur some four years after the supposed ban came into force that would send shockwaves through the hunting community. On 9th March 2009, hunt monitor Bryan Griffiths was spending another day monitoring the Warwickshire Hunt from high above in his gyrocopter, this time at their last meet of the season. He had been shot at numerous times before whilst flying above the hunt and the aggression shown by hunt supporters that day was no less apparent. The hunt had organised a plan to ambush the monitors at the earliest opportunity and after having had to land to refuel at Long Marston airfield near Stratford-Upon-Avon, Griffiths was confronted by a Land Rover steaming straight towards him. Driving the vehicle was 48 year old Trevor Morse, a long-standing supporter of the Warwickshire, accompanied by another fervent supporter, Julie Sargeant. Morse was furious that his hunt was being monitored to ensure that it kept within the Hunting Act and headed over to confront the pilot. Fearful that Morse was about to seriously and violently attack him, Griffiths proceeded to take off. The numerous warnings were ignored by Morse as he stood close to the gyrocopter and was sliced through the head by a spinning rotor blade travelling at around 200mph. He was virtually decapitated and died instantaneously. Griffiths was originally charged with murder but this was later lessened to manslaughter. He was subsequently cleared of all charges at Birmingham Crown Court as the court heard from an impartial plane spotter at the airfield who initially believed the incident involved a drugs dispute due to the nature of Morse's 'intrusive and aggressive' attitude.

Top: Turncoat Miles Cooper with the body of a baby muntjac killed by the Vale of Aylesbury Foxhounds on Coleshill Common, 7th March 1992

Opposite page top: Princess Anne exchanges insults with a saboteur

Opposite page bottom: Saboteurs prevent a hound from searching for quarry

Otis the Fox

Among the countless animals saved by hunt saboteurs, another lucky fox would gain fame after being rescued from the Ledbury Hunt's hounds in 2008. On Saturday 15th November, saboteurs from Bristol and South Wales heard the sound of hounds in cry and followed the noise down a lane just in time to see a fox (who was later christened Otis, after Otis Ferry the notorious huntsman and son of singer Brian Ferry) attempting to get through a hedge. They stepped aside to let the animal cross the lane but before he could, two hounds appeared and one of them locked their jaws around Otis' face. The saboteurs raced in to free the fox as more and more hounds joined the chaos. Some of them used the sound of their whips to keep most of the pack at bay whilst Otis bit one of his rescuers in the panic that ensued. Otis was later taken to the Vale Wildlife Rescue in Evesham where he was found to be suffering from extreme shock as well as several deep puncture wounds. Miraculously Otis survived, but due to the severity of his injuries, it was a month before he was released back into the wild.

Swapping Sides...

Over the years there have been those who have switched sides from the different ends of the hunting issue. Whilst it is true that some have abandoned what ethics they ever had in regards to animals and have joined the pro-hunt community, there has been a far greater number jumping ship the other way. The Countryside Alliance likes to periodically champion Miles Cooper, who sabotaged hunts in the late 1980s before working for the League and later became a master of the Highmoor Hunt (a bloodhound pack in Yorkshire). Cooper was even present as a member of Oxford HSA when the Vale of Aylesbury Hunt killed a baby deer in full view of children who were playing nearby. The hunt, despite numerous protestations from local residents, were drawing a common and wildlife sanctuary near the village of Coleshill in Buckinghamshire. Within minutes a baby muntjac leapt from the undergrowth and was quickly grabbed around the neck and hindquarters by two hounds and a tug-of-war ensued. The hunt staff present were unable to control the hounds and when the deer was finally released she fell back into the undergrowth to die. Even this incident showing the callous disregard for life that hunters have was not enough to stop Cooper from betraying his former colleagues and friends to live a life of cruelty. James Barrington, a one-time hunt saboteur and former Executive Director of the League Against Cruel Sports, switched sides in 1995 before joining the Countryside Alliance as an 'animal welfare consultant' in 2009.

Amongst those who have found compassion and have denounced their cruel past was Clifford Pellow, an ex-huntsman of numerous hunts across England and Wales for over 20 years, most notably with the Tredegar Farmers Hunt. Growing considerably uneasy with the abuse of foxes he was ordered to carry out that went against the hunting community's own codes of conduct, he protested and was subsequently fired. Pellow then went on to work with the League and provided invaluable knowledge about the cruel sport and anecdotes of the true barbarity of fox hunting, including an incident where his hounds had torn apart a pregnant vixen and on seeing that the three pups were still alive, the hunt master simply crushed them under the heel of his boot. A booklet entitled *A Brush With Conscience. Why a Huntsman Abandoned His Sport* was published in 1997 and detailed the shocking cruelty that Pellow was party to.

One extract read:

> *In advance of hunting days, he says, foxes were caught in traps, put into sacks and, after being dragged across a couple of fields to get up a good scent, released for the hounds to slaughter. In one incident, a milk churn rather than a sack was used. In another, the terrified fox bolted from the bag into a farm where he fell into a manure pit. The farmer's son shot him.*

Another read:

> *He [Pellow] remembers one fox, caught and handed over by a local farmer, who was kept for a week in a 40 gallon bone bin, where he was sustained on liver and water. "I remember looking in on him on the Friday, looking at this beautiful creature, which he was, and thinking; tomorrow this time you'll be a thing of the past, ripped to pieces. Seventeen and a half couple of hounds will be biting at you, each hound with 32 teeth.*

In October 1982, hunt servant Paul Woodhouse exposed his former colleagues in an article from the *News of the World.*

He stated:

> *In every hunt there are always one or two people, particularly the terrier men, who get a sadistic pleasure from torturing foxes. I regard such people with disgust and have vowed never again to have anything to do with them or the so-called 'sport' of foxhunting.*

Working on information Woodhouse provided, a fox named Tag, who was regularly baited by the Derwent Hunt's terrierman, Fred Jackson, in order to train his terriers, was liberated from the garden shed in which Jackson had kept him for eight years and taken to a sanctuary in the South West. Among the atrocities that Woodhouse described in his exposé was an incident near the kennels at Snainton, Scarborough. A fox had gone to ground and was dug out. On the orders of the huntsman, Roderick Ando, Jackson cut the animal's paws and released the fox who only managed to run for 200 yards before being pulled down by the hounds. This was a common occurrence in the hunt during Ando's joint mastership.

Woodhouse also stated that the Derwent Hunt and the five other hunts that he had worked with all dropped bagged foxes in front of hounds when there were visiting dignitaries present. For example, when Prince Charles visited the Derwent a fox was caught prior to hunting, was bagged and subsequently released in front of the hounds on the day so that the prince was shown 'good sport'.

Perhaps the most high profile campaigner to have denounced their hunting past was Lynn Sawyer. Sawyer's hunting career began in 1982 at the Essex Foxhounds at the age of only fourteen and by 1990, she had hunted with many different packs, including foxhounds, minkhounds, staghounds and coursing clubs. Between the years 1984 and 1990, much of her time was spent gathering information on anti-hunting activity for the British Field Sports Society. This included taking vehicle registrations (over 130 were on file by 1990), photographing saboteurs, sifting through animal rights literature, attending animal rights meetings and gigs as well as liaising with the police to ascertain as much information as possible.

However, through this process, Sawyer began to realise the reality of the situation; that the saboteurs' sole intention was to stop harm to animals and that the vast majority of the violence dished out at hunt meets came from the hunt itself. In an attempt to reconcile her concerns over hunt violence, she turned to various important figures within the hunting community including Nick Herbert of the BFSS and the director of the British Association for Shooting and Conservation, John Swift. However, she later said of the meetings, "it became clear that I could not permeate their rather narrow-minded way of thinking or change or influence any of them without being patronised or being singled out as a trouble-maker." After four years of soul-searching, she decided to write an open letter to her former friends that detailed the reasons for her abandoning her "position of neutrality on the hunting issue in favour of the animal rights movement."

Top: Undercover police officer, John Dines (with beard)

Opposite page: Saboteurs, including undercover police officer 'Christine Green' (front), at a Vale of Aylesbury Hunt's cub hunting meet near their kennels at Princes Risborough, 1997

An extract read:

> *Whilst maintaining my deep respect for the sanctity of human life and dignity, I have extended my concern to ALL sentient beings. I now believe that it is abhorrent to kill, unless in exceptional cases such as euthanasia, or to cause suffering to any living creature for our own benefit. This means that I am now a dietary vegan and I will be boycotting leather, silk, wool, etc. in the future. I can no longer ignore my remorse at the large amount of suffering that I have caused, nor can I ignore what is happening in the abattoirs, in the laboratories, in the oceans, down on the farm and out in the field.*

Sawyer later went on to become a dedicated hunt saboteur and animal rights activist.

Undercover

Hunt saboteur groups, alongside many other animal rights organisations, have also been targets for undercover police officers wanting to gain information and stop the growing animal liberation movement. Among those who have been found out are Bob Lambert (cover name: Bob Robinson) who was based in North London during the 1980s, John Dines (cover name: John Barker) who was also active in North London in the late 1980s, Jim Boyling (cover name: Jim Sutton) who was based in London in the late 1990s and 'Rod Richardson' whose real name remains unknown and was active in Nottingham in the early 2000s. Another undercover officer, 'Christine Green', also managed to infiltrate West London Hunt Saboteurs during the 1990s. Interestingly, Green also took part in an ALF raid in 1998 in which 6,000 mink were released from a fur farm in Hampshire. Whilst on deployment, Green began a relationship with Tom Frampton, a prominent member of West London Hunt Saboteurs and Chair of the HSA.

Frampton was a committed hunt saboteur and was even jailed for his anti-hunting activities after allegedly head-butting a terrierman. The ALF Supporters Group said of the incident:

> *On 19th March Thomas Frampton was convicted of actual bodily harm (ABH) on a terrier man of a fox hunt. He was sentenced to three months in prison. Tom is known to most people as Joe Tax and was on the HSA committee as chairperson a short while ago. In the same week as Tom was sent down the huntsman of the Surrey Union fox hunt, who was under a suspended sentence, was also convicted of ABH. He received a £61 fine! Tom has a release date of 30th April.*

After her deployment had ended, Green and Frampton remained together and moved to remote cottages in both Cornwall and Scotland.

The South Cornwall Folds...

The South Cornwall Hunt folded in February 2004 after sustained pressure from hunt saboteurs. Throughout the 1990s the South Cornwall Hunt was a particular target. The pack originally hunted three times a week but this was dropped to just Saturdays as field support dwindled to around ten riders. The huntsman was given the sack for not providing enough 'sport' and the local saboteur group made the choice to hit other larger hunts in the area now that the South Cornwall was on its last legs. At the turn of the millennium, sabotage became a regular feature to the hunt's season again. The hunt was a complete shambles and in March 2001, 11 hounds were hit by a train as they ventured onto the busy Par to Newquay railway, three of whom were later shot due to their injuries. This complete lack of compassion for the dogs under his control was something that huntsman Steve Parkin showed time and again and was

Top left: The Hampshire Hunt's huntsman, Bob Collins, trespasses on a railway line, 1999

Top right: Pytchley Hunt staff drag a dead hound along the A43, near Sywell, Northamptonshire, 4th February 2019

Bottom: Guilford HSA alert the train driver and prevent hounds being killed on the Guildford to Dorking line at a meet of the Surrey Union Hunt, 11th March 2000

Opposite page top: A liberated Wye College beagle settles happily into his new home, 6th January 2001

Opposite page middle: Exeter saboteur Jane Finch with Silverton foxhound, Baby, rescued from the Bristol to Exeter railway line, 1984

Opposite page bottom: Lanyard, a North Ledbury foxhound found straying by Pete Hardy, 1984

to prove to be the hunt's final undoing. Parkin was arrested in September 2003 on animal cruelty charges after one of the hunt's hounds was found unable to stand and weighing just 12.3 kilograms, under half the suitable weight of a hound her size. The pack was also kept in filthy conditions, having to lay in sodden, urine-soaked bedding. He was convicted and was banned from keeping dogs for five years. An emergency meeting was called by the committee of the South Cornwall Hunt in which it was agreed the hunt would close and the rest of the pack split between the Four Burrow Hunt and the North Cornwall Hunt.

The Sad Life of a Hound

Sadly, it's not uncommon for hounds to be killed on train tracks and roads as hunters recklessly place them in danger in their crazed pursuit of their quarry. On New Years Eve 2009, six hounds from the Beaufort Hunt were killed outright by a speeding train after straying onto the railway near Wootton Bassett. Two Fitzwilliam hounds were hit by a train on the Peterborough to Kings Cross Line at Wood Walton in 1995. That same year, the Cottesmore Hunt was fined £12,000 by Railtrack for a trespass incident that ended in the deaths of two of their hounds. In 2008, two hounds were hit by a car and killed after the Crawley and Horsham chased a fox across the A281 near Partridge Green. That same year one of the Britannia Beagles was also killed as the pack caused chaos on the busy dual carriageway of the A380 at Ideford Dip in South Devon. In 2006, a hound from the Cotswold Hunt was killed outright after being hit by a car whilst chasing a fox across the A417 near Daglingworth. In 1998, ten hounds from the South Pembrokeshire Hunt were killed by a train. That same year, two Cheshire Forest hounds and a further two from the South Shropshire were killed on the tracks. On Boxing Day 1983, eight of the Brighton and Storrington Hunt beagles are electrocuted on a live railway line. On the same day, six of the Blean beagles were killed on a railway near Seasalter Marshes. Indeed, in a statement in the *Big Issue* after these incidents, the League noted that between 1986 and 1998, a grim total of 120 hounds had been killed as a result of rail and road accidents. Trespassing on a railway line is a criminal offence, yet one that the British Transport Police seemingly don't take very seriously when it comes to hunts. The Cheshire Foxhounds were the only hunt to have been successfully prosecuted for the offence when three members of the hunt were fined a meagre £25 each. These few examples are sadly just the tip of the iceberg when it comes to the tragedies that hunt hounds suffer.

These accidents are routinely blamed on saboteurs by the hunts whenever they are present but not one hound death has ever been caused by an anti-hunt activist. In the 1980s, the Masters of Foxhounds Association even issued a press release to effect that it was a new tactic of members of the HSA to deliberately call hounds away from the hunt and then claim to the press that they had rescued the animals from the path of oncoming trains or cars. In reality, quite the opposite is true. There have been countless times where saboteurs have had to prevent hounds from careering across busy roads. The South Dorset group were even thanked by hunters for running onto the A35 and stopping traffic after the South Dorset Hunt chased a fox across the road on Boxing Day 1997. In a not dissimilar case, saboteurs from Exeter were waiting at a meet of the Stoke Hill Beagles next to the main railway line linking Exeter and Bristol in late 1984. Waiting for the hunt to leave, they spotted a pack of hounds from the nearby Silverton Hunt chasing a fox across the tracks and promptly took them off the scent. Half an hour later, the saboteurs noticed a lone hound (who they nicknamed 'Baby') running along the railway. She was grabbed and subsequently spent the next week living at the house of six of the saboteurs before being eventually collected by two policemen exchanging her for £6 paid by the hunt for her food! Not long before this incident, a North Ledbury hound named Lanyard was found alone some hours after the hunt had passed. He was then picked up by the driver of a car that had almost run him over and taken home. When the hunt were notified of his whereabouts and two hunt servants arrived to the house to pick Lanyard up, they were duly greeted by an anti-hunt campaigner wearing a League Against Cruel Sports shirt!

Top: Fitzwilliam Hunt staff carry a dead hound along the A14, 8th December 2018

Bottom: A hound killed and dumped by the Cambridgeshire Hunt

Opposite page top: An HSA member has a read of *HOWL*

Opposite page bottom: The Fabulous Mrs Fox bubble bars, sold in aid of the HSA

More recently, in 2018, a hound from the Fitzwilliam Hunt was killed after being struck by two cars whilst running onto the A14 dual carriageway near Thrapston, Northamptonshire. The pack of hounds chased a fox along the hedgerow adjacent to the A14 before the tragic incident occurred. Images taken by North Cambs Hunt Saboteurs of two hunt staff carrying the dog's lifeless body went viral across social media, showing this dark side of hunting with hounds to huge numbers of the general public.

Life for a foxhound is an unnaturally short one. Despite the life expectancy of an English Foxhound being ten to thirteen years, hunt hounds rarely live past six or seven seasons. When they become too old or too slow, or don't work as part of the pack, the thanks they get for providing 'sport' is a bullet to the temple. Indeed, it is estimated that around 4,000 hounds are killed by hunts each year.

Hunts are very aware that this practice is quite rightly viewed as abhorrent by the public and so do their very best to hide this particularly cruel aspect, especially as they like to promote the idea that 'huntsmen love their hounds' at many country shows during the summer months when the public get the chance to see them. Despite this, some do come clean about it. For example, West Country hunter George Hyatt is quoted as saying, "when I put down a good seasoned hound it is awful. I almost feel like an anti. I cry for days. But when I put down a hound that is detrimental to the pack, one that is a babbler and shouts, or one that runs off, then I can do it without any problem." Ex-huntsman Clifford Pellow also testified over this shady practice when he stated, "we see plenty of images of young hounds and hound puppies being cuddled. What people don't realise is that, if those young animals don't 'enter' when they're introduced to hunting, they will be shot. I should know, I've had to do it myself. In my day, out of a pack of 40 hounds, I would say that 10 would be shot in a year." Indeed, in his book *Foxhunting,* the Duke of Beaufort wrote:

> *Lord Henry Bentinck hunted the Rufford and Burton countries for thirty years [...]. He also said that the secret of his success was to breed a great many hounds and then to put down a great many. If you can afford to follow this example so much the better for your pack.*

He also described the reason why some hounds are 'put down':

> *Now we come to the decisions that must be firm and may sound ruthless, [...] if one hound outruns all of the rest, then he must go. A skirter [a hound who cuts corners rather than following the actual line the quarry has taken] will have to be culled, as must one that runs mute. [...] This stringent rule also applies to a babbler [a hound who speaks on anything but the right scent].*

Various attempts have been made to get footage of hunt workers killing hounds and on 30th October 1996, Joe Hashman achieved what seemed almost impossible. Whilst on a secret investigation for the League Against Cruel Sports, Hashman videoed the Cheshire Foxhounds kennelman shooting two of the hunt's hounds and dumping them in a metal bin at their kennels in Sandiway. On Boxing Day the following year, the BBC's *Under the Sun* programme included a scene in which workers from the Ludlow Foxhounds shot a three year old hound who was no longer required and dumped the animal into an incinerator without even bothering to check that the hound was dead.

It was not only the quarry and the hunt's own hounds that were suffering but many companion animals were also being attacked by the hunt. Two hounds from the Tiverton Staghounds mauled and killed Pippa, a Jack Russell, as her owner tried desperately to form a human shield over the terrified animal. Outrageously, Catherine Hodgson was offered compensation on the condition that she kept the attack quiet. To further compound the brutality of the incident, the hunt shot both of the hounds involved straight afterwards. Flopsy, a pygmy goat, was savaged to death by the East Cornwall Hunt after 26 hounds burst into a back garden. Moppet, an 18 year old deaf tabby, was killed by 27 of the Goathland Hunt's hounds. The cat's body was later returned to the distraught owners in an empty bag of dog food. In 2016, the Ross Harriers killed a cat named Fluffy in front of her owner as four hounds strayed into their garden in Marlas near Kilpeck. The few incidents listed here barely scratch the surface of non-quarry species killed by hunts. The list could go on and on.

Soap Dodgers

Throughout the 2000s, although there were less saboteurs out in the fields than in the previous decade (mainly due to the public's perception that hunting no longer took place after the ban), the HSA continued to garner support. The high street soap company, Lush, fully threw its support behind the actions of hunt saboteurs and in 2009 launched a nationwide campaign to raise awareness that despite hunting with hounds having been banned some four years previous, hunts across the UK were still killing wildlife. 'The Hunts Are Still At It' campaign saw Lush produce a bubble bar called 'Fabulous Mrs Fox' (after the much-loved Roald Dahl book) with the profits going straight to the HSA. It was a bold move by the soap company to so publicly link itself with a group that took direct action for animal rights but the support from Lush towards hunt saboteurs has remained steadfast throughout the years. When the 'Fabulous Mrs Fox' bars were launched, a small number of shops had visits from various disgruntled bumpkins that included 'FUCK YOU' being scratched into the Maidstone store's window and a kebab smeared across it, along with threatening phone calls made to the Manchester store and to the Taunton store during an in-store children's party. Rather unsurprisingly, the pro-hunt threats never actually materialised as it quickly became clear that the campaign had very large public support, especially in the cities surrounding the huge number of shops making the point that fox hunts are openly flouting the ban. After years of shouting insults such as 'soap dodgers' and 'the great unwashed', hunt supporters were now desperately racking their brains for new quips to throw at the (now sweet-scented) antis!

Although the movement was still consoling itself to the fact that since the Hunting Act had come into force, hunts were still continuing to kill with impunity, there remained a strong core of those heading out each week to save wildlife. It is true to say that many stopped sabotaging hunts after the act, believing that the battle had been won. However, despite a decrease in numbers of saboteurs over the latter half of the 2000s, the movement would slowly begin to expand again as the rise of the internet and video technology allowed the public to see the farce of 'trail' hunting. Indeed, the HSA had come a long way over the years, so much so that a government -backed project called *Icons Online* released 120 English 'icons' to spark a debate over national identity. Fox hunts were sadly included in the list but only with the inclusion of hunt saboteurs as well.

The iconic nature of the hunt saboteur was again further recognised in February 2015, when long-standing Radio 4 programme, *The Archers,* included hunt sabotage in a storyline. Rob Tichener, a wholly unpleasant character who was out hunting with the fictional 'South Borsetshire Hunt', punched a saboteur and tried to steal his camera after the hunt had just killed a fox. In a later police interview, Tichener put forward the story that Vince Murphy (the saboteur) had thrown the first punch but (as is all too often the case in reality) it later transpired that he was lying. This storyline was by no means the first time that hunt saboteurs had featured in fiction. In 1995, for example, one episode of *A Touch of Frost* centred around the murders of two hunt saboteurs after a confrontation with hunt stewards. It is a testament to the tenacity and determination of the thousands of hunt saboteurs throughout the years that the status of the saboteur has become almost as well known as fox hunting itself and that even fictional stories about fox hunting more often than not contain plots of sabotage.

BADGER CULLING

Top: A Nottingham saboteur surveys a sett entrance, 2014

Bottom: A haul of cage traps found by Sheffield Hunt Saboteurs, 2015

Opposite page top: Badger killers stop shooting for the night after they are confronted by Liverpool and Manchester Hunt Saboteurs, 2015

Opposite page middle: A trapped badger found and released by Devon County Hunt Saboteurs, 13th September 2017

Opposite page bottom: A saboteur decommissions a badger cage trap, 2020

Meles Meles

The badger has for a long time been persecuted both as sport and as a scapegoat for the dairy industry. Despite becoming a protected species in 1992 with the introduction of the Protection of Badgers Act, this much loved British mammal has borne the brunt of the callous cruelty of dairy farmers for many years. In the 1990s, Lord Krebs ran a ten year badger culling trial known as the Randomised Badger Culling Trial. This cull was designed to see whether or not killing badgers had any effect on the levels of bovine tuberculosis in cattle. Outraged that not only were cattle being routinely abused but now also badgers, many animal rights activists headed to the West Country to sabotage the killings. Despite being small in number, the activists were extremely effective. As reported in *HOWL*, 50 badger cages belonging to the Ministry of Agriculture, Fisheries and Food were found on a farm near Wotton Bassett and trashed on one night alone. This was after locals had discovered that over a hundred badgers had been trapped and killed on the site.

One activist who was working against the culls around Devizes at the turn of the millennium described her experience:

> *I saw two distressed badger cubs in traps and another cub was running around the traps confused at why his family had been captured. I approached the traps and immediately the cubs changed from being confused to being terrified. One cub, who was half grown, backed into a corner and hissed at us. We soon released him and he ran to freedom. When we opened the door to the other trap, the badger inside sat at the back of the cage rigid with fear. I find it unbelievable that MAFF workers can look these beautiful young badger cubs in the eyes and callously shoot them dead.*

Ben Bradshaw, the Under Secretary of State for the Department of Environment, Food and Rural Affairs (DEFRA), was forced to state in Parliamentary Questions that, "between December 1998 and 10th October 2003, during which 15,666 traps were sited, there were 8,981 individual occasions where a trap was interfered with, and 1,827 individual occasions when a trap was removed." The cull's leader, Professor John Bourne, even decided to call the cull off early after a marked increase in the number of cattle herds with bTB was found in cull areas.

A Second Slaughter

Eager to be seen to be doing something to tackle the spread of bTB, the Conservative government later decided to push ahead with another, much larger badger cull and completely ignore the Krebs Trials' findings that:

> *[...] while badgers are clearly a source of cattle TB, careful evaluation of our own and others' data indicates that badger culling can make no meaningful contribution to cattle TB control in Britain.*

The cull was due to start in 2012 but was postponed a year due to the police being tied up with the London Olympics and the threat of mass direct action by a multitude of campaigners under the banner Stop the Cull. Such was the general feeling against the cull that in 2012, even the RSPCA's chief executive, Gavin Grant, was moved to state:

> *The spotlight of attention will be turned on those marksmen and on those who give permission for this cull to take place. They will be named and we will decide as citizens of this country whether they will be shamed.*

Never before had the RSPCA taken such a hardline stance on the issue of animal rights and although Grant's statement caused much controversy it proved just how deeply unpopular the slaughter of thousands of badgers was.

The badger cull was now a cited campaign of the HSA and many local groups from all across the UK were travelling into the two pilot cull zones (in Somerset and Gloucestershire) to survey the land for badger activity and ready themselves to do whatever it took to bring the cull to a halt. The locations of the cull zones were kept secret but were found by activists phoning around dairy farmers whilst posing as journalists. The culls eventually started in August 2013 and were originally intended to last six weeks. Camps were set up in both the zones and armed with the knowledge of where the badgers were living and therefore where the shooters were going to be, saboteurs, together with hundreds of local people, set about disrupting the night time shooters by using bright torches, whistles, alarms and various other equipment to make it impossible for them to kill. Although the cull was initially set up to test whether the method of free shooting badgers was 'safe, humane and effective' (with no mention on whether culling actually has any effect on bTB rates), before long the cull companies were forced to use traps as well to catch badgers due to the sheer efficacy of the saboteurs' actions. A huge police presence was seen across both zones, with police officers often acting as a private security firm for cull contractors. Details of saboteurs were even passed onto the National Farmers Union (NFU) by Gloucestershire Police following stop searches. According to a later police investigation, employees of HNV Associates Ltd (the cull company responsible for the Somerset zone) directed the deployment of police officers against activists and on at least one occasion, half of the personnel inside the police's night time control centre in Somerset were from either HNV Associates Ltd or the NFU. However, despite both the police and the cull contractors doing everything they could to ensure that the targets were met, after six weeks both cull companies had failed to reach their targets to kill 70% of the local badger population, due solely to the disruption caused by animal rights activists.

Instead of abandoning the culls, Natural England (the body responsible for licensing the culls) granted an extension of three weeks to the Somerset zone and five weeks and three days to the Gloucestershire zone. However, both zones again failed to reach their revised targets even after the extensions were over. In the Gloucestershire cull zone, 921 badgers had lost their lives, a total of 40% of the local population. In Somerset this number was 940 (65% of the local population), with only 90 more badgers being shot during the additional three week extension.

Although these statistics do indeed tell the story that saboteurs were hugely successful during this period, much can be lost when the lives of hundreds of individuals are turned into numbers. Each badger killed was a unique individual with their own wants and needs, their own family and their own home. For those on the ground fighting this insane cull, attachments inevitably grew with the particular setts that they were protecting and for many the resistance became personal. One saboteur tells of the first time he encountered a badger trap in the first year of the cull:

> *As we walked towards the sett, a sense of wonderment came over me. The location was beautiful. The lack of light pollution in this remote corner of Somerset meant that a multitude of stars lit up the cloudless sky and bounced off the reservoir below. The traps were positioned not too far from the sett, on pathways that its inhabitants used to get to places of food or water. My heart raced as the bolt cutters sliced through the metalwork, putting an abrupt end to the night's silence as its echoes travelled down the valley. The crashing of the two halves of the cage as we threw them down the riverbank to their harmless resting place filled the air, but thankfully the surrounding farms were too far as to be a problem. The night returned to its still beauty and the badgers who knew this wood as home were out there somewhere, oblivious of just what a narrow escape they had had.*

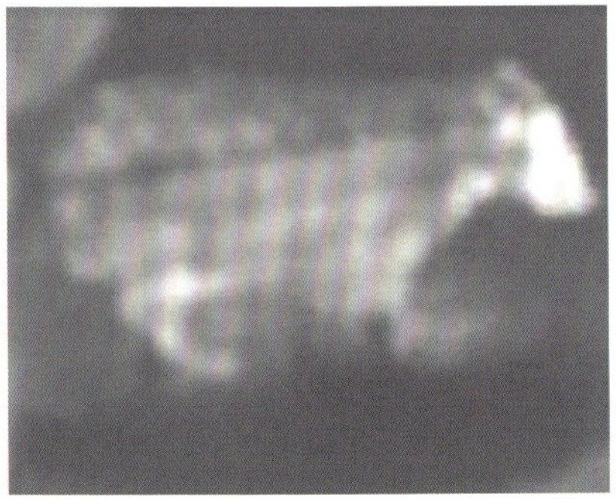

Top: A caged badger found by Manchester Hunt Saboteurs using thermal imaging equipment, 2017

Bottom: A caged badger who was found and set free by Severn Vale Hunt Saboteurs, October 2018

Opposite page left: A West Country saboteur liberates a badger from a trap in the Avon cull zone, 2019

Opposite page right top: The body of a shot badger recovered from a shooter's Land Rover, 2017

Opposite page right bottom: Manchester Hunt Saboteurs escort badger killers away from a sett, 2nd October 2015

Both policing and logistics costs skyrocketed as the cull companies truly felt the effect of well organised and dedicated action. The cull was huge news in the national media with many news outlets acknowledging the work of hunt saboteurs on the ground such as in this extract from *The Guardian,* dated 3rd April 2014:

> *The cull also cost far more than projected [...] - largely because of the highly disruptive actions of hunt saboteurs. Although small in number, they represented the concerns of many in society.*

The official cost to the taxpayer of the first year of the cull was put at £6.3m. This, however, excluded policing costs which were estimated at £3.5m, bringing the overall cost to kill each badger to £5,200.

Expansion

A motion in the House of Commons that stated that the culls had 'decisively failed' and called for a halt to the programme received overwhelming support from MPs as it was passed by 219 votes to one. However, the vote was non-binding and the government callously ignored it and pressed ahead with further culls. A second year of culling began in 2014 but only in the original Somerset and Gloucestershire zones despite the government previously stating that it would roll the cull out to ten zones that year. This postponement of the rollout was largely caused by the hugely disruptive actions of saboteurs on the ground. A third zone was added in North Dorset the following year in which nearly 1,500 badgers were killed and a greater rollout took place in 2016, extending the massacre further into Devon, Cornwall, Herefordshire and the Cotswolds.

In 2017, the situation proved even harder for saboteurs and yet more desperate for badgers as eleven new cull zones were added to the 10 existing ones. Despite this inevitably leading to the dispersal of anti-cull activists over a much larger area, a fierce resistance was put up and the lives of countless badgers were saved. A total of 19,274 badgers were sadly killed that year, although nine out of the eleven new zones failed to reach their original target forcing DEFRA to revise the target numbers down in order to claim that the culls were 'successful'. The cull was further rolled out in 2018, when 32,601 badgers lost their lives. In 2019, following yet more new culling zones, 35,034 badgers were killed, bringing the total death toll of the cull to 102,349.

Despite the heartbreaking loss of over a hundred thousand badgers, the culls did provide a mechanism whereby the HSA was able to forge long-lasting links with local people living in the areas where culling was taking place. Prior to the culls, many living in the zones viewed hunt saboteurs with suspicion and had, in part, been taken in by much of the media's false narrative that hunt saboteurs were violent, mindless thugs. However, through the process of working together in the interests of these most enchanting of mustelids, valuable skills were shared and deep friendships made as many saw hunt saboteurs for who they really were; ordinary people taking action against animal abuse. As well as forging links with locals living in the cull zones, the badger culls also proved to be a way in which much of 'Middle England' would change their minds over the HSA and more direct forms of campaigning. Those that attended the badger patrols (walking footpaths at night to deter marksmen) often worked hand in glove with the saboteur groups in their area with each group learning skills from one another and providing assistance if needed. Many new local groups were also formed as a result of the badger culls, including Beds and Bucks Hunt Saboteurs, Kernow Hunt Saboteurs and Somerset Hunt Saboteurs.

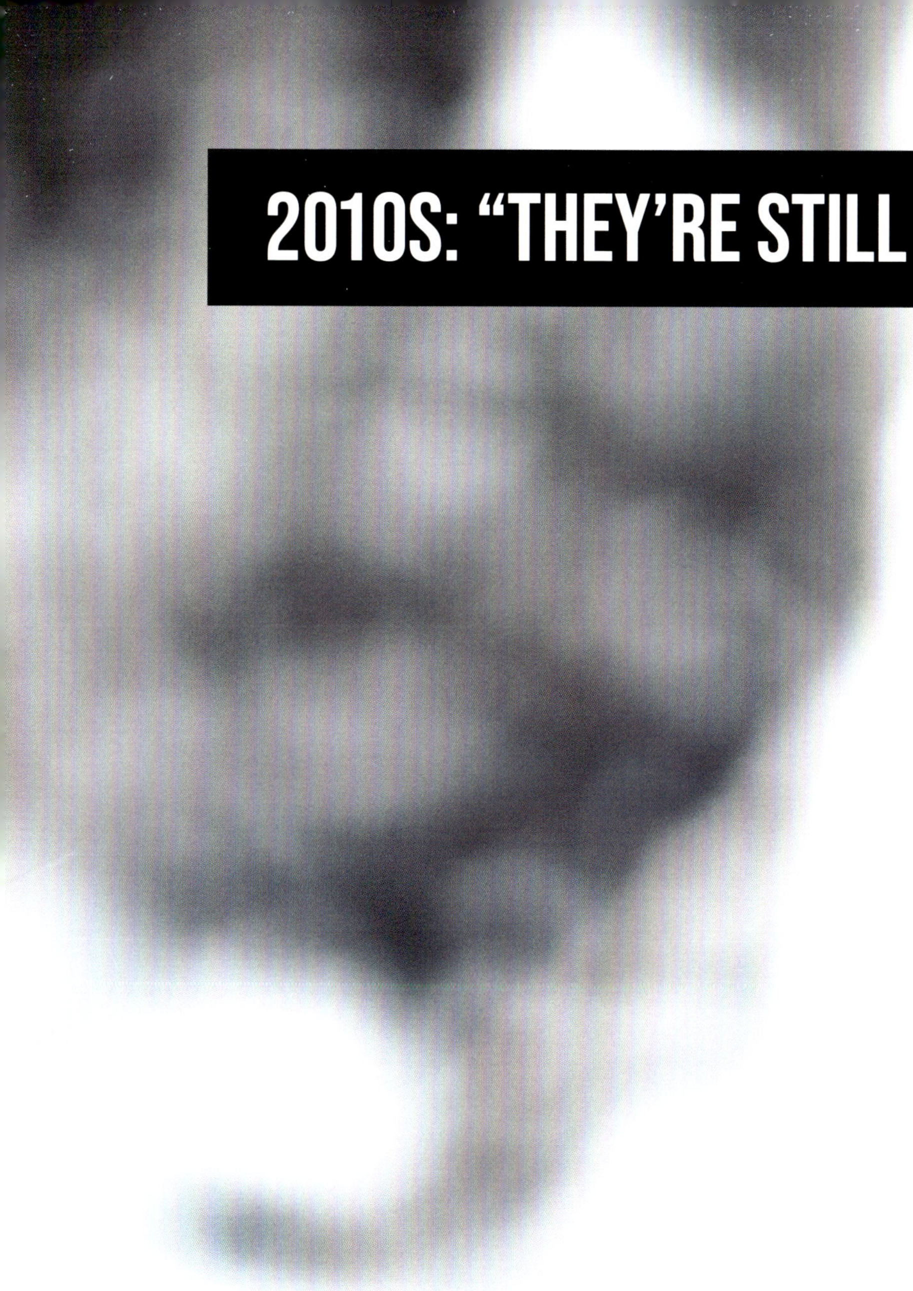

2010S: “THEY’RE STILL HUNTING, WE’RE STILL SABBING”

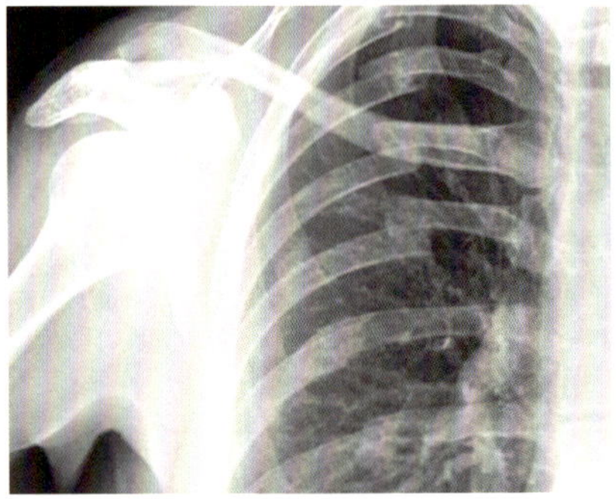

Top: X-ray showing Nid's seven broken ribs, 2014

Bottom: A Devon County saboteur cradles a fox killed by the Silverton Hunt near Cullompton, 1st January 2018

Opposite page: Bristol Hunt Saboteurs, 2017

In the West Country...

Despite the numbers of saboteurs out in the field being considerably lower than in the perceived heyday of the 1980s and 1990s, the efficacy of hunt sabotage continued to prevail. The rise of social media meant that local groups now had a way in which to show their hit reports directly to the public and to fundraise much more effectively, meaning that many more were now becoming much more self-sustaining. The number of local groups stood at around 50, with battle-hardened veterans being joined by fresh-faced and keen youngsters. In the South West, Bristol Hunt Saboteurs were regularly taking on the Cotswold Vale Farmers and the Ross Harriers with great success. The sustained campaign on both of these hunts escalated into violence quite frequently, but the Bristol group had a fierce reputation amongst hunters in the area and never backed down whenever they were attacked. The scuffles on the Ross Harriers were more often than not started by their huntsman, Lee Peters, whose quick temper regularly saw him jump from his horse and wade into saboteurs as soon as any intervention occurred. A scumbag of the lowest order, Peters was believed to be a keen supporter of the far-right English Defence League and on one occasion was even convicted of racially aggravated harassment after he called one of the Bristol saboteurs a "fucking wog" (although this was later overturned on appeal). Come the 2015/16 season, however, both the Cotswold Vale and the Ross Harriers were extremely soft hunts with dwindling support bases, their main troublemakers having either left or died, and years of constant action by saboteurs had pushed them to such a sorry state.

Fourteen years after the running over of Steve Christmas, a West Country saboteur became another victim to be pushed close to death by the hunt. Dorset Hunt Saboteurs were paying a visit to both an evening cubbing meet and a pony club meet (where children aged seven to fourteen are invited to ride with the hunt) of the Blackmore and Sparkford Vale Hunt near the Somerset village of Charlton Horethorne. As three members of the group were stood at a field gateway observing the hunt, huntsman Mark Doggrell galloped straight through them on his way into the field, riding down one saboteur and throwing her up into the air with the force of the blow. 'Nid', an NHS worker, suffered seven broken ribs, a collapsed lung and shoulder damage. An ambulance was called but was blocked in by hunt supporters, delaying it getting to the unconscious saboteur. 'Nid' subsequently spent two weeks in hospital. Two days after the incident, Doggrell handed himself over to the police where he was arrested and investigated for causing grievous bodily harm. Five months on, however, and the CPS once again dropped the charges. This decision not to prosecute a man who had so blatantly and deliberately rode down a saboteur caused public outcry, further aided by a campaign to get the CPS to overturn their decision under the banner 'Justice for Nid'. Following a large petition and the process of the victim review scheme, Doggrell eventually found himself before Taunton Crown Court charged with maliciously inflicting grievous bodily harm. Outrageously, the jury acquitted him after a mere three days of the trial.

The Infamous Buckhounds

Further south, the Devon group was doing good work in very difficult circumstances, there being so many notorious hunts in the area. Things were not helped when a small number of the group barred the majority from access to their email account, social media accounts and even the group's Land Rover after a dispute. The HSA, having paid for the vehicle, was forced to take the unprecedented step of taking the splinter group to court in order to recover the vehicle and funds donated to the group so that they could be used where they were needed (although the judge ruled against the HSA), out in the field. The original group renamed themselves Devon County Hunt Saboteurs and with a £5,000 grant from the HSA to purchase a new vehicle, carried on their actions against both fox hunting and the badger cull which had by now been extended into the county. One visit to the Chelden Buckhounds ended in a vicious attack by supporters, some of whom wore motorbike helmets as they launched their assault. 53 year old saboteur Andy Cain was left with blood pouring down his face whilst his friend, Ollie Richmond, required staples in his head after

CATEGORY 2
MATERIAL:
NOT FOR ANIMAL
CONSUMPTION
CAT.2

he suffered a fractured skull for attempting to pull the supporters from Cain. The police response was shameful as three supporters received cautions for their involvement in the assault and this was only as a result of video footage and media coverage gained by saboteurs. The hunt gained notoriety in 1993 (a mere three years after their formation) when Jeremy Gibbs, a member of the hunt, leapt on an exhausted deer, slashed the animal's throat and sat on him for 15 minutes while he slowly bled to death. The deer had attempted to jump the fence that the Devon and Somerset Staghounds had erected to stop deer from gaining access to the League Against Cruel Sports' Baronsdown Sanctuary, but was left dangling from the fence by his antlers. The Chelden Buckhounds were expelled by the Masters of Deer Hounds Association and the BFSS were even moved to state that hunting roe deer was not a legitimate 'fieldsport'.

Scuffles in the South East

In the South East, the Brighton, South Coast and Croydon groups regularly met up to take on the Southdown and Eridge, the Crawley and Horsham and the Old Surrey and Burstow, all three of whom had been continually sabotaged for the past 30 years. All three hunts were by now a shadow of their former selves. That being said, violence did sporadically break out such as on Boxing Day 2012, when a group of terriermen smashed the windscreen of the South Coast group's Land Rover and bent its door back on its hinges before launching a sustained attack on the driver and stealing both the keys and an iPad from inside. Ambulance staff were told by the police to not attend the scene due to the danger to their medics. Shockingly, the two men arrested for the attack were later found not guilty despite evidence from one defendant naming his co-defendant as participating in the attack as well as being a paid terrierman for the hunt. One of the three magistrates also admitted outside of court that she stabled her horses at the same location as one of the men named in the paperwork but did not excuse herself. At the same hunt in November 2015, a group of hunt supporters attacked three saboteurs from behind near Eridge Green. Little did they know, however, that the main body of 20 or so saboteurs were behind them and a large fracas took place as the activists rushed to protect their friends. The attackers came off far worse, although whilst attempting to flee, one hunt supporter pulled out a knife and stabbed one of the South Coast saboteurs in the hand. Despite the rare escalations into violence, both the Southdown and Eridge and the Old Surrey and Burstow have been sabotaged to such a state that, on Saturdays when saboteurs turn up, they have resorted to often actually following a trail. Indeed, on 2nd December 2017 the Southdown and Eridge field master even handed a copy of the map showing where they had laid their trails to one saboteur and perhaps even more amazingly, the hunt actually stuck to it. However, on a later meet at the same location, the hunt had drafted in a contingent of its former terriermen and when Brighton Hunt Saboteurs first made contact with the hunt, they were digging out an active badger sett in which a fox had gone to ground. Trail hunting is also not the cruelty-free 'sport' that some animal welfare campaigners make it out to be as foxes are still killed to obtain the liquid used for the scent, not to mention the abuse of the hounds and horses.

One South Coast saboteur would gain worldwide fame after being struck on the head 17 times by an irate rider of the East Sussex and Romney Marsh as he took hold of her reins after she attempted to ride down several members of the group. Footage of the assault received millions of views and news outlets as far as Germany, USA and Japan reported on the attack. The story gained further traction when it was revealed that the rider involved was Jane Miller, the wife of Richard Goring of the Goring Hotel dynasty (a luxury hotel in Belgravia that the Queen and other royals regularly frequent). Unsurprisingly, despite the clear evidence of the assault, Sussex Police decided to take no further action and proved to the public that once again those with power and privilege are able to break the law with impunity. A private prosecution was later set up against Miller, however in a strange turn of events, she died from a fall whilst riding with the Mid Surrey Farmers' Draghounds before she was due to appear in court.

Opposite page: A Northants saboteur confronts the huntsman of the Cotswold Vale Farmers Hunt, 2011

Top: Terriermen from the Eggesford Hunt retrieve their badly injured terrier from an active badger sett after being confronted by Devon County Hunt Saboteurs, 20th January 2018

Bottom: Southdown and Eridge Hunt terriermen attack South Coast Hunt Saboteurs' Land Rover, 26th December 2012

HUNT SABOTEURS
ASSOCIATION

Further east, the East Kent group generally kept themselves to themselves focusing mainly on the Ashford Valley Hunt and the East Kent with West Street Hunt. West Sussex Hunt Saboteurs continued to hit the Crawley and Horsham and the Chiddingfold on an extremely regular basis, more often than not going out twice a week or more.

Breaking the Atherstone

Meanwhile, the West Midlands group decided that the best strategy was to focus solely on one hunt and by doing so, eventually forced them to disband. This is the story of their campaign against the Atherstone Hunt in their own words:

The Atherstone Hunt was one of a few local hunts we sabbed during the 2013/2014 season. The following season however we decided to focus completely on the Atherstone. We wanted to document and expose the activities of one hunt and show that if this is what one hunt gets up to, imagine what all hunts around the country are doing. We decided to do this by fully exploiting the power of social media, by filming everything that we do and everything the hunt does and then uploading it to social media. A lot of the videos went viral and reached tens of thousands of people and in some cases hundreds of thousands. We also wanted to reach out to new audiences and dispel some of the myths about hunt sabs by showing that we are ordinary people. The age of affordable good quality camcorders and social media means that fox hunts have nowhere left to hide.

On Boxing Day 2014, we covertly filmed the Atherstone Hunt terrierman Rob Pickering and another terrierman putting a terrier down an active badger sett and then blocking all the entrances to the sett. This is an illegal act in itself under the Protection of Badgers Act but a few hours later we also filmed Atherstone huntsman Stuart Barton taking his hounds over the badger sett. We also saw a fox running away from the same area. The fox would have been unable to seek refuge down the sett so had to keep running, providing the Atherstone with a chase. The evidence was handed over to Leicestershire Police who conveniently didn't hand the evidence over on time to the CPS so the case had to be dropped. They never even bothered to charge the second person filmed blocking the sett despite being given his details.

Our first full season with the Atherstone clearly had an impact as during the summer after the season had finished, one sab had her car burnt out at her home address and the tyres of another car all slashed. Supporters of the hunt later admitted they knew where she lived and implied they were responsible.

It was also during this summer that Leicestershire Police handed Police Information Notices (PINs) or 'harassment notices' to two sabs based on false allegations made by Atherstone Hunt member Luke Smith. The two sabs spent the rest of the summer running a high profile campaign to get the PINs overturned with both of their MPs getting involved to help them. Only the police can impose and revoke PINs and don't need any actual evidence to issue them. Eventually, thanks to this campaign, Leicestershire Police were forced to overturn the two PINs and issue an apology to the two sabs.

We filmed the Atherstone Hunt killing foxes on two separate occasions, both of which were covered by the national media and both of which had the investigation into illegal hunting dropped by the police. At the first kill, sabs were too far away to be able to stop the hounds. We saw the fox running for its life, looking left and then right as it saw hounds either side of it before it was taken down and killed. Female sabs were physically held back by male hunt supporters and had to watch as a third fox was killed. A member of the public also contacted us saying they

Opposite page: South Coast Hunt Saboteurs celebrate a successful hit with a cup of brandy coffee

Top: A West Midlands saboteur snatches a fox from the Atherstone's hounds, 2017

Bottom: The Atherstone's huntsman, Stuart Barton, rides onto a busy A road, 2015

Top: Sheffield Hunt Saboteurs stop a dig out at the York and Ainsty (South) Hunt at Escrick Park, 28th December 2013

Middle: The Battle for the Thornby Rabbits, 22nd March 2014

Bottom: Saboteurs from Manchester, Nottingham, Sheffield and West Yorkshire at the Badsworth and Bramham Moor Hunt

had witnessed the Atherstone Hunt killing a fox in front of them in a pub car park whilst they were having lunch at the pub. They told us that Leicestershire Police had not logged the incident but after repeatedly asking them to, it was eventually given a proper crime reference number but again no further action was taken. That fourth fox was killed whilst sabs were busy saving another fox from a few hounds that had split from the main pack.

Not long after this, we revealed that the huntsman of the North Warwickshire Beagles (who share the same kennels as the Atherstone Hunt), Brett Parker, was also a serving police officer with Warwickshire Police. Clearly no conflict of interest there then! This might explain some of the biased policing we've experienced. It also later emerged that Leicestershire Police's wildlife officer rode with the Belvoir Hunt.

The pressure was clearly getting to the Atherstone, their numbers were down which that meant less money was coming in and by the end of the season meant they were close to collapse. They were in so much financial trouble that they had to be bailed out by a member of the Master of Foxhounds Association who offered to pay the wages of huntsman Stuart Barton for the following season.

Terrierman Rob Pickering would also leave at the end of this season, the constant threat of being exposed blocking another badger sett proving too much as in his own words: "there's too many cameras about". The hunt failed to find anybody willing to replace him as terrierman because of this issue. During the next season, we noticed a dramatic drop in the number of foxes we were seeing, showing just how important terriermen are to hunts. Without anyone to block badger setts and release bagged foxes, Barton had to find the foxes himself which he often failed to do and when he did they were now free to escape down setts.

Our third season with the Atherstone saw them trying to rebuild the hunt from scratch. Every Saturday during cub hunting was spent not hunting but just riding around fields in an attempt to attract new riders. Unfortunately for the hunt, we were there demonstrating at the meet, reminding everyone exactly what this hunt was all about.

By the end of the season there were so few riders left that sabs would often outnumber the hunt. One of the hunt's masters put out a public statement on Facebook as part of an attempt at crowd funding, saying that the Atherstone had seen a dramatic drop in riders due to the consistent sab presence. A second attempt at crowd funding was taken down after people contacted the hosting website and asked why they were allowing people to raise money for illegal activities. More public pressure resulted in the hunt's ball being pulled from a well known theme park and local landowners began to talk to each other and stand up to the hunt by refusing to allow them on their land. Stuart Barton was given notice towards the end of the season too. He subsequently decided to sue the hunt for lack of earnings and missed one of the last meets due to him having a job interview elsewhere which effectively cancelled that day's hunting. We managed to get our hands on the Atherstone Hunt Ltd accounts before they were published which showed that the hunt was making huge financial losses and several EGMs were called towards the end of the season.

The Atherstone somehow managed to limp over the line and finished the season without collapsing completely. They were effectively bailed out again with new masters joining for the next season and putting money into the hunt. Old Atherstone Huntsman Mike Lane was roped back into rejoining but as an amateur huntsman to reduce the costs as he wasn't paid.

The sheer tenacity and determination of the West Midlands group eventually paid off however, as in 2019, the news finally came that the 200 year old Atherstone Hunt had disbanded. This was a momentous victory for the whole of the anti-hunt movement. In the six years that West Midlands Hunt Saboteurs campaigned against the hunt, almost every meet was visited by saboteurs. Dave Graham, a spokesperson for the group stated:

> *We've received death threats, had our tyres slashed, cars burnt out and have been hospitalized. We have also faced a hostile campaign of police harassment from Leicestershire Police who have actively sabotaged investigations against the Atherstone Hunt whilst constantly seeking to prosecute members of our group at all costs. We persevered and never backed down.*

This amazing achievement also attracted the praise of TV presenter Chris Packham who commented: "good riddance, top work. Let's move onto the next one."

Battling the Rabbit Hunters

Sheffield Hunt Saboteurs proved themselves to be a very capable and sturdy group, providing a strong base amongst the northern groups. On 22nd March 2014, 40 saboteurs from Sheffield, Liverpool, Manchester, Nottingham and the West Midlands hit the Ryeford Chase Rabbit hounds who were being hosted by the Pytchley Hunt near Thornby. The groups were well aware that they were making history as they headed to the meet as the Ryeford Chase had never been sabotaged before. Almost as soon as the saboteurs entered the meet, some of the 250 hunt supporters began attacking the group with sticks and a huge fight (later dubbed the Battle for the Thornby Rabbits) broke out as the antis firmly defended themselves. Not long after, the Ryeford Chase's huntsman, Nick Valentine, put his hounds back into the trailer before they had even left the meet and started the long drive back to Gloucestershire. Northamptonshire Police quickly attended the scene, sending a helicopter and three patrol cars along with three firearms officers. As was becoming depressingly familar, the police's actions were incredibly biased in favour of the hunt, attempting to confiscate mobile phones and video cameras from saboteurs and even cancelling an ambulance that had been called to attend to injured saboteurs. The Ryeford Chase claimed to be able to kill between 20 and 60 rabbits in a single afternoon and so the saboteurs' actions were extremely successful in saving the lives of many lagomorphs that day. After packing up one hunt, the saboteurs headed to the almost pitifully small Woodland Pytchley Hunt who were hunting nearby and made sure no more foxes were killed. Following the attack at the Ryeford Chase, hunt supporter Jacob Whalley pleaded guilty to three counts of battery, contrary to section 39 of the Criminal Justice Act 1988, and was ordered to pay £450 in compensation to his victims. The Ryford Chase Rabbithounds are a private pack of Petit Basset Griffon Vendéen, a breed who were originally bred to hunt hares in the thick brambles of the Vendée district of France. As the pack only hunts on invitation of other hunts it has proven to be quite a challenge to locate and sabotage them. However, on 3rd March 2019, the Ryford Chase were due to hunt the first day of the Ilminster Hare Week, a week-long 'festival' of hare hunting hosted by the Ilminster Beagles near Taunton. Word of this soon reached the HSA, and a mass hit was organised which saw 50 saboteurs from across the South West swamp the meet, forcing Nick Valentine to immediately abandon the day's hunting.

The Berkshire group would build themselves a reputation as skilled savours of hares as they focused almost exclusively on beagle packs. Norfolk and Suffolk Hunt Saboteurs also became highly skilled in saving hares, targeting the Easton Harriers and the Waveney Harriers. Hare hunting, much like fox hunting, is suffering a terminal decline with most beagle packs consisting of just a small hardcore of supporters. Indeed, the Vectis Beagles, the Claro Beagles and the North Warwickshire Beagles all disbanded in 2019 due to a lack of support.

Top: A master of the Easton Harriers attempts to conceal the body of a freshly killed hare, 2016

Middle: The remains of the chopped rabbit killed by the Royal Artillery Hunt, 2020

Bottom: Norfolk and Suffolk calls off the Waveney Harriers, 2018

Top: A Scottish saboteur grabs the body of a fox from the Lanarkshire & Renfrewshire Foxhounds, 5th November 2016

Bottom: Iain Dickson from the Fife Foxhounds points a loaded shotgun at a saboteur after Grampian and Perthshire Hunt Saboteurs stopped the hunt from digging out a fox, 17th December 2014

Opposite page top: Saboteurs at the HSA's 50th anniversary hit against the South Devon Hunt, 18th January 2014

Opposite page bottom: The HSA's 50th anniversary logo

The Beds and Bucks, North Cambridgeshire and South Cambridgeshire groups took on the Oakley Hunt and the Fitzwilliam Hunt with regular success. The Fitzwilliam even regularly took a golden eagle out with them in an attempt to circumvent the Hunting Act by pretending to use the bird of prey exemption. Indeed, an incident on New Year's Day 2016 in which a fox was killed by the Fitzwilliam whilst saboteurs were in attendance even resulted in the then huntsman, George Adams, being convicted of illegal hunting. In a separate incident, the hunt's 'falconer', John Mease, was incredulously found not guilty of causing unnecessary suffering to an animal in 2018 after he killed a fox caught by the golden eagle by driving a knife through the animal's eye.

Dealing With the Gunmen

Since the passing of the Protection of Wild Mammals (Scotland) Act back in 2002, saboteurs in Scotland have come across differing challenges to their English and Welsh counterparts, not least in the presence of a gunman in the scenario. The act allows for a pack of hounds to be used to flush a fox from cover in order to be shot, and as such many Scottish hunts have a person with a gun present to claim that their activity is within the law. The addition of a gun into already heightened confrontations between hunters and saboteurs is highly dangerous as was the case in December 2014, after the Fife Foxhounds had just chased a fox to ground into an active badger sett:

With sabs on the scene quickly we managed to stop the hunt putting a terrier down the sett to try and flush out the fox. Before the hunt knew it there were sabs coming out of thickets everywhere, bringing the whole incident to a standoff. The terrier boys had to stop their disgusting work and figure out what they were going to do next. One of the terrier boys called Iain Dickson stood with his gun - made safe - away from the sett so a sab decided to go and join the others sitting on top of the badger sett to protect the fox and as he walked past Dickson, the man raised his loaded gun, snapped it into position and pointed it at the sab as he lunged towards him. Despite this reckless and intimidating attempt by Dickson, the sabs stood firm and refused to move and ultimately help save that fox.

This was a big and defining moment for Scottish hunt saboteurs because now all the hunters in Scotland knew we meant business and that we were not going to go away, no matter how hard they tried to intimidate and bully us. Their days of illegally hunting in Scotland unopposed had come to an end.

Tough Times in Wales

At this point in time, there were only two HSA groups covering the entirety of Wales. Whilst the Flint and Denbigh Hunt regularly became victims of sabotage due to the efforts of North Wales Hunt Saboteurs, South Wales Hunt Saboteurs chose a much larger number of hunts to hit such as the Llangeinor Farmers Hunt, the Banwen Miners Hunt and the South Pembrokeshire Hunt. Both the Banwen and the South Pembrokeshire could be sabotaged with only a handful of activists. The group often used their small numbers to great effect, always working out which way a fox would be likely to break from cover and positioning themselves accordingly. During one meet of the South Pembrokeshire Hunt, the South Wales group had stopped all attempts of the huntsman to get onto the scent of a fox and due to this, the hunt phoned the police and told them that the saboteurs had a rifle and were pointing the firearm towards them from inside their vehicle! The 2015 Paris terrorist attacks had recently occurred and this had led to an increased terror threat level in the UK. A carload of armed police officers sped onto the scene and lapping up all of the hunt's lies, surrounded the saboteurs' Land Rover and ordered its occupants out with their hands above their heads before searching the vehicle for this mysterious weapon. On realising that they had been made

fools of, the police quickly let the group go and all of the huntsman's hopes that he had given the antis the slip were soon dashed as the group immediately caught up with him again, putting an end to the last draw of the day. A huge success was also gained in the valleys in 2019 when the Tredegar Farmers Hunt, who had been visited on numerous occasions by South Wales Hunt Saboteurs during the previous season, disbanded.

Half a Century of the HSA

To celebrate 50 years of the Hunt Saboteurs Association, the organisation returned to Dartmoor for a national hit of the South Devon Hunt, which had been on the receiving end of the HSA's very first act of sabotage back in 1964. On 18th January 2014, around one hundred saboteurs spread themselves across the moor, forcing the much-depleted numbers of hunters to keep on the move. As is often the case with mass hits involving large numbers of groups, communication and strategic planning on the day proved to be somewhat difficult but such was the large numbers of antis that the day went relatively successfully. Towards early afternoon, members of the South Wales group spotted a fox running from the hounds. After having ducked behind a dry stone wall at the perimeter of the field that the fox was in, so as not to scare the frightened animal back towards the hounds, the group hopped over the wall and immediately formed a line across the path of the fox. The hounds, just some 30 or so seconds behind, stopped immediately when greeted with the cloud of citronella and the solid wall of whips cracking. The huntsman was forced to call the hounds off and no more attempts at hunting were made that day.

A lot had changed since 10th January 1964. The Criminal Justice Act, the intention of which was to make hunt sabotage illegal, had come into force, so too had the Hunting Act which was supposedly the end of fox hunting. When questioned about the fact the police were taking no interest in the blatantly illegal hunting taking place in front of them, one officer attending on the day answered, "hunting is an issue for DEFRA, not the police". Clearly, it is not, but this is the precise reason why hunts have been able to kill with impunity even since the bloodsport was made illegal in 2005.

HUNT SABOTEURS 50 years still saving wildlife 1963-2013

Every hardened saboteur knows that the road to animal liberation is a long and hard fought one and as such a great respect is due to those who have stuck it out for long periods of time, facing severe hunt violence, police disinterest or bias and many hours of organisational work. It is all worthwhile, however, when one sees that fox run free.

Hunts were struggling though, and as the pressure against bloodsports continued to build, the good news came in 2015 that the Farndale Hunt, located in North Yorkshire, had disbanded.

Surveillance

As advances in technology progressed, some anti-hunt activists were now beginning to turn to the use of covert cameras to expose the various sick practices of the hunt to the wider public and to prove some of the rumours about what exactly hunts were getting up to away from the Saturday saboteurs. One such rumour, that hunts regularly feed fox cubs to the hounds in order to encourage their thirst for blood of that particular species, was to be proved by a small group of people named the Hunt Investigation Team. The group's focus was the South Herefordshire Hunt and in May 2016, they hit the jackpot. After weeks of intelligence gathering and surveillance work, HIT managed to gather footage of the huntsman storing fox cubs and heading into the kennels, cub in hand, to throw the petrified baby to the jaws of the pack of hounds. This was not the first time hunts had been exposed for keeping captive fox cubs; the League Against Cruel Sports had obtained video evidence of fox cubs being kept in a barn by the Middleton Hunt in 2015, but it was the first time the practice of throwing live cubs to the hounds was laid bare for the public to witness. Following the initial exposé, five people connected to the hunt (including the huntsman and his wife) were arrested for animal cruelty offences. A huge public outcry was heard against the South Herefordshire and the hunt didn't go out at all that season, in part due to the knowledge that if they did, vast numbers of saboteurs would join them. It was later found that the neighbouring Ledbury Hunt would hunt the South Herefordshire's country and that the South Herefordshire had no plans to begin hunting again. In May 2017, a year on from the initial investigation, HIT received a tip off from someone very close to the hunt that all but four of the hounds had been shot, some hugely sad news marring the positive outcome that the South Herefordshire Hunt was no more. Desperate to salvage something from the situation, the ex-master of the South Herefordshire Hunt and High Sheriff of Herefordshire, Major Patrick Darling, later formed a new pack named the Ledbury South which met at his home of Caradoc Court near Ross-on-Wye. The hunt was mostly formed of the neighbouring Ledbury Hunt (even the huntsman was the same) and proved to be a complete shambles every time they were visited by saboteurs from Bristol, Bath and the Three Counties. Over three years after the cub killing incident, huntsman Paul Oliver and kennel maid Hannah Rose were convicted at Birmingham Magistrates Court for multiple counts of animal cruelty but, to the outrage of many on the anti-hunt side, they were only given 16 week and 12 week suspended prison sentences respectively. Both Julie Elmore and Paul Reece (of the nearby Curre and Llangibby Hunt) both pleaded guilty after they were found to have supplied Oliver with foxes.

Another national scandal involving captive fox cubs again occurred in 2018 when the huntsman, master and founder of the Dwyryd Hunt, David Thomas, was jailed for 22 weeks following an RSPCA investigation. An artificial badger sett used for badger baiting was found at the hunt's kennels, along with two captive fox cubs kept in cages who would have been lured to the hounds.

Captive Quarry

Also keen to capitalise on the internet's growing capacity to spread the sordid (and now illegal) activities of hunts far and wide were two activists who managed to infiltrate the Pytchley Hunt, based in Northamptonshire. Posing as hunting enthusiasts, the two were able to follow the hunt for

Top: South Herefordshire huntsman Paul Oliver takes a captive fox cub to throw to the hunt's hounds, May 2016

Bottom: The central chamber of an artificial fox earth belonging to the West Norfolk Foxhounds located near the village of Horningtoft

Opposite page left: A Kernow saboteur sprays the ground with citronella oil to mask the scent of a fox

Opposite page right: Kernow Hunt Saboteurs in action

Top: A Liverpool saboteur makes friends with some hounds

Bottom: Members of Hunt Saboteurs Ireland after a hit of the Galway Blazers, 14th September 2019

Opposite page: Melbourne Hunt Saboteurs head towards the Oakley Hunt Club, 9th September 2017

four seasons before they were finally outed. Key to the investigation was the hunt's use of artificial earths to breed fox cubs in a specific wood to be hunted later in the season. Damning footage, released by the HSA, was obtained showing hunt workers feeding fox cubs in a cage attached to an artificial earth. Further footage showed the hunt drawing the very same covert with the terriermen bolting the fox out of the earth and the fox fleeing from the hounds, completely disproving the claim that fox hunting has anything to do with 'pest' control.

Ever since the bloodsport of fox hunting began, hunts have used artificial earths to rear foxes and keep them in a particular covert for hunting. These earths usually comprise of two tunnels leading to a central chamber. When the huntsman wishes to bolt a fox from the earth, a terrier is put down one tunnel thus forcing the fleeing fox to escape via the other. Artificial earths are normally situated close to the edge of a covert and facing out towards the fields so that the fox will escape across open country, giving the spectators a long chase. This abhorrent activity is something done in secret as the general public are rightly outraged by such practices but numerous exposés have happened over the years detailing the widespread use of artificial earths. A *Newsnight* programme that aired on 9th June 2000, showed footage of a Duke of Beaufort Hunt employee putting out food for foxes at two artificial earths. The Disciplinary Committee of the MFHA met five days later to consider whether the hunt had broken their rule referring to, 'the hunting of the fox in its wild and natural state and that no one shall be allowed to hunt a fox in any way inconsistent with this precept.' The committee, of which Ian Farquhar (the Beaufort's huntsman) was a member, came to the absurd but unsurprising conclusion that:

> *The situation arose because throughout hunting's history members of the public have sometimes come to hunts to ask for their help in looking after foxes which have been orphaned or are in difficulties. Our rules have therefore allowed, within certain parameters, for this to happen.*

The anti-hunt movement has come to expect such blatant lies and cover-ups over the years as the hunting community become increasingly desperate and aware that their 'sport' is viewed as abhorrent by the vast majority of people. Indeed, Ian Farquar cares little about the suffering he inflicts upon wild animals as in October 1998 he was fined £6,000 for polluting a river with chemicals used for treating mange in foxhounds and subsequently causing the deaths of 10,000 crayfish.

The HSA would again highlight the use of these artificial earths in a national scandal that saw two members of the Kimblewick Hunt convicted for animal cruelty offences. On New Year's Day 2019, Ian Parkinson was filmed using drain rods to force a captive fox out of an artificial earth, before Mark Vincent pulled the animal out by their brush and threw the terrified fox in front of the hunt's hounds. This abhorrent cruelty only resulted in suspended prison sentences for the pair, despite huge public outcry after the HSA released the footage.

Hunt Sabotage Goes International

As the 2010s were nearing a close, hunt sabotage was beginning to flourish again and hunts were severely suffering across the board. Groups were also springing up outside of the UK too as the movement spread its wings further afield. In 2017, with help from both the HSA and South Coast Hunt Saboteurs, a group was set up on the opposite side of the world, in Australia. As was the case with the Isle of Wight, foxes were introduced to Australia so that they could be hunted for 'sport'. Although some laws surrounding fox hunting and hunt sabotage differ, the core principles remain the same between the UK and Australia, in that a fox is chased by a pack on hounds hunted by red-coated huntsmen. Fox hunts are much more secretive down under and as such much of Melbourne Hunt Saboteurs' first season was spent gathering intelligence. The first hit of the newly-formed group was on 9th September 2017 when they took on a joint meet of the Oaklands Hunt Club and the Findon Harriers Hunt Club in Nulla Vale, Victoria.

Top: A saboteur after ruining a day's hunting for the North Norfolk Harriers, February 2018

Bottom: Reading Hunt Saboteurs fuss hounds of the Hampshire Hunt, 2019

In 2019, the Republic of Ireland would see a resurgence in anti-hunt activity when a number of new groups sprang into action. Groups in Munster, Connacht and Leinster joined forces to form Hunt Saboteurs Ireland, an association structurally based on the successes of the HSA. Fox hunting sadly remains entirely legal in Ireland which adds an extra hurdle for these incredibly dedicated activists to face.

Webinars

2020 was to be a momentous year, not only for the HSA, but for the whole anti-hunting movement as yet another nail in the coffin for fox hunting came in the unlikely form of a series of online webinars. On 13th November 2020, the HSA published two leaked online training sessions held in August that year by fox hunting's governing body, the Hunting Office, to around 150 hunt staff from across the UK. The coronavirus pandemic meant that such events, as well as the Hunting Office's usual meetings, were being held online rather than in person.

The infamous webinars, chaired by Conservative Peer Lord Mancroft, involved extensive discussions on how to continue to break the Hunting Act and evidenced a huge criminal conspiracy at the highest level of the hunting world. The Director of the Masters of Foxhounds Association, Mark Hankinson, described 'trail hunting' as merely a 'smokescreen' to hide traditional fox hunting. He even went further and described use of the bird of prey exemption as a 'terribly good wheeze' to disguise 'holding up', a practice during cub hunting in which riders surround a covert to prevent foxes from escaping the wood.

Paul Jelley, a committee member of the Association of Masters of Harriers and Beagles (AMHB) and a retired police officer, even suggested that hunt staff used 'burner' phones to avoid prosecution.

Astonishingly, Lord Mancroft, who has sat in the House of Lords since 1988, commented that "[…] there are no friendly interviews with police officers."

As well as evidencing a vast conspiracy not only to break the Hunting Act but to commit perjury, the webinars also proved just how effective saboteurs were. Indeed, Richard Tyacke, the Director of the AMHB advised beagle packs to simply head home when saboteurs were spotted:

> *Currently most beagle packs go home if sabs or monitors are present. This is the safe and sensible course of action. […] What is not acceptable is to carry on regardless with them all around you as if they weren't there.*

Dejectedly, he went on to concede:

> *Even if your hunt has never seen sabs before, sooner or later they will turn up.*

The impact of the leaks was enormous and a huge public outcry ensued. The story was covered far and wide by the national and local press as well as being featured on ITV News' television programme three nights in a row. A police investigation was soon launched by Devon and Cornwall Police, who led the UK's police response to hunting. Following this, landowners were quick to stop hunting on their land, with the National Trust, United Utilities, Forestry England, the Lake District National Park Authority and Natural Resources Wales all suspending hunting licences within a matter of days. It was estimated that over two million acres had been put out of bounds to the hunts.

Luke Pollard MP, Labour's Shadow Environment Secretary, was even moved to raise the issue in the House of Commons, suggesting that the Hunting Act needed strengthening.

In February 2021, three months after the HSA published the webinars, Hankinson was charged with intentionally encouraging or assisting others to commit an offence under the Hunting Act 2004, contrary to Section 44 of the Serious Crimes Act 2007.

The publication of the Hunting Office webinars proved to be a watershed moment. The myth of 'trail hunting' was well and truly blown out of the water; donations to the HSA soared; and with most of the hunting season cancelled due to coronavirus restrictions, 2020 was a year the hunting fraternity would most definitely wish to forget.

Until Wildlife Are Free

The resilience, determination and tireless work by hunt saboteurs over more than 50 years is truly remarkable. It is quite amazing that the HSA has provided a such highly organised structure that has supported direct action against animal abuse over such a sustained period of time and in so doing, has provided the backbone for the grassroots animal liberation movement over many decades. As of 2017, *Baily's Hunting Directory* listed a total of 198 fox hunts, this number being considerably lower than in the time of the HSA's inception in 1963 when this number stood at around the 250 mark. Slowly but surely, the determination of ordinary people who go out and take action to stop hunting is forcing this most disgusting of traditions into a terminal decline.

From the early days of the 1960s, when new techniques and strategies were being tried and tested; through the 1970s when the network of local groups was truly starting to solidify; into the late 1980s and early 1990s when the burgeoning squatting culture and ease of living on the dole turned hunt sabotage into a lifestyle; to the Hunting Act and its ultimate failure to stop hunting with hounds; up to the present day where the internet has proven to be an invaluable tool in casting light onto the murky world of fox hunting, the Hunt Saboteurs Association has always remained steadfast in its active opposition to bloodsports. Although fox hunting remains the main focus of the HSA, many species of wildlife have benefitted from the actions of saboteurs. The scope of tactics employed against many forms of hunting is as wide as those used by hunters themselves.

As the pages of this book testify, the grassroots anti-hunt movement has been (and continues to be) formed of people from a wide range of backgrounds, skills and ideologies, yet are brought together by a compassion towards animals in need and a willingness to take action to stop their suffering. It is this diversity that truly strengthens the saboteur network throughout the UK and beyond.

It should be noted that the stories told within these previous pages barely scratch the surface of the movement's vast history, one that is far too huge to be written in the pages of a single book. Every single week, for almost 60 years, hundreds of saboteurs have headed out into the killing fields to save wildlife. Countless lives have been saved throughout the decades and the work of the HSA shall continue until wild animals are finally able to live their lives free from persecution.

Top: A saboteur fusses hounds during an afternoon cub hunting meet of the West Norfolk Foxhounds, 2018

Bottom: The Vine and Craven Hunt openly displaying their intentions during an early morning cub hunting meet in Berkshire, September 2020

HUNT SABOTEURS
SAVE LIVES

CREDITS

ALFSG: page 155.
Animal Welfare Information Service (AWIS): pages 5, 7, 8, 12, 13, 14, 15, 18, 34, 36 and 92.
Deidre Barlow: page 146
Tarquin le Bear: pages 119, 121, 161 and 163.
Richard Bowler: pages 1, 10, 11, 16, 17, 18, 34, 35, 50 ,51 ,78, 79, 92, 93, 138, 139, 157, 158, 163 and 164.
Iain Brown: pages 38 and 39.
Aitor Garmendia: front cover image and back cover image.
The Great Unwashed: pages 161, 173, 180 and 181.
Harrison: page 90.
Hunt Investigation Team: page 177.
Noah Ortega: page 167.
Adam Parker: pages 40, 48, 49 and 80.
PG: pages 104, 105, 108, 113, 141, 143, 147, 152 and 153.
Mark Skid: page 120.
Amy Schouwenburg: pages 42 and 176.
Andrew Testa: pages 104, 111 and 112.
Rob Todd: pages 96, 115, 123 and 127.
Murray Turner: pages 67, 80 and 116.
Simon Wild: pages 87 and 125.
We Animals (Jo-Anne McArthur): page 168.

All attempts were made at tracing photographers.
Apologies for any photographs used without credit.

Sincere thanks to all those who contributed to the making of this book.

Protest at the hunt ball
HUNT saboteurs heckled members of the Ledbury Hunt as they arrived for last night's hunt ball at Hatherley Manor, near Gloucester.
Fox cub hunting under fire from protest group
Flare-up at hunt demo
A HUNT for hares left saboteurs and hunters with egg on their faces when they clashed at a Whitminster weekend.
Villager saves red deer from hunstsman
Masters in cruelty row suspended
Hunt disrupted
Hunt saboteurs threw meat, blew hunting horns and sprayed aerosols to disrupt a hunt at Linton on Saturday.
Police say there were no serious incidents and no arrests when around 40 people
Cotswold Vale Hunt.
Cruelty protest at hunt's first
the ball gestures to a y
council-owned
"Regardless
county council's
will continue to
wherever they
The Hatherley
25/11/93
Independent
BAN BLOOD SPORTS
BAN HUNTING
KILL OFF HUNTING NOT OUR WILDLIFE
18/1/9
Call for ban on 'cruel' hunting
Saboteur is hurt during hunt fracas
Saboteurs strike again
Queen's men take on hunt wreckers
STORMY START
ANTI-BLOOD sports protestors vented their fury outside the Cotswold Vale Farmers' annual hunt ball at Cheltenham town hall.
Story by Independent reporter Matthew Carpenter
Celebrating
Prince foxes saboteurs
Hunt clash as saboteurs bid to end killing
By John McJannet
Saboteurs scent victory
ANTI-BLOOD sport campaigners are
Worcester put hounds off the scent.
the Cotswold Hunt, Mr John Whitehouse,
Foxhounds kill Cassy the cat